Indefensible Weapons

INDEFENSIBLE WEAPONS

The Political and Psychological Case Against Nuclearism

ROBERT JAY LIFTON

RICHARD FALK

Basic Books, Inc., Publishers

For

Chris, Dimitri, Karen, Ken, and Noah,

and their children

and all children

CONTENTS

Section I

Imagining the Real

Robert Jay Lifton

Contents

Section II

Political Anatomy of Nuclearism
Richard Falk

PREFACE

In the early 1980s something extremely important has happened to nuclear weapons. They have begun to emerge from the shadows. While they have been among us since World War II, it is only now that they have become psychologically and politically visible to the common man and woman.

They are no less dangerous to us; they are in fact more dangerous than ever. But it is no longer possible, we believe, to reinstate the universal numbing that has so long maintained such distance between them and us, and at so great a cost.

One result of this welcome exposure is that world leaders feel constrained to address nuclear dangers and to present themselves as nuclear peacemakers. Surely that is a desirable step, because it contains possibilities for treaties that restrict or reduce weapons systems.

But whatever the extent of that kind of reduction, the problem of what we call nuclearism remains. By nuclearism we mean psychological, political, and military dependence on nuclear weapons, the embrace of the weapons as a solution to a wide variety of human dilemmas, most ironically that of "security." Our goal in this book is to explore this fundamental deformation of *attitude* toward the weapons, as well as their immediate dangers. We are equally concerned with pressing toward the kind of awareness that can reverse, even cast off, this syndrome of nuclearism.

Nuclearism, then, is the disease. Our focus on the underlying disease process does not make us unmindful of the symptoms—nuclear weapons stockpiles and policies. In this case symptoms can not only kill but kill all. What is required is an examination of both symptoms and disease, a double awareness, which could lead to steps in the direction of cure.

We feel deeply encouraged by the shifting context around nuclearism, the broad revulsion toward nuclear weapons now visible in Europe, North America, and Japan. And we take the 1982 Special Session of the United Nations on Disarmament—and the massive nuclear weapons protest that accompanied that session—to be manifestations of this revulsion. We are all too cognizant of the danger that this worldwide trend can lull us into false reassurance. For the weapons remain, and indeed their numbers dangerously expand.

The recent book by Jonathan Schell, *The Fate of the Earth*, was a landmark document in its consolidation of knowledge about the nuclear threat. His book came at an opportune time, entering into and significantly furthering the revulsion of which we speak.

Our intention in this book is to examine more systematically the psychological, historical, and political dilemmas around nuclear weapons, and to suggest the beginnings of a way out. We seek to raise fundamental questions and yet to consider where we are now and how we might proceed from there. We are perhaps unusual collaborators, coming from very different intellectual disciplines, but converging in shared sensibility, joint public stands, and close friendship. We see this book as part of a sequence of collaboration. We published *Crimes of War* in 1971 and are planning a subsequent book on issues of war and peace. In the sequence, we follow a convention of alternating the order of our names from book to book.

In the first half of the book, Lifton explores the mind's struggle to "imagine the real." The approach is primarily psychological (or psychohistorical) but inevitably leads to political and tactical issues. Similarly, Falk's subsequent examination of "the anatomy of nuclearism" is primarily political and historical (including military and tactical considerations) but raises its own psychological and sociological issues. Over the course of many detailed conversations, moreover, each of us has had considerable influence on the other's section. Hence, the two sections converge on the book's central issues: nuclear weapons attitudes and their self-deceptions; contradictions around "security"; various forms of entrapment through reliance on the weapons; their many forms of malignant influence on us; and our imaginative capacities to reverse these trends and transform our individual and collective existence. Without attempting anything on the order of systematic philosophical or moral analysis, we try to remain sensitive to insistent ethical questions.

We write as Americans, mostly about the American situation, although we are also concerned about Soviet-American mutuality in nuclear matters, and as members of a species endangered by itself.

We know that no mind—or pair of minds—is adequate to this problem of problems. Yet we insist upon the importance of bringing to bear upon it whatever knowledge we can call forth.

In this we are not neutral. We have both long been involved in the antinuclear weapons struggle. We believe that involvement to be consistent with, indeed necessary for, useful scholarship on this subject. In any case we offer a set of ideas that begin in pain and proceed toward hope.

Richard Falk
Robert Jay Lifton
June 1982

ACKNOWLEDGMENTS

Jane Isay has been a guiding presence for us throughout, infusing our efforts with form, clarity, and warm friendship. Colleagues and friends from the Wellfleet Psychohistory Group, Physicians for Social Responsibility, and International Physicians for the Prevention of Nuclear War have contributed much to our understanding, as have Michael Carey and Eric Markusen. Joe Swain and Eric Villeponteux provided useful research and editorial assistance. Lily B. Finn and June Garson prepared the manuscript with dedication. Florence Falk and Betty Jean Lifton offered loving sustenance and crucial comradeship.

Section I

Imagining the Real

Robert Jay Lifton

CHAPTER 1

The World of
the Bomb

We are just now beginning to realize that nuclear weapons radically alter our existence. It is true that none of our actions, problems, or symptoms is caused by nuclear weapons alone. But it is also true that nothing we do or feel—in working, playing, and loving, and in our private, family, and public lives—is free of their influence. The threat they pose has become the context for our lives, a shadow that persistently intrudes upon our mental ecology.

We would hardly expect the influence to be a salutory one, but we have been slow to come to terms with how malignant it is. At the heart of the matter are ways in which the bomb impairs our capacity to confront the bomb. The presence of these mass-killing devices in the world, that is, creates staggering new problems for us and at the same time distorts our thinking and blunts our feeling about precisely these problems.

My concern in these chapters, then, is our mental relationship to the instrument we have created and our altered relationship to life and death resulting from its presence among us. This means identifying a specific set of illusions about the weapons themselves and the ultimate deception (or "psychologism") around the concept of "security" as well as related issues around secrecy, credibility, and stability. I will then go back in time and briefly reexamine the Hiroshima experience and what it means for us now. That will take us to an exploration of evidence of the bomb's impingement on our lives, both in terms of earlier nuclear folkways (the nuclear air-raid drills of the 1950s) and the far-reaching psychological consequences of our continuing imagery of extinction. These consequences include individual-psychological responses to a sense of futurelessness, as well as certain forms of collective behavior such as widespread fundamentalism on the one hand and psychic numbing on the other. Finally I will suggest hopeful beginnings toward casting off our obeisance to the bomb, beginnings of awareness and action on behalf of a human future.

But before proceeding with those explorations, we need to take a look at our immediate predicament. That predicament can be summed up by a single word: absurdity. Perhaps existentialist philosophers are correct in their assertion that human existence, in the face of our knowledge of death, has always been absurd. But we live now in a very special realm of absurdity. We are haunted by something we cannot see or even imagine, threatened by something we call "nuclear holocaust."

Our absurdity, then, has several layers. First, there is the idea that organizations of human beings (we usually think of the Soviet Union and the United States, but they are hardly the only ones) stand poised to destroy virtually all of human civilization—destroy humankind—in the name of destroying one another. That is our basic structural absurdity.

Our second absurdity is the knowledge on the one hand that

we, each of us, could be consumed in a moment together with everyone and everything we have touched or loved, and on the other our tendency to go about business as usual—continue with our routines—as though no such threat existed. This is the absurdity of our double life.

A third layer of absurdity has to do with the mind's relationship to the "thing." We simply cannot locate in our images anything like this "nuclear holocaust." Here is the special absurdity of the mind, our struggle with our limited capacity to (in Buber's phrase) "imagine the real." With the appearance of nuclear weapons, doing just that has become uniquely difficult and at the same time a prerequisite for collective survival.

This absurdity of the mind readily leads to self-deception, and here two images come to mind. The first is of the seven-year-old school girl, following her teacher's advice in the midst of a nuclear air-raid drill (of a kind that used to be required in American schools) and holding a sheet of paper over her head to protect herself from fallout. The second image is of a scene conjured up by Herman Kahn, in which the bomb has fallen; one survivor who feels weak and complains of radiation effects has his individual radiation meter (everybody has one) read by another survivor: "You look at his meter and say, 'You have only received ten roentgens, why are you vomiting? Pull yourself together and get to work' "[1]

Images like these—and I shall have more to say about them later—are products of desperate conventionality. They cling to the basic mental habits associated with war, with "air raids" one can prepare for and recover from. Our minds balk at the simple truth that we are no longer talking about war or weaponry but about a technology of destruction so extreme, of such a quantum jump from anything we have known, as to border on the absolute.

Still another order of absurdity lies in the stance of the civilization and species threatened with annihilation—waiting for it to happen, indeed using much of its resources toward making it happen and virtually none of its resources toward preventing it. There is nothing on the order of vast, collective effort in which governments, leaders, gifted artists and thinkers, and ordinary people struggle together to head off the ultimate catastrophe.

I am part of a university. And from that vantage point I must acknowledge an absurdity, and a moral and intellectual scandal of similar magnitude, in the failure of our centers of knowledge and learning—of scholars, teachers, and students—to address seriously our general predicament. Precisely this absurdity was expressed by the provost of a small college in a recent letter to me. He wrote of a "minor nightmare" of his of hypothetical survivors in the year 2050 "looking in disbelief at our 1980 catalog," and added: "Living on the edge of a cliff, the academy seemed not to care."

There are of course reasons for this neglect, some of which have to do with our conventions about categories of knowledge and academic "departments." But at the heart of the matter is the violation by the subject matter itself of traditional patterns of teaching and learning. We generally understand our teaching function as one of transmitting and recasting knowledge, in the process of which we explore a variety of structures and narratives. We have no experience with a narrative of potential extinction—of ourselves as teachers and students, of our universities and schools, our libraries and laboratories. Our pedagogical impulse understandably shies away from such a narrative. And we thereby contribute to the general absurdity of the disparity between threat and response.

The mind perceives but suppresses each of these levels of absurdity. Yet we also know that a sense of absurdity, if acknowledged and confronted, can lead to something beyond itself. And from that very struggle to transcend absurdity can emerge the most powerful kinds of teaching and learning. I speak here not of teaching and learning as substitutes for action but as themselves forms of action that lead to further action.

In any thinking or action around our nuclear predicament we do well to *insist* upon its absurdity in the extreme—its objective social madness, its insanity of consequences. At the same time we need to function within that absurdity (and accept it only to that extent) sufficiently to conduct methodical day-to-day efforts of negotiation, education, and other kinds of organized activity to bring about change. The insistent awareness of absurdity gives us the incentive for radical new approaches and at the same time energizes even the more limited, methodical efforts. It is when we lose our sense of nuclear absurdity that we surrender to the forces of annihilation and cease to imagine the real.

Given these levels of absurdity, and given the simple extravagance of nuclear weapons consequences, it is all too easy to view them as existing outside of human history. Our sense is that a force capable of *destroying* human history must not be of it but beyond it. Similarly, weapons that can obliterate virtually all of human mind (in both its individual and collective cultural expressions) seems to us to be, in Otto Rank's term, "beyond psychology." The weapons so encompass and diminish us as to seem not of us but to have entered our realm mysteriously from somewhere "outside" and "beyond."

But the difficult truth is that they are both of us and among us. That they exist all too obtrusively in the shared narrative we call our history no less than in the tissues of our minds.

Consider our overall nuclear weapons predicament as I complete this manuscript during the early spring of 1982. The first general trend is the clearly increasing danger of nuclear war. This is the opinion of virtually everyone who has been close to national and international weapons buildup and nuclear weapons policies and negotiations, and who is free to speak out. There are many reasons for this increasing danger, some of them quite familiar: the proliferation of such large numbers of powerful nuclear warheads within the two great superpowers, the United States and the Soviet Union; the proliferation of nuclear weapons, already occurring or else imminent, to an increasing number of additional countries, some of them with limited governmental stability; the destabilizing technological developments in the mutual sequence of new weapons systems against which there is little possibility of defense, with an increasing tendency toward first-strike capability, temptation, and policy; talk of fighting and winning a "tactical" or "limited" nuclear war, especially in the United States; the breakdown of the policy of détente between the United States and the Soviet Union with increasing open conflict between the two nations, as well as international policies on the part of both that are adventurist and suppressive; and an expanding, worldwide arena of antagonisms, so that conflicts in the Middle East, Europe, Black Africa, South America, or East Asia, no matter how they originally develop, can quickly involve the two superpowers.

An additional source of increasing danger lies in the relationship between people and weapons. I refer here to the widespread sense, at least in the United States and probably in the Soviet Union as well, that weapons systems have so expanded, technologically and bureaucratically, that no one person or group has the capacity to control them completely. This point was made most compellingly for me by Philip Morrison, who as a young physicist literally helped put together (along with a few colleagues) the first atomic bomb tested near Los Alamos and who did the same for the next plutonium bomb built, that used on Nagasaki. Morrison has critically monitored our weapons systems ever since, and speaks of the extreme contrast between those nuclear weapons beginnings when people closely involved knew all the necessary details about the single weapon existing at any particular moment, and the contemporary sense of our weaponry as a series of structures so extensive, elaborate, and intricate as to be virtually unmanageable. The problem is partly one of increasing automation, of computers making "decisions" about when one is attacked and what one does in return; but ultimately it is a matter of the difficulty of human minds, individually or collectively, maintaining control over these vast man-machine constellations they have created. As such control becomes more tenuous, the likelihood of nuclear war becomes greater, whether by design, accident, or the kind of curious mixture of the two that may be most dangerous of all.

The problem is compounded by refinements in nuclear technology. The present-day nuclear warheads are small and light enough to be fired from tanks and sufficiently compact in their destructive potential so that warheads from a single Poseidon submarine, within minutes of being released, could annihilate all major Soviet cities and destroy the Soviet Union as a functional entity. Needless to say, a Soviet submarine could do the same to the United States. Faced with these facts, the mind can lose its bearings. It can come to view nuclear warheads as merely another weapon or "option" rather than as a step toward oblivion. Technology comes to shape and render belligerent the mind-set, rather than the mind-set controlling and restraining the technology.

But there has been an opposite trend taking shape during the late 1970s and early 1980s—an increasing concern about the real danger of nuclear war on the part of large numbers of people throughout the world. In the United States one encounters an expanding skepticism toward the scenarios and rationales put forward to justify the nuclear arms race; the collective numbing no longer holds. People are worried and afraid, increasingly distrustful of assurances that stockpiling more weapons is the path to safety. I will have more to say in chapter 11 about this shift in consciousness. But we need to start out by emphasizing this seeming contradiction of increasing danger of nuclear war and increasing resistance to the world of nuclear weapons. Not long ago I tried to convey this duality by means of an image of two trains, hurtling through the night, the one speeding toward nuclear extinction, the other toward a destination of prevention and peace. But I was quickly reminded that the metaphor is misleading: We are all on the same train, and the question is whether we can pull the emergency cord in time.

The official response to this emerging skepticism, at least in the United States, has tended to be a new call for nuclear numbing—for an end to doubt and protest, for leaving everything to leaders and experts. The continuing nuclear weapons cycle in any country depends on the collusion, or at least compliance, of most of the people. It depends, that is, on maintaining the degree of collective numbing necessary for that compliance.

We can now identify a certain psychological combination taking shape in many people, in something like the following sequence: Fear and a sense of threat break through prior numbing; these uncomfortable (potentially shattering) feelings in turn raise the personal question of whether one should take some form of action to counter the danger; that question becomes an additional source of conflict, associated as it is with feelings of helplessness and doubts about efficacy; and one seeks a psychological safe haven of resignation ("Well, if it happens, it happens—and it will happen to all of us") and cynicism ("They'll drop it all right and it will be the end of all of us—

that's the way people are, and that will be that!"). That stance prevents one from feeling too fearful, and, equally important, it protects one from conflict and anxiety about *doing something* about the situation. If the situation is hopeless, one need do nothing. There is a particularly sophisticated version of resignation-cynicism that one encounters these days mainly at universities, which go something like this: "Well, what is so special about man? Other species have come and gone, so perhaps this is our turn to become extinct." This is perhaps the ultimate "above the battle" position. Again nothing is to be done, one is philosophically—cosmically—detached from it all. All of these add up to a stance of *waiting for the bomb* and contribute to a self-fulfilling prophesy of universal doom.

A poem by Alia Johnson, called "Why We Should Drop the Bombs," captures those sentiments and others with sardonic brilliance:[2]

> it would be so exciting
> it would be so powerful
> it would punish us for our sins
> things wouldn't be so boring anymore
> we could get back to basics
> we would remember who we love
> it would be so loud
> it would be so hot
> the mushroom clouds would rise up
> we could start over
> we wouldn't have to be afraid of it anymore
> we wouldn't have to be afraid anymore
> we would finally have done it
>   better than Raskolnikov
> it would release our anger
>   in the ultimate tantrum
> then we could rest

11

In this stance of waiting for the bomb, then, we encounter various combinations of resignation, cynicism, and yearning—along with large numbers of people, some of them very talented, going about tasks that contribute to this potential holocaust. And here I confess that my perception of the danger of our situation has been intensified by recent research on Nazi doctors. There one could observe (in a very different kind of situation, to be sure) how very ordinary men and women who were in no way inherently demonic could engage in demonic pursuits; how professionals with pride in their professions could lend themselves to mass murder; how in fact the killing process itself depended on an alliance between political leaders putting forward particular policies and professionals making available not only technical skills but intellectual and "moral" justifications.

In the case of nuclear weapons, policies and justifications that might contribute to the killing process are products of specific illusions.

CHAPTER 2

Nuclear Illusions

Nothing lends itself more to illusion than our perceptions of nuclear weapons. This is so because of the quality of fear they inspire, their special mystery, their relationship to the infinite, and our sense of profound helplessness before them.

Our *fear* of them is amorphous, but contains Hiroshima-like images of extraordinary destruction and of extraordinarily grotesque forms of collective dying. Our fear is heightened by the invisibility of the added lethal component, the radiation.

This invisibility is part of the weapons' *mystery*. But the mystery also is importantly associated with our sense that we do not know, and cannot ever know, exactly what the weapons will do. Their action—above all their destructiveness—is beyond our grasp. Hence the weapons are readily perceived as a kind of revenge of nature on us for our tampering; or as being outside of nature in the sense of possessing more-than-natural (supernatural) destructive power.

This sense of mystery is bound up with the weapons' relationship to the *infinite.* We sense we are tapping an ultimate force of destructive energy—from atomic nuclei, from the sun itself. We sense their destructive power to be equally infinite. Again there are Hiroshima images: a single object from a single plane destroying a whole city; poisonous effects from radiation remaining throughout one's life and extending *endlessly* over subsequent generations. And that first "tiny bomb," we know, is the progenitor—the direct ancestor—of a "doomsday machine"—a nuclear weapons structure, or set of structures, that could literally destroy the earth.

In the face of such perceptions we feel immediately, excruciatingly, overwhelmingly *helpless.* Compared to the bomb's infinite, mysterious killing power, we feel ourselves to be nothing—to be vulnerable creatures whose lives and very humanity can be snuffed out instantaneously. We feel ourselves unable to break out of the death-trap we know to be of our own making.

Now I would stress that these are not "irrational" or "pathological" reactions. With the exception of viewing the bomb as supernatural, all of the perceptions I have described can be considered more or less appropriate mental formations or symbolizations of a particular entity.*

There is first, then, the overriding *illusion of limit and control.* Virtually all false assumptions about the bomb are related to this most fundamental of nuclear illusions. But here let us look at the militarized version of it: the concept of "tactical" or "limited nuclear war." One could say that the United States fought such a war during the final days of World War II but

---

*There is even a measure of appropriateness in viewing the bomb as "more than natural" or "supernatural," in the sense of the degree to which nature must be disturbed making it, with the utilization of elements (plutonium and uranium isotope 235) not ordinarily present in nature as separate, functional elements. But this supernatural symbolization can itself become quite pathological, when it takes the form, as we shall later discuss, of worship of the bombs themselves. Moreover—and this seems to me crucially important—these images haunt everyone from about the age of six or seven, at least in the United States. This includes nuclear strategists, who deny them and put forward seemingly opposite assumptions, such as that of the possibility of limited nuclear war.

14

that nuclear war could stay limited because the enemy had no atomic weapons and because no one had thermonuclear weapons. During the 1950s, nuclear scenarios bandied about very frequently assumed "rational" decisions of limitation—you destroyed Moscow so we must destroy New York, but let us stop there (Why? Because we are gentlemen!)—made in the midst of nuclear conflict. The leading nuclear scenarists of the time were Herman Kahn and Edward Teller, each of whom published books in the early 1960s advocating readiness for limited nuclear war. Teller in particular provides psychologically astounding scenarios demonstrating the thesis.[1] In one sequence, for instance, there are two outcomes. The scenario includes a Communist uprising in a small, fictitious democratic country with whom the United States has a mutual defense treaty. American indecisiveness and oversensitivity to Soviet nuclear threat combine to prevent the United States from making a declaration of war or taking effective action of any kind. The Communists win, and the war becomes "the beginning of the end of world leadership for the United States," following which "the Near East [is] abandoned," and "three months later . . ."

But in the second scenario, when there is a similar Communist revolution and the Soviet Union sends paratroopers, the United States acts swiftly, making effective use of small nuclear weapons, and when the U.S.S.R. threatens a nuclear attack on the U.S., this is met with a "nationwide atomic alert" and immediate second-strike readiness, which quickly aborts the Soviet threat. The U.S.S.R. withdraws its forces, free elections are held under United Nations auspices, and the Loyalist officials are returned to office. The clear moral is that nuclear restraint will lead to our downfall, while limited nuclear war brings complete success. But the psychological key is the assumption that a preplanned combination of bold, limited nu-

15

clear action and equally bold, more or less *unlimited* nuclear threat can enable us to *control* the situation and keep it *limited.* That assumption defies virtually all psychological experience. Having nuclear weapons dropped on one or even on a close ally can readily be perceived as threatening to a nation's overall existence. A response to that kind of threat is likely to include full expression of one's potential for violence,*which means full use of one's available nuclear arsenal.

Hence a number of careful studies over the years, even when posed in essentially military and political terms, have expressed grave doubts about limited nuclear war. One of the most recent, reported by the International Institute for Strategic Studies in London in November 1981, concluded that it would be "most unrealistic" to expect "a relatively smooth and controlled progression from limited and selective strikes to major counterforce exchanges or a breaking off of the war prior to large-scale attacks on urban-industrial areas" Controlled nuclear war is described as a "chimera,"[3] that is, an illusion.

But the concept, while frequently out of favor, has persisted, at least among some American and presumably Soviet strategists. In the late 1970s and early 1980s it has even had a bit of a revival. President Jimmy Carter, after first rejecting the concept, somehow embraced it toward the end of his administration. And it has been still more belligerently articulated by President Ronald Reagan and his military advisors. But a closer look at Reagan's statements reveal much of the way in which the illusion is maintained. On October 16, 1981, the president told a group of visiting editors at the White House that a nuclear exchange could occur "without it bringing either one of the major powers to pushing the button." When asked twenty-

---

*In *The Broken Connection,*[2] I emphasize the perception of a threat to one's existence, whether in terms of ultimate human connections or immediate death or its equivalent, as central to individual and collective violence.

five days later at a press conference whether he still held to that belief, he became uncomfortable, made a long rambling response, concluding with the statement that limited nuclear exchange was a "possibility" that "could take place" and adding: "You could have a pessimistic outlook on it or an optimistic. I always tend to be optimistic[4]"

We get the sense here that Reagan is not willing to insist that a nuclear exchange can *with certainty* be kept limited, but rather that it was a "possibility" one could believe in by staying "optimistic" (leaving aside the grotesquery of considering millions of deaths an "optimistic" outcome). Nor would one *with certainty* contest that statement, for it is at least conceivable that a nuclear war, as Reagan says, *could* stay limited. The overwhelming psychological—as well as military and political—likelihood is that it would *not.* Yet not only Reagan but many strategists cling to the remote possibility of a limited nuclear war and build a vast set of policies around it. Various motivations, including the need to *feel* in control, as well as specific deep-seated attitudes toward nuclear weapons (which we will discuss later) are at issue here. What results is a reassertion, in the face of all evidence, of the illusion of control and limitation.

The second great nuclear deception is the *illusion of foreknowledge.* At Hiroshima we know that people were deeply confused and had no idea of what had hit them or (with the occurrence of acute radiation effects) what was happening to them. Now we know what the bombs are and do, it is argued, so that we can teach people what to expect. The model here is the known value of such knowledge for helping people to withstand ordinary disasters, such as a tornado, a flood, or, in wartime, an air raid with conventional bombs. But if people who had been told the truth about current nuclear weapons—their radius of destructiveness and the consequences of radiation fallout—would they, as survivors of the initial blast, be strengthened by that knowledge? I think not. Indeed the reverse is probably true. Knowledge of what the weapons really are and do is likely to evoke in the survivor an appropriate sense of doom. Genuine knowledge of the weapons is essentially incompatible with belief in the efficacy of any kind of preparation for attack.

The third deception, then, is the *illusion of preparation.* Preparation consists of such things as evacuation plans, extensive shelter systems, and assignment of particular people to carry out various responsibilities in a nuclear attack. These "preparations" presuppose that the attack will be "limited," but the extent and destructive power of current nuclear arsenals render the idea of preparation something on the order of a psychotic fantasy. That is, each assumption logically follows upon the other, but each is at the same time patently absurd (people would not gather at the gathering places because they would either be dead or preoccupied with finding family members; the cars, buses, or trains designated to transport them to rural areas would hardly be functional, etc.), and the entire constellation is radically divorced from actuality. When such a fantasy structure becomes fixed, we call it a delusion. This fantasy or delusion is a product not of individual but of *social madness.* We thus encounter the kind of situation in which individual people who are psychologically "normal" (in the sense of being functional in a given society) can collude in forms of thought structure that are unreal in the extreme, in this case based on assumptions relevant to prenuclear crises and insisting— against all evidence—on their implementation as a way of managing—again controlling—nuclear destruction.

Closely related is the *illusion of protection.* This is the idea that something we call "shelters" will live up to their name, again in willful disregard of such truths that, in a large-scale nuclear war, very few people would have the time or capacity to arrive at such shelters; once there most would be incinerated in them; and those few who were still alive would emerge into a "dead world" of lethal radiation fallout.

It is often said that the Soviets must be planning for a nuclear war because they have built an extensive fallout system. To the extent that they have, we may say that they are as contradictory as we. But I can vividly remember a full delegation of Soviet doctors at a recent convocation of International Physicians for the Prevention of Nuclear War joining American and European delegations in rejecting shelters or any other "protection" against nuclear war and insisting on a perspective of "preventive medicine" in approaching the overall problem of nuclear war.

Next is the *illusion of stoic behavior under nuclear attack.* Herman Kahn has here provided us with a classic illustration. Kahn is concerned with minimizing fear of radiation, hypochondriacal behavior, and psychological contagion ("If one man vomits, everyone vomits") during a thermonuclear attack. That is why he recommends individual radiation meters and boy-scout stoicism ("You have only received ten roentgens, why are you vomiting? Pull yourself together and get to work!"). But contrast that picture with what I consider a much truer one, as portrayed in a short paper by Kai Erikson and myself, included in this book as an appendix. We anticipate in survivors psychic numbing so extreme that the mind would be shut down altogether.

One's answer to Kahn, then, is that nuclear weapons make either corpses or, at best, hypochondriacs of us all. Kahn's absurd image is again based on other, more genuinely manageable disasters, where accurate estimates of physical capacity can combine with discipline to produce genuinely stoic and constructive behavior. But the image has nothing to do with the kind of destruction and lethal radiation effects that would occur in nuclear war, and little to do with the way people react to radiation fears in general.

There is also the related *illusion of recovery*. The supposition behind this illusion is that there will be an outside world to come in and help. Again the projection Kai Erikson and I made is relevant. We anticipate the most extreme form of collective trauma stemming from a rupture of the patterns of social existence, with no possibility of outside help.

The international doctors antinuclear movement has devoted itself to dispelling the medical side of the illusion. In our systematic presentations of the overwhelming medical consequences of nuclear war, we have rejected outright the concept of medical contribution to recovery. The concept itself is more a product of prenuclear times and wars: the injured would be treated by doctors, who would do their duty and stay at their posts, healing all those who could be healed. Our message in the doctors' movement is, in effect: In a nuclear war, don't expect us to patch you up. You'll be dead and we'll be dead too. And whatever tiny bands of survivors might exist will, at least for a while, be at a stone-age level of struggle for the means of maintaining life, with little capacity either to heal or to be healed.

Not surprisingly, these various illusions tend to accompany one another, as again illustrated in the convictions of Edward Teller and Herman Kahn. Teller informs us that "rational behavior" consists of "courage," "readiness," and being "prepared to survive and all-out nuclear attack." For this we must "have adequate shelters for our entire population" as well as "plans and stockpiles [food and equipment] so that after an all-out attack, we could recover"; and also maintain "secure retaliatory forces to make sure that any all-out attack against our nation could be answered with a crushing counter-blow." And he reassures us:

> . . . this much is certain: Properly defended, we can survive a nuclear attack; we can dig out of the ruins; we can recover from the catastrophe. . . . As a nation, we shall survive, and our democratic ideals and institutions will survive with us, if we make adequate preparations for survival now—and adequate preparations are within our reach and our capabilities.[5]

Kahn also tells us that a "reasonable" individual (by which he means nonhypochondriac) who survives a future nuclear war "should be willing to accept, *almost with equanimity* [italics added], somewhat larger risks than those to which we subject our industrial workers in peace time. We should not magnify our view of the costs of the war inordinately because such postwar risks added to the wartime casualties"[6] (emphasis added).

One could claim that these strange words were written twenty years ago, but in 1980 Colin S. Gray and Keith Payne wrote an article entitled "Victory Is Possible," in which they insist that "If American nuclear power is to support U.S. foreign policy objectives, the United States must possess the ability to wage nuclear war rationally." That means that "The United States should plan to defeat the Soviet Union and to do so at a cost that would not prohibit U.S. recovery . . . [and] identify war aims that in the last resort would contemplate the destruction of Soviet political authority and the emergence of a postwar world order compatible with Western values."[7]

In these three stated attitudes we encounter another fundamental deception, the *illusion of rationality.* In these last three statements we encounter assumptions about the "reasonable individual," and we are urged toward "rational behavior" and told (by Gray and Payne) to be ready to "wage nuclear war rationally." The illusion is of a "systems rationality"—of a whole structure of elements, each in "logical" relation to the other components and to the whole. We are dealing here with nothing less than the logic of madness—of the social madness and collective "mad fantasy" we spoke of earlier.

In all nuclear weapons' discourse we must be on guard for such bootlegging of claims to reason and rationality. For the builders of such "rational systems"—of weapons and ideas— are, like the rest of us, confronted by an image they really do not know how to cope with, and seek desperately to call forth, however erroneously, the modern virtue of reason.

CHAPTER 3

Security – The Ultimate Psychologism

The central existential fact of the nuclear age is *vulnerability*. The simple physics of nuclear devices render everyone, everywhere, susceptible to instant destruction. That kind of vulnerability creates the strongest possible psychological impulse toward reclaiming the opposite and infinitely more comfortable state of security.

And here we come upon the central psychological and political confusion of the nuclear age.

Psychologically, security means feeling safe, experiencing one's environment as reliable and, generally speaking, life enhancing. The earliest sense of security is made available to the newborn by the adults who structure the environment in a way that renders it safe and dependable. That sense of security becomes inseparable from anticipation—the sense that one's environment will remain safe, that one can thrive, experiment, try new things, take chances, and still be safe.

But that sense of security is never total: The young child undergoes separations, momentary or prolonged, from nurturing figures; feelings of insecurity take hold. And in that way, over time, one's relative sense of feeling safe or threatened is a matter of one's internal legacy—all of prior life experience—as well as of the relative safety or threat associated with a particular environment.

In early life security is provided. While the infant is never completely passive, he anticipates being taken care of. But as one moves toward adulthood one becomes increasingly responsible for one's own security—for making choices about one's environment, above all about the significant relationships that bolster one's inner capacity for a *sense* of security.

All this takes place within a society and a nation-state. And we depend increasingly on social and national institutions to maintain a context of security within which we can play out our individual struggles. We then collectivize the concept and speak of "social security" and of something we call "national security."

National security concerns the safety of the governmental structure or polity, the safety of the nation-state. But in our perceptions it comes to include the safety of every individual and family within that nation-state. That is what renders the image of national security so powerful and personal.

Yet, in fact, "national security" no longer exists. Every nation-state is in some degree haunted by the possibility of extinction, the United States and the Soviet Union all the more so, because they are the main targets for each other's nuclear technology.

Now something odd and dangerous occurs. Those most responsible for political and military decisions that keep their nation safe inevitably sense, at some level of consciousness, that they are simply unable to carry out that responsibility. Ordinary people also have doubts and fears. But once more nuclear actuality becomes unacceptable to those in power. And we encounter a burgeoning of a national security industry and of what Richard Barnet called "national security managers." The task they embark upon is that of reestablishing a *sense* of security in both themselves and their followers. To create that *psychological* sense of safety they follow a course that objectively increases the danger: they build more nuclear weapons. Americans (and Soviets) are told that their expanding nuclear weapons technology protects them from the enemy's aggressive designs. And to an extent the method works; psychological security is purchased at the expense of escalating danger of extermination.

This discrepancy between actual threat and psychological quest for security surely constitutes our most dangerous contemporary dislocation. We depend on a kind of psychological thermostat to detect the "heat" of external threat. But imagine a house in which the heat is rising to the point of near conflagration and the thermostat has been so manipulated that it registers increasingly low temperatures. Should that thermostat, for whatever reason, show a beginning rise in temperature (people getting worried and a little anxious about nuclear weapons), the custodians again turn the heat higher, in order to get the thermostat down to "safe" readings. We are, however belatedly, beginning to suspect the accuracy of our thermostats.

Within this general realm of psychological misreading of security we may look further at issues of secrecy, credibility, and stability. Earliest American perceptions of security in relation to the bomb focused on keeping a secret. That meant no one else could know fully what it was, or possess the knowledge to make it. As in so many cases, an attitude associated originally with a kernel of truth (it was reasonable to invoke military secrecy around a weapon of such magnitude and importance) became the center of a persistent *mystique*—though in the case of the bomb it is probably more correct to say that the mystique of the secret held powerful sway from the very beginning. There was the secret race with the Nazi enemy to make the bomb first; the policy of keeping the secret even from our allies during World War II (even in part from Great Britain, with whom we collaborated closely in making it); from the American people and most of our political leaders; and from scientists not involved in making the bomb and even from those who were (through Leslie Groves's policy of "compartmentalization of knowledge," meaning that "each man should know everything he needed to know about doing his job and nothing else").

From the beginning it is possible that mystique took precedence over need. Los Alamos, New Mexico, was chosen as the place to make the bomb because of its isolation; but that isolation was so extreme that it presented formidable difficulties in the way of supplies and living accommodations. In any case, its choice had much to do with Robert Oppenheimer's knowledge of the area through camping trips into the wilderness as a boy—that is, with the secrets of childhood. As a sensitive novelist of those events has written, "The secret times of that time are the most secret of all, the most everlastingly private, the safest in retrospect. . . . Hence the physicist's proposal must have given an almost sentimental sanction to the choice of the mesa of Los Alamos for the secret gestation of the bomb."[1]

The term "bomb secret" suggested the equation of the image of the absolute weapon with the image of total possession of its know-how around the inclusive image of security. Hence the shock of the discovery that scientist spies (Klaus Fuchs, Alan Nunn May, and Bruno Pontecorvo) took it upon themselves to "tell the secret" to representatives of another country that was both ally and adversary. The resulting sense of extreme vulnerability—of threat to national security and collective existence in general—clearly influenced the extraordinary application of capital punishment to Julius and Ethel Rosenberg, nonscientists whose espionage roles were never established with certainty.

Hence Edward Shils calls his study of that period *The Torment of Secrecy: The Background and Consequences of American Security Policies.* In it he emphasizes how difficult it was for Americans to feel themselves endangered by nuclear threat in a perpetual crisis they could not end. For "it is infuriating to feel that what one holds sacred is rendered insecure by hidden enemies who through indifference or design would give away the secrets on which survival rests"[2] Shils goes on to point out that "The secret . . . became the central issue," equated directly with "security" and "national survival." The Soviet Union's designation as the stealer of the secret became inseparable from the threat it posed. Throughout the inquisitory hearings the stress was on "telling all" and "naming names"—on revealing all personal secrets that might somehow be useful to "the enemy." For the ultimate secret rendered all lesser secrets more dangerous. The whole process, according to Shils, was intensified by "the faint trace of guilt" over having first used the bomb, as well as by transcendent fear over the possible future use of nuclear weapons by anyone. Hence the desperate intensification of the mythological constellation of secrecy and security—in the face of the ultimate availability to all of the principles of nature on which nuclear weapons are based.

To understand how this mythology could take shape one must again turn to childhood themes. Victor Hugo claimed that "No one keeps a secret so well as a child," but it may be more accurate to say that no one is more enthralled by the *idea* of the secret. The secret begins with what adults presumably know and the child does not—the mystery of life's origin (Where did I come from? Who was the first man?) and end (What happens to old people? When you're dead, can you wake up again?). From within the framework of those ultimate mysteries emerge early sexual secrets (what adults— parents—do in the bedroom). No wonder the young child is so drawn to having secrets of his own. For *any* secret becomes associated with forbidden knowledge of ultimate mysteries and therefore with a transcendent life-power. The child's evolving sexual secrets (the pleasures of one's own body and early erotic feelings toward family members) are likely to become associated with "bad" secret wishes (for the death of a sibling or a parent) or bad behavior (stealing a penny or striking another child). The secret, then, takes on a trinity of forbidden knowledge, special power, and hidden badness (guilt and shame). At the same time the secret's possessor is likely to associate it in some way with virtue—the virtue of keeping it and of thereby supporting the person or group with whom one shares the secret.

The secret is always held (by the child especially but by the adult also) under active psychic tension; to hold on to it means struggling against one's impulse to reveal it. That impulse may be related to guilt, or to the wish to please or merge with those who want to know the secret, or to conditions causing a diminution of power or reward derived from holding on to it. But it is probably fair to say that without this conflict over retention, one cannot properly speak of a secret. Indeed precisely that tension invests the secret with a sense of ultimate consequences: To hold on to it is to hold on to life itself; to reveal it is to risk attack, annihilation, loss of life—until the appropriate moment, should there be one, at which time revealing it enhances life.

The unique existential intensity of the secret is inseparable from its association with the idea of conspiracy. A conspiracy requires a secret *plan* for doing harm of some kind to those from whom vital information is held. But any situation in which two or more people share a secret can prefigure a conspiracy. To share a secret, then, is to begin to conspire. And to conspire evokes profound emotions and ultimate forms of behavior, as the derivation of the word suggests: It is related to the Latin *spiritus* and to words such as spirit, inspire, respire [respiration], and expire. To conspire, then, is to extend one's secret into a harmful, possibly lethal, plan and to do so in closest spiritual communion with others.

Moreover, the association of the secret with the idea of conspiracy can take on endless variations and reversals. The conspiracy may lie in holding the secret, or in telling it surreptitiously—secretly—to someone else, or in telling part of it and holding on to part of it, or in replacing an old secret with a new one (thereby selectively subverting the power of those privy to the old one). Overall, the idea of a conspiracy causes the secret to be associated with the most intense and threatening forms of transgression and heresy.

From the beginning, the idea of atomic energy was associated with all these dimensions of the secret. It was of course a "secret of nature," but the image was typically (as H. G. Wells put it) "the secret powers of the atom." That power, as Frederick Soddy, (a Nobel Prize-winning British chemist) stated as early as the turn of the century, could not only "destroy the earth" but could also provide a "transmutation" similar to that of the alchemists (of base metal to gold but also, symbolically, of the human spirit), a source of "inexhaustible" power of a kind that could "transform a desert continent, thaw the frozen poles, and make the whole world one smiling Garden of Eden"[3] *This* secret could provide utopia or doom, equally absolute.

Over time, the wonders of radiation became the manifest image; its dangers became the secret. Consider the life and death of Marie Curie. Embraced by the world not only as a great woman scientist but as the romantic "lady of radium," she was looked upon as a discoverer of a substance that might provide secrets of creation—possibly even the means of overcoming death. What was little commented upon—and still does not occur in most accounts of her life—was her radiation death. Apparently careless in exposing herself to radioactive matter, "she . . . grew more feeble year by year . . . [but] refused to believe that her wonderful radium was killing her by inches" Nor did the deaths of other laboratory workers (including one in her own institute), of uranium miners, or watch-dial painters, of radiologists and X-ray technicians bring about much acknowledgment of the destructive potential of radiation. Here maintaining the secret depended on massive denial and numbing.

With the construction, testing, and use of actual atomic bombs, that secret was out. But still, secrets were needed. They took the form of knowledge needed for each "advance" in the technology of destruction, each new bomb and delivery system. Only rarely is a truth-haunted soul able to say, with David Lillienthal in early 1946 *"What* is there that is secret?. . . . in the real sense there are no secrets . . ."[4] There was a struggle to maintain "faith in the atomic secret" because that faith made possible "the assumption of an enduring monopoly on the bomb." Dexter Masters saw very early that obsession with the secret was a way of covering over one's genuine dilemmas—one's own "disease." His fictional protagonist thus speaks of "fears and suspicions all over . . . a sickness," and adds that "If you are sick and do not wish to know the progress of your disease, you cover it with secrecy," concluding that "one dies anyway . . . perhaps sometimes even faster"[5]

The myth of the "bomb secret" is integral to the entire structure of illusion and deception around security. It enables a small group of bomb managers to assume a priestlike stance as exclusive possessors of secrets too arcane and too sacred to be made available to the rest of us. And, the assumption goes, by their vigilance in protecting those secrets from everyone, their own countrymen as well as foreign adversaries, they guarantee everyone's safety. The process perpetuates itself because the technology and bureaucracy of nuclear weapons constantly generate new secrets as older ones become known, new esoteric mysteries known only to the nuclear priesthood. What the mythology actually guarantees is a perpetuation of dangerous self-deception and the prevention of the kind of informed exchange that might result in more constructive policies.

Looking more briefly at the themes of credibility and stability, we find contradictions analogous to those already described. In regard to credibility, there is a specific contradiction between intent and others' perception of that intent. American policymakers (and everything I said here applies to their Soviet counterparts as well) cannot avoid being aware of the potential range of nuclear destruction, and have repeatedly acknowledged that all-out nuclear war cannot be (as even Henry Kissinger once wrote) "a meaningful instrument of policy." Yet they insist upon constructing Draconian nuclear weapons systems in order to threaten their potential enemies with precisely that "meaningless" (because mutually suicidal) action. The excruciating dilemma is "that nuclear weapons, the most powerful instruments of violence ever invented, tend . . . to immobilize rather than strengthen their possessors"[6] But a major reason for continuing to build them *ad infinitum* is to create what an internal Defense Department memo once described as "psychological impact . . . on the countries of the world."

A way out of the dilemma was the development of a doctrine

of limited conventional war. Indeed the Vietnam War grew out of a shift from the Eisenhower-Dulles policy of "massive nuclear retaliation" for even minor enemy transgressions (because that doctrine was not considered "credible") to a new Kennedy Administration policy of "counterinsurgency war." One had to fight that war, it was said again and again in military and political circles, in order to demonstrate American will and determination in fighting communism—and affirm the "credibility of American power." But the Vietnam War demonstrated, if nothing else, precisely the opposite—the *non*credibility of American power. And the reembrace of the concept of limited *nuclear* war is partly an effort to reassert the "credibility" of that power by retaining the nuclear option, together with the illusion of limit and control. Here the unacceptable actuality that had to be denied at all cost was the self-image of the United States as the "pitiful, helpless giant" so bitterly articulated by President Nixon.

These contradictions create in any American president an anxious sense of executive impotence. Hence the tendency of the Nixon Administration (as later exposed in the Watergate scandal) to be pathologically sensitive to opposition, to see opponents as "enemies" and domestic issues as nothing short of "war." Precisely this struggle around the persistent, never-realizable quest for nuclear weapons–based "credibility" "drove two presidents into states of something like madness and led to the near-ruin of our political system." And the illusory claim to nonexistent credibility, in turn, tended to "draw the government into a world of fantasy, for the images, like the theories that had given rise to them, could not be tested against experience."[7]

There is a simple psychological point to be made here. Credibility means believability or plausibility. Again going back to early life, we know that the child's effort to convince others of his intent depends largely on the actuality of that intent—his own belief in what he says he will do. Should he make an overall threat to a significant adversary that is not carried out, for whatever reasons, he is likely to become uneasy in the face of others' and his own sense of being something of a fraud or an imposter. He may subsequently feel impelled to take dramatic steps to carry out that threat, now basing his actions on the kind of adversary behavior he had previously been willing to tolerate. And he may do this even where the likely consequence is that he will suffer as much as, or more than, that adversary. Here we have a model, crude but I think appropriate, for the gravest danger surrounding the nuclear credibility contradiction.

But there is also another possibility. That same child could hold back from such action despite difficult, often losing struggles with adversaries, and as a consequence move increasingly into an uncomfortable and confused style of self-process. The constellation would include strong elements of the imposter and (assuming the child was big and strong) of the "pitiful, helpless giant," along with various kinds of erratic, compensatory behavior. I am suggesting the emergence of a national political identity within which we significantly disbelieve our self-judgments, until we find ourselves (in the manner of the imposter) becoming ever more deeply involved in false roles in order to find ways to believe what we cannot believe. Nuclear weapons, that is, make of their possessors either mass murderers or else deceivers and self-deceivers who fluctuate between feelings of omnipotence and impotence, as they gradually lose their hold on ethical tradition and existence itself.

Stability is another conceptual victim of nuclear age thought. In brief, stability becomes confused with inertia. Inertia means resistance to motion, action, or change; its Latin root, *iners*—inert—means lack of skill or idleness. Stability, in contrast, implies achievement of a certain amount of strength and balance. Its meanings include resistance to sudden change, dislodgment, or overthrow; and constancy or steadfastness of character or purpose; as well as reliability and dependency. Its Latin root is *stabilis*, meaning standing firm; in essence, it signifies the capacity to stand and is related to such words as stance and stature. A stable person is neither inert nor subject to absolute flux but is, rather, in some form of psychological equilibrium that permits him to remain significantly constant while experiencing growth and change. By this definition many we consider to be mercurial, bold, or experimental—or what I call "Protean" (See p. 105)—have, at the same time, areas of constancy (in the work process, in specific relationships, or in political or moral commitment) that give their lives a form of stability.*

For individual people, this kind of ideal stability is hard won. To achieve it one must develop, beginning in childhood, sufficient inner confidence in one's place—one's "standing" in the world—to be flexible in the face of challenge. For nations too stability is difficult to come by. Political and military rigidity is often called stability; and when confronted with various forms of instability, too many politicians and generals (or self-proclaimed moralists) are likely to confuse symptom with cause and to attack vehemently those who seek sufficient change to overcome the instability. Fear of nuclear instability, then, increases trends toward the militarization of society and toward acceptance of that process or what has been called psychological militarization. And here we encounter the problematic relationship between stability and the sense of *control*.

*Actual instability tends to be associated not only with inconstancy but with intolerance for genuine change. An unstable person may deal with pressures toward change by calling forth extreme numbing (becoming inert); by erratic or explosive behavior; or by a form of continuous flux in which the absence of engagement precludes a real change.

The individual, faced with a breakdown of his stability, may call forth compulsive or obsessive maneuvers to maintain control over what is perceived as virtually uncontrollable. In such a situation, spontaneity or unpredictability can be so threatening as to be equated with death itself.

In a world of nuclear weapons, that perception takes on more than a kernel of truth. That is, instability in the form of unpredictable behavior around nuclear weapons could indeed be fatal to extremely large numbers of people, if not our entire civilization. From the beginning, then, nuclear instability was a dreaded image.

That image could lead to strange proposals. One such proposal was described to me by a former colleague at Yale, Eugene Rostow, who now (April 1982) serves as head of the Arms Control and Disarmament Agency. Rostow said that, toward the end of World War II, he circulated a memo within the Office of Stragetic Services advocating that we issue an ultimatum to the Soviet Union that we would drop an atomic bomb upon it unless it took active steps to open up its society. Rostow's rationale—and he was surely not the only one who felt this way at the time—was that we had to take that step while we alone possessed the bomb, since the world would be rendered too dangerous when a closed society such as the Soviet Union eventually acquired it. Subsequently Bertrand Russell and Harold Urey made proposals that we should similarly threaten the Soviet Union with preventive nuclear war, should it fail to accept a reasonable proposal toward controlling or getting rid of nuclear weapons. And one must remember that Russell became one of the world's most prominent spokesmen for the abolition of nuclear weapons and Urey one of the World War II nuclear scientists most sensitive to the dangers of the weapons.

The image of nuclear instability was also at play in what

Walter Lippmann spoke of as the "dangerous from of self-delusion" leading Americans toward "the conception of ourselves as the policemen of mankind." That American self-delusion has had many disastrous consequences. These include our role in the Vietnam War and our support of oppressive, dictatorial regimes in various parts of the world because they have the appearance of "stability" in the face of social forces (often seen as potentially Communist, and sometimes actually so) threatening that "stability." There are always many other factors involved, of course, but our one-sided image of terrifying nuclear instability directly fuels and intensifies all such situations. I say one-sided because responses to the image all too often, and all too willfully, avoid confronting the part our own policies play in perpetuating precisely these dangers around nuclear instability.

Thus we dubiously invoke the principle of stability even as we conduct a nuclear arms race that is inherently destabilizing, not just to us and the Soviet Union but to all of humankind. And we then look elsewhere for targets for our increasing terror about nuclear instability and find such targets in countries with pressures toward social change or revolution. We thus contribute to an atmosphere of extreme polarization that favors technological terrorism: either the use of threat and violence by governments in possession of high technology, or the attempt of small, oppositionist groups to invoke violent threats by interrupting that technology (airplane hijacking). And now the image of nuclear instability extends to both of those situations—the dropping of a nuclear weapon by a country possessing them in order to impose its will somewhere in the world; or the furtive creation and possibly furtive use of a nuclear weapon by a small terrorist group. What is sometimes overlooked is that the most extreme technological terrorism of all is conducted by the two great nuclear superpowers in their very stockpiling of genocidal devices and in their threats to use them, whether on one another or elsewhere in the world.

In between, of course, there are the manifold possibilities of proliferation of weapons to countries of varying domestic and international stability. These dangers are all too real and require the most careful political evaluation and policies. But we do nothing toward diminishing the danger until we recognize the inherent, deadly instability in the very existence of large numbers of these lethal instruments.

CHAPTER 4

Is Hiroshima Our Text?

I arrived in Hiroshima in the early spring of 1962. I intended no more than a brief visit. But very quickly I made a discovery that I found almost incomprehensible. It had been seventeen years since the dropping of the first atomic weapon on an inhabited city—surely one of the tragic turning points in human history—and no one had studied the impact of that event. There had of course been research on the physical aftereffects of the bomb, and there had been brief commentaries here and there on behavior of some of the survivors at the time of the bomb and afterward. But there had been no systematic examination of what had taken place in people's lives, of the psychological and social consequences of the bomb.

I came to a terrible, but I believe essentially accurate, rule of thumb: the more significant an event, the less likely it is to be studied. Again there are reasons. One reason, certainly relevant to Hiroshima, has to do with the fear and pain the event arouses—the unacceptable images to which one must, as an investigator, expose oneself. To this anxiety and pain I can certainly attest.

Is Hiroshima Our Text?

But another source of avoidance is the threat posed to our traditional assumptions and conventional ways of going about our studies. We would rather avoid looking at events that, by their very nature, must change us and our relation to the world. We prefer to hold on to our presuppositions and habits of personal and professional function. And we may well sense that seriously studying such an event means being haunted by it from then on, taking on a lifelong burden of responsibility to it.

I was able to stay in Hiroshima and conduct interview research with people there over a six-month period. The best way I know to describe a few of my findings that might be of use to us now is to look at the Hiroshima experience as taking place in four stages.

The first stage was the immersion in the sea of dead and near-dead at the time the bomb fell. This was the beginning of what I have called a permanent encounter with death. But it was not just death; it was grotesque and absurd death, which had no relationship to the life cycle as such. There was a sudden and absolute shift from normal existence to this overwhelming immersion in death.

Survivors recalled not only feeling that they themselves would soon die but experiencing the sense that *the whole world was dying.* For instance, a science professor who had been covered by falling debris and temporarily blinded remembered: "My body seemed all black. Everything seemed dark, dark all over. Then I thought, 'The world is ending.' " And a Protestant minister, responding to scenes of mutilation and destruction he saw everywhere, told me: "The feeling I had was that everyone was dead. The whole city was destroyed. . . . I thought all of my family must be dead. It doesn't matter if I die. . . . I thought this was the end of Hiroshima, of Japan, of humankind." And a writer later recorded her impressions:

I just could not understand why our surroundings change so greatly in one instant. . . . I thought it must have been something which had nothing to do with the war, the collapse of the earth, which was said to take place at the end of the world, which I had read about as a child. . . . There was a fearful silence, which made me feel that all people . . . were dead.[1]

As psychiatrists, we are accustomed to look upon imagery of the end of the world as a symptom of mental illness, usually paranoid psychosis. But here it may be said that this imagery is a more or less appropriate response to an extraordinary external event.

In referring to themselves and others at the time, survivors used such terms as "walking ghosts," "people who walk in the realm of dreams," or as one man said of himself: "I was not really alive." People were literally uncertain about whether they were dead or alive, which was why I came to call my study of the event *Death in Life*.

Indicative of the nature of the event is the extraordinary disparity in estimates of the number killed by the bomb. These vary from less than 70,000 to more than 250,000, with the City of Hiroshima estimating 200,000. These estimates depend on who one counts and how one goes about counting, and can be subject at either end to various ideological and emotional influences. But the simple truth is that nobody really knows how many people have been killed by the Hiroshima bomb, and such was the confusion at the time that nobody will ever know.

The second stage was associated with what I call "invisible contamination." Within hours or days or weeks after the bomb fell, people—even some who had appeared to be untouched by the bomb—began to experience grotesque symptoms: severe diarrhea and weakness, ulceration of the mouth and gums with bleeding, bleeding from all of the bodily orifices and into the skin, high fever; extremely low white blood cell counts when these could be taken; and later, loss of scalp and bodily hair—the condition often following a progressive course until death. These were symptoms of acute radiation effects. People did not know that at the time, of course, and even surviving doctors thought it was some kind of strange epidemic. Ordinary people spoke of a mysterious "poison."

But the kind of terror experienced by survivors can be understood from the rumors that quickly spread among them. One rumor simply held that everyone in Hiroshima would be dead within a few months or a few years. The symbolic message here was: None can escape the poison; the epidemic is total—all shall die. But there was a second rumor, reported to me even more frequently and with greater emotion: the belief that trees, grass, and flowers would never again grow in Hiroshima; that from that day on the city would be unable to sustain vegetation of any kind. The meaning here was that nature was drying up altogether. Life was being extinguished at its source—an ultimate form of desolation that not only encompassed human death but went beyond it.

These early symptoms were the first large-scale manifestation of the invisible contamination stemming from the atomic particles. The symptoms also gave rise to a special image in the minds of the people of Hiroshima—an image of a force that not only kills and destroys on a colossal scale but also leaves behind in the bodies of those exposed to it deadly influences that may emerge at any time and strike down their victims. That image has also made its way to the rest of us, however we have resisted it.

The third stage of Hiroshima survivors' encounter with death occurred not weeks or months but years after the bomb fell, with the discovery (beginning in 1948 and 1949) that various forms of leukemia were increasing in incidence among survivors sufficiently exposed to irradiation. That fatal malignancy of the blood-forming organs became the model for the relatively loose but highly significant term "A-bomb disease." Then, over decades, there have been increases in various forms of cancer—first thyroid cancer, and then cancer of the breast, lung, stomach, bone marrow, and other areas. Since the latent period for radiation-induced cancer can be quite long, and since for many forms it is still not known, the results are by no means in. Researchers are still learning about increases in different cancers, and the truth is that the incidence of virtually *any* form of cancer can be increased by exposure to radiation.

An additional array of harmful bodily influences have been either demonstrated, or are suspected, to be caused by radiation exposure—including impaired growth and development, premature aging, various blood diseases, endocrine and skin disorders, damage to the central nervous system, and a vague but persistently reported borderline condition of general weakness and debilitation. Again the returns are not in. But on a chronic level of bodily concern, survivors have the feeling that the bomb can do anything, and that anything it does is likely to be fatal. Moreover, there are endless situations in which neither survivors themselves nor the most astute physicians can say with any certainty where physical radiation effects end and psychological manifestations begin. There is always a "nagging doubt." For instance, I retain a vivid memory of a talk I had in Hiroshima with a distinguished physician who, despite injuries and radiation effects of his own, had at the time of the bomb courageously attempted to care for patients around him. He spoke in philosophical terms of the problem of radiation effects as one that "man cannot solve," but when I asked him about general anxieties he smiled uneasily and spoke in a way that gave me the strong sense that a raw nerve had been exposed:

Yes, of course, people are anxious. Take my own case. If I am shaving in the morning and I should happen to cut myself very slightly, I dab the blood with a piece of paper—and then, when I notice that it has stopped flowing, I think to myself, "Well, I guess I am all right."[2]

Nor does the matter end with one's own body or life. There is the fear that this invisible contamination will manifest itself in the next generation, because it is scientifically known that such abnormalities *can* be caused by radiation. There is medical controversy here about whether genetic abnormalities have occurred: They have not been convincingly demonstrated in studies on comparative populations, but abnormalities in the chromosomes of exposed survivors have been demonstrated. People of course retain profound anxiety about the possibility of transmitting this deadly taint to subsequent generations. For instance, when I revisited Hiroshima in 1980, people said to me: "Well, maybe the next generation is okay after all, but what about the third generation? The fact is that, scientifically speaking, no one can assure them with certainty that subsequent generations will not be affected. Again, nobody knows. So there is no end-point for possible damage, and for anxiety.

No wonder, then, that a number of survivors told me that they considered the dropping of the bomb to be a "big experiment" by the United States. It was a new weapon; its effects were unknown; American authorities wanted to see what those effects would be. Unfortunately, there is more than a kernel of truth in that claim, at least in its suggestion of one among several motivations. More important for us now is the idea that any use of nuclear warheads would still be in a related sense "experimental."

The fourth stage of the Hiroshima experience is its culmination in a lifelong identification with the dead—so extreme in many cases as to cause survivors to feel "as-if dead" and to take on what I spoke of as an "identity of the dead." Hiroshima and Nagasaki survivors became, in their own eyes as well as those of others, a tainted group, one whose collective identity was formed around precisely the continuous death immersion and the invisible contamination we have been discussing. The identity can include what we may think of as paradoxical guilt—the tendency of survivors to berate themselves inwardly for having remained alive while others died, and for not having been able to do more to save others or combat the general evil at the time of the bomb. In connection with the latter, the sense of "failed enactment"[3] can have little to do with what was possible at the time or with what one actually did or did not do.

More than that, survivors underwent what can be called a second victimization in the form of significant discrimination in two fundamental areas of life: marriage and work. The "logic" of the discrimination was the awareness of potential marriage partners (or families and go-betweens involved in making marriage arrangements) and prospective employers that survivors are susceptible to aftereffects of the bomb, making them poor bets for marriage (and healthy children) and employment. But the deeper, often unconscious feeling about atomic bomb survivors was that they were death-tainted, that they were reminders of a fearful event people did not want to be reminded of, that they were "carriers," so to speak, of the dreaded "A-bomb disease."

At the end of my study of these events, I spoke of Hiroshima, together with Nagasaki, as a last chance, a nuclear catastro-

Is Hiroshima Our Text?

phe from which one could still learn. The bombs had been dropped, there was an "end of the world" in ways we have observed, yet the world still exists. And precisely in this end-of-the-world quality of Hiroshima lies both its threat and its potential wisdom.

Is Hiroshima, then, our text? Certainly as our *only* text, it would be quite inadequate. We know well that what happened there could not really represent what would happen to people if our contemporary nuclear warheads were used. When the Hiroshima and Nagasaki bombs were dropped, they were the only two functional atomic bombs in the world. Now there are approximately 50,000 nuclear warheads, most of them many times—some a hundred or a thousand or more times—the destructive and contaminating (through radiation) power of those first "tiny" bombs. While those early bombs initiated a revolution in killing power, we may speak of another subsequent technological revolution of even greater dimensions in its magnification of that killing power. The scale of Hiroshima was difficult enough to grasp; now the scale is again so radically altered that holding literally to Hiroshima images misleads us in the direction of extreme understatement.

Yet despite all that, Hiroshima and Nagasaki hold out important nuclear age truths for us. The first of these is the *totality of destruction*. It has been pointed out that Tokyo and Dresden were decimated no less than Hiroshima. But in Hiroshima it was one plane, one bomb, one city destroyed. And the result of that single bomb was the incalculable death and suffering we have noted.

A second Hiroshima truth for us is that of the weapon's *unending lethal influence*. Radiation effects were (and are) such that the experience has had no cutoff point. Survivors have the possibility of experiencing delayed but deadly radiation effects for the rest of their lives. That possibility extends to their children, to their children's children, indefinitely into the future—over how many generations no one knows. And we have seen how the physical and psychological blend in relation to these continuing effects.

A third truth, really derived from the other two, has to do with Hiroshima and Nagasaki survivors' identification of themselves as *victims of an ultimate weapon*—of a force that threatens to exterminate the species. This sense had considerable impact on Hiroshima survivors, sometimes creating in them an expectation of future nuclear destruction of all of humankind and most of the earth.

And there is still something more to be said about Hiroshima and Nagasaki regarding our perceptions of nuclear danger. The two cities convey to us a sense of *nuclear actuality*. The bombs were really used there. We can read, view, and if we will allow ourselves, *feel* what happened to people in them. In the process we experience emotions such as awe, dread, and wonder (at the extent and nature of killing, maiming, and destruction)—emotions surely appropriate to our current nuclear threat. Such emotions can transform our intellectual and moral efforts against nuclear killing into a personal mission—one with profound ethical, spiritual, and sometimes religious overtones. Hiroshima, then, is indeed our text, even if in miniature. And we have hardly even begun to take in what Hiroshima has to teach us.

The argument is sometimes extended to the point of claiming that this sense of nuclear actuality has prevented full-scale nuclear war; that in the absence of the restraining influence of Hiroshima and Nagasaki, the United States and the Soviet Union would have by now embarked upon nuclear annihilation. The claim is difficult to evaluate, and while I feel some of its persuasiveness, I do not quite accept it. In any case, one must raise a countervailing argument having to do with another dimension of Hiroshima's and Nagasaki's nuclear actuality: namely, the legitimation of a nation's using atomic bombs on human populations under certain conditions (in this case wartime). Once anything has been done, it is psychologically and in a sense morally easier for it to be done again. That legitimation can then combine with an argument minimizing the effects of the Hiroshima bomb: the claim that one has unfortunately heard more than once from American leaders that Hiroshima's having been rebuilt as a city is evidence that one can fight and recover from a limited nuclear war.

Here we may say that part of Hiroshima's value as a text is in its contrasts with our current situation. One crucial contrast has to do with the existence of an outside world to help. Hiroshima could slowly recover from the bomb because there were intact people who came in from the outside and brought healing energies to the city. Help was erratic and slow in arriving, but it did become available: from nearby areas (including a few medical teams); from Japanese returning from former overseas possessions; and, to some extent, from the American Occupation. The groups converging on Hiroshima in many cases contributed more to the recovery of the city as such than to that of individual survivors (physically, mentally, or economically). But they made possible the city's revitalization and repopulation.

In Hiroshima there was a total breakdown of the social and communal structure—of the web of institutions and arrangements necessary to the function of any human group. But because of the existence and intervention of an intact outside world, that social breakdown could be temporary.

Given the number and power of our current nuclear warheads, can one reasonably assume that there will be an intact outside world to help? I do not think so.

CHAPTER 5

The Bomb in Our Schools—and in Us

We know that nuclear illusions sustain the image of the existence of precisely that postbomb "intact outside world." But we are just beginning to understand the relationship of that particular illusion to our general psychological responses to the bomb.

Over the decades since World War II, many of us have been concerned with the effects of our psyches of the mere existence of the bombs among us, along with talk of their being used. But only recently has there emerged empirical evidence of those effects based on systematic research.

One of the most important studies was done by Michael Carey,[1] a writer-researcher with psychoanalytic and historical training and a former assistant of mine. Carey remembered all too vividly the nuclear air-raid drills he had experienced as a primary school pupil in the 1950s and decided to do a study of the psychological impact of those drills on people of his generation. During the early and mid-1970s he interviewed more than forty young men and women (then in their twenties and thirties) and extended his inquiry from drills to early and subsequent imagery about nuclear weapons and other threats, to more general feelings about death, the future, and various aspects of living. I was able to discuss Carey's results with him along the course of the work and to join him in conducting a few of the interviews. I was profoundly impressed, as was he, by the ubiquitous presence of the bomb at some level of people's minds.

Those participating in the drills (held in schools throughout the United States during the late 1950s and early 1960s) described a general sequence from amorphous death anxiety to sustained numbing to periodic contact with anxious death imagery. They remembered, as preparation for the drills, a kind of pep talk, whose theme was, yes, the bomb was formidable and very destructive, but it could be overcome—defeated, so to speak—by means of an American spirit of cooperation, discipline, and goodwill. One was trained to go down to the basement together with other students and teachers, or else to duck under desks or cover one's head with a book or a paper (all in order to avoid fallout) and to avoid looking out the window (lest one be blinded by the flash). And participants remembered, as the initial phase of their response, a sense of a dreadful and mysterious entity known as "the bomb" or "the thing," which was so powerful it might even blow up the world. While they varied in how closely or strongly the bomb entered their fears, they had frequent dreams or fantasies of people and neighborhoods and cities destroyed by explosiosn and fires, with desperate efforts to reach the sanctuary of shelters or find family members—all of this often in the form of disjointed images of terror and destruction.

Then came the second phase, the disappearance of these

conscious images with little remembered awareness of the bomb. This phase was quite lasting, and could extend over much of childhood and adolescence, with of course great personal variation. Many people told Carey that they sensed they were supposed to avoid thinking about the bomb, that they sensed that their teachers, often their parents, and the culture in general did not want them to be troubled by it. If the subject did come up, it was often dealt with lightly—there might be talk, for instance, about sex play in the shelters and other good things. But even during this phase of sustained numbing, there could be frightening dreams related to the bomb. The more Carey probed the more evidence he found of imagery of extinction that was constant and close to the surface of the mind.

During the third phase, perhaps beginning in adolescence or early adult life, that imagery would periodically emerge in the form of conscious fear or nightmares of nuclear war, often in response either to a specific international scare or to more personal death equivalents (ordinary experiences of separation or loss, of stasis or entrapment, or of disintegration or "falling apart"). In this third or "normal adult" phase, periods of nuclear fear would alternate with numbness and absence of that fear. But whether people described themselves as *always* preoccupied with nuclear dangers, as *never* thinking about them, or as part of the in-between majority who think about them but only on occasion, all were subject to some of those fears, often in response to Carey's mere raising of the issue. The fears included the sense that one's own life and those of one's children could well end suddenly and violently; or else the more vague sense of living under a nuclear shadow, a sense that could not be equated with any particular life decision but just hung over one and would never quite go away.

Certain shared psychological themes emerge from Carey's study, themes that turn out to have significance far beyond the nuclear air-raid drills themselves. The first theme is the equation of death with grotesque, absurd annihilation. Just as these young people (often from the ages of five to ten) were struggling to absorb the concept that death is final—that one does not "lie down and wake up" as children (and not only children) often seek to believe—they were confronted with the idea of massive, meaningless extermination. They—we—are divested of our individual deaths, and at a cost. For our already troubled relationship to death (troubled because of impairment of many traditional symbols around living and dying) now becomes still more deformed. And that deformation around the anticipation of death inevitably extends to our relation to life.

A second theme is the sense that nothing can be depended on to last, that the threat of extinction renders life unmanageable. This "new ephemeralism" includes doubts about the lasting nature of anything and similar doubts about the authenticity of virtually all claims to achievement.

A third theme is the perception of craziness. The youngest school child was usually too intelligent to believe fully in what he was told. His memories are of a weird and strange constellation, including both the anticipated holocaust and the means of preparing for it. It was, at the very least, an introduction into radical absurdity, and that sense of absurdity—and its accompanying principle of mockery—were to manifest themselves vividly, and sometimes brilliantly, during the worldwide protest movements of the late 1960s and early 1970s.

A fourth theme was an unhealthy extension of the third—an identification with this weird, all-powerful device, with the bomb itself. One's own "craziness" joined that of the bomb, and fascination could extend to a wish that it be dropped so that one might witness this strange spectacle, experience the ultimate "nuclear high," and put an end to anxious wondering (and everything else, of course).

And a final theme, encompassing all the others, is that of the double life. The people Carey spoke to knew that everything—themselves, their families and friends and teachers, all that they had ever touched or known or loved—could be extinguished in a moment. Yet they and everyone else seemed to go about business as usual. To some extent they felt they had to; how else could they get through the day, pursue their lives, do what they had to do? But some sensed it was at a price, a price that had to do with the expansion of numbing to other areas of life, with gaps between what one knew and what one felt and did.

It is clear by now that these themes—Carey's findings in general—have relevance for all of us. The air-raid drills are metaphors for the nuclear age. We all go through sequences of nuclear terror, numbing, and periodic return of the terror. We all experience confusion between death and massive nuclear death, the new ephemeralism and unmanageability of life, as sense of nuclear-related craziness that sometimes can extend into dangerous forms of "nuclear madness." Above all, we all live a double life.

The relevance of Carey's findings to the subsequent generation has been confirmed by questionnaire research with adolescents performed by a special Task Force of the American Psychiatric Association. Reports by John Mack and William Beardslee[2] have movingly demonstrated that, during the late 1970s and early 1980s, children were aware early of nuclear dangers and retained fearful and confused images of nuclear devastation. For instance, in response to the question about what the word nuclear brings to mind:

Bombs, the world is nothing, completely wiped out.
Danger, death, sadness, corruption, explosion, cancer, chidren waste, bombs, pollution, terrible, terrible devaluing of human life.

The Bomb in Our Schools—and in Us

All that comes to mind is the world's final demise. A total kind of holocaust. The world will be killed by all nuclear devices. Also, I think of very dangerous unlimited energy.

In response to the question about the importance of nuclear weapons to national security:

The whole idea of nuclear weapons makes me shudder. They will only serve to wipe man off this planet. The bombs and nuclear warheads are only garbage. National security wouldn't be important if people had more understanding.

About surviving a nuclear attack:

I really don't think we could and even if some of us did, the side effects from it would be awful. Remember, there are still people today suffering from the affects of Hiroshima.

I think about that often. I really don't think they could survive one whereas I am so close to one. My city would be demolished and the country in big trouble. We really don't know. It hasn't happened yet. Let's hope and pray it doesn't.

And about thoughts on the future and general view of the world:

I don't really worry about it, but it's terrifying to think that the world may not be here in a half-hour. But I'm still going to live for now.

I think that, unless we do something about nuclear weapons, the world and the human race may not have much time left (corney, huh?)

I feel that everyone's views of the world and ideas of the future have changed somewhat. I feel that the future is very unsettled and a nuclear war could destroy the world in a short time.[3]

To be sure, there were other responses much less dire, and some even optimistic about nuclear advances, but the research leaves no doubt about the powerful psychological threat posed by the bombs, right now, to the capacity of adolescents—and the rest of us too, one must presume—to imagine a human future.

Adolescents with whom I conducted workshops on "living with the bomb" expressed themselves similarly. I was especially impressed with currents of hopelessness:

We feel ourselves to be doomed.

And of anger:

It makes me so angry when I think that these people [our political leaders] are making decisions that affect all of us. They don't even know what they are doing!

And (from a girl):

It makes me so mad—it's a masculine thing—competing with each other to see who's got the biggest bomb.

There will be more such research reports. At last people are getting interested in what the bombs are doing to us psychologically and spiritually. And that is a hopeful sign. Just as Carey did (and as the APA Task Force did to a certain extent), some of this work will inevitably focus on attitudes toward civil defense measures. For these reveal ultimate nuclear-weapons con-

The Bomb in Our Schools—and in Us

tradictions. Indeed, the kind of impulse we now encounter in the United States (in early 1982) to extend civil defense measures can be viewed as a desperate effort to shore up the vast nuclear weapons illusory system against its increasing exposure as such. It is as if our leaders are saying: Stop doubting us so much. We can, with our evacuation plans, remove you from danger. Our shelters can protect you. We are still all secure. But what is one to make of evacuation plans that include such details as postal arrangements for change of address and orderly instructions—odd-numbered license plates must wait for even-numbered ones to go first—for driving out of the bombed city? Or of the assurances of a leading civil defense official to the effect that we can fully recover from an all-out nuclear war with the Soviet Union in two to four years and "everybody's going to make it if there are enough shovels to go around" and "Dig a hole, cover it with a couple of doors and then throw three feet of dirt on top. It's the dirt that does it"[4]

Perhaps the main point to be made here is that projections of civil defense inevitably reveal the entire absurd system of nuclear weapons rationale—a kind of final common pathway of deception and delusion. As Admiral Noel A. Gayler, former commander of the American forces in the Pacific, has refreshingly commented: "Their civil defense program is a turkey, as they are beginning to realize." Those doubts can lead some people—some leaders—to cling to their "turkey" even more desperately.

In the process, these deadly absurdities seep through our psychological tissues. Questions arise among the young about adults' capacity to keep them, and the world, alive. Generational ties, depending as they do on a sense of the future, are further impaired. In different but parallel ways the young and the old become frightened, angry, confused. And we begin to see the truth of the contention that nothing in our lives is unaffected by these demonic technological entities.

But to look further at the bomb's impact on our mind and spirit, we need to examine the extremity of imagery and feeling they inevitably evoke in us.

CHAPTER 6

The Image of
Extinction

When I first heard that the United States had dropped an atomic bomb on a Japanese city, I reacted in a way I am not proud of. I remember telling a friend that, if a single American life were saved, dropping the bomb was the right thing to do. Then nineteen years old and a medical student, I wanted very much, like other Americans, for the war to end quickly in victory.

I find it painful to recall that sentiment now. But I do so not only to suggest the terrible nature of wartime acquiescence to mass killing but also the special difficulty in coming to terms with what was then a new image.

For with the two American atomic bombings in 1945 there came into the world a special image: that of exterminating ourselves as a species with our own technology. I certainly had no sense of that image at that moment. But I also remember reading a description of the bomb in the *New York Herald Tribune* the next day in which it was referred to as "weird, incredible and somehow disturbing," so that "one forgets the effect on Japan or on the course of the war as one senses the foundations of one's own universe trembling."[1] I had to begin to reexamine my initial callous naiveté—my own psychic numbing at the time—and I have been continuing with that self-examination ever since.

The image in question, really *imagery of extinction,* *has never taken on sharp contours for me. Rather than experience the ready psychic flow associated with most lively images, I must struggle amorphously to encompass the *idea* of violently attained nothingness. Further blurring occurs around the *process* by which this happens—and here the imagery contains scenes and description from Hiroshima, pictures of later thermonuclear explosions, consuming fire storms, decimated cities, and variable additional suggestions of total destruction. All of this, however, never fully coheres and never takes a clear place among the many more limited and specific images that regularly connect with my mind's continuing encounters with prosaic events and larger matters. Yet that image, amorphous though it may be, is never entirely absent from my ongoing mental activities.

To grasp something of the image we need to approach it a bit indirectly and to make a few comparisons. We know that religious images of the end of the world go back to the beginnings of history: for instance, images of Armageddon or "final judgment." These have undoubtedly been terrifying to many people, but they are part of a worldview or cosmology. Humankind is acted upon by a higher power who has his reasons, who

---

*Since my Hiroshima study in 1962, I have been exploring the psychological consequences of imagery of extinction. In 1964[2] I spoke of the "prospect of being severed from virtually all of our symbolic paths to immortality" and of the "potentially terminal revolution" in which we felt ourselves. In *The Broken Connection,* I explored more specifically some of the ramifications of imagery of extinction. And Jonathan Schell, in *The Fate of the Earth* has taken up that theme more recently from essentially a philosophical standpoint.[3]

destroys only for spiritual purposes, such as achieving "the kingdom of God." For the believer, terror is accompanied by a structure of meaning; there is a larger purpose and even an image of a future—again the kingdom of God.

Extinction by technology would seem to be from a different tradition. Technological prophets have envisioned this modern, secular version of the world's end from at least the time of the Industrial Revolution. This is the literary tradition of the "mad scientist" who either, like Frankenstein, creates world-destroying technological monster or else invents equally lethal "death rays" (this image predating but much influenced by the discovery of radiation).

Perhaps the greatest exemplar of this tradition was H. G. Wells, who not only projected technological world destruction, but invoked something he named the "atomic bomb" as the agent of that destruction. In his 1913 novel, *The World Set Free*, Wells describes a world war of the 1950s in which the world's great cities are destroyed, each by an individual atomic bomb the size of a bowling ball. Ironically enough, it was through reading H. G. Wells in the mid-1930s that Leo Szilard became convinced that actual atomic bombs could indeed be built.

But there is much more to the story. Wells himself had been greatly influenced by Frederick Soddy, collaborator on radioactivity studies with the great physicist Ernest Rutherford, and a man with sufficient vision to declare as early as 1903 that anyone who controlled nuclear energy "would possess a weapon by which he could destroy the earth if he chose." Wells, who had a background in science and had taught biology for a number of years, could fully grasp Soddy's ideas. So much so that in *The World Set Free,* he even described the radioactive chain reaction making possible the atomic bombs.[4]

Soddy himself, much earlier had also been deeply impressed by this Wells novel, which seemed to give greater reality to his own nuclear fear. Soddy's increasing concern about nuclear weapons, as well as his reaction to World War I and the death in battle of a friend and fellow scientist, caused him to change his life focus and devote his remaining years to social and economic studies on behalf of world peace. But when Szilard came to H. G. Wells, the nuclear chain reaction was not merely a scientific projection; it had been specifically identified and demonstrated. We may assume that Wells's images brought to awareness Szilard's already-existing preconscious knowledge that such a bomb was not only possible but imminently feasible. And from that moment on Szilard's life actions were dominated by that awareness: first in trying to prevent scientists from publishing findings that might lead to the making of a bomb; next by initiating (through a letter to President Roosevelt he convinced Einstein to sign) the American Manhattan Project, largely out of fear that if that were not done the Germans would produce one first; then, in his desperate efforts (with other scientists) to prevent the bomb from being dropped on a populated city without warning; and finally in his heroic post-World War II leadership of the scientists' movement to bring about nuclear disarmament.

In any case, the actual use of the weapons on the two Japanese cities gave substance to the image and disseminated it everywhere, making it the dubious psychic property of the common man and woman. Moreover, other events have contributed to imagery of extinction. Here I would include Nazi genocide during World War II; various nuclear accidents involving weapons (the coming apart of a bomb in Arkansas in 1980) or energy (Three Mile Island, in 1979); the idea of destroying the environment or its outer supports (the ozone layer); or of the depletion of the world's resources (especially food and energy). Nuclear weapons are simply the destructive edge of our technology gone wild in its distorted blend with science—or what Lewis Mumford calls the final apotheosis of the contemporary megamachine. But the weapons remain at the heart of our fear as the most extreme expression of that aberration.

Undoubtedly these technological versions draw upon emotions that went into earlier theological images. Or to put the matter another way, the technological version of the end of the world probably owes a great deal, imaginatively speaking, to its theological predecessor. Moreover, just as we have seen that literary and scientific versions influence one another in back-and-forth ways, the same can be said of theological and scientific image structures. In that sense traditions are not so distinct after all. (We will return to this merging of imagery in the discussion of "nuclear fundamentalism" in chapter 9.)

But there are several special features to this contemporary, technical end-of-the-world imagery. There is first the more specific suggestion of the end of our species, of something on the order of biological extinction. Second, it is related to specific external events of recent history, namely Hiroshima and Nagasaki, as well as the Nazi death camps. And third, unlike earlier imagery—even that associated with such external events as the plagues of the Middle Ages—the danger comes from our own hand, from man and his technology. The source is not God or nature but we ourselves. Our "end" is perceived as a form of self-destruct, and try as we may we are hard put to give it purpose or meaning.

What does such imagery do to us? Until recently psychological science had no reason to ask such a question. And now, when the *question* comes to haunt us no less than the end-of-the-world imagery itself, psychologists, like others, remain mostly silent. Yet there is every reason to believe that we are indeed affected by this imagery in ways that are both ambiguous and profound.

CHAPTER 7

A Way of Seeing

To discern the effects of the nuclear image, we need a sense of what to look for and how to look for it. We require a model or "paradigm"—an overall "controlling image" that sets the terms of investigation and provides a set of assumptions about human behavior around which to work. For instance, the controlling image of Freud's paradigm was that of instinct (mostly sexual, but also aggressive) and defense (mostly repression). But it is difficult indeed to apply this model—with its stress on demonic instinctual forces and intrapsychic efforts to stem and recast those forces—to the general question we have posed: that of the impact of imagery of extinction.

We need different emphases: upon image formation and symbolization that are in turn sensitive to historical process. And we need a focus on the relationship between death, or threat of death, and the continuity of life. The paradigm I have used in most of my work includes those emphases around the general principle (or controlling image) of symbolization of life and death.*

We can see how historical forces impinge upon not just what

*I would argue that Freud, in his later formulation of "life instincts" versus "death instincts," was moving toward the kind of paradigm I suggest. That is, he was establish-

we study but the assumptions and methods we make in going about our studies. For instance, Freud's focus on sexual repression had much to do with historical struggles around just that, which took such intense form during that late Victorian era. Similarly, our own focus on symbolization of life and death emerges from threats posed by our own history that have to do with the massive destruction of life and with fundamental disorders in our relationship to life and death.

The fact that we are creatures of our history in this way does not necessarily limit the relevance of our findings to a particular historical moment. Freud's observations on sex and neurosis have universal significance. And similarly, our own struggles to give psychological form to massive twentieth-century absurd death, actual or threatened, can also have more general significance for our understanding of human function. All the more so when we consider the neglect of life-death issues in most psychological theory, even when (as has been the case in the United States lately) focusing on aging, the dying patient, and other death-related matters.

To consider the significance of imagery of extinction we need a model that not only includes immediate everyday experience, as addressed in most psychological work, but also questions of larger human connectedness—of what Paul Tillich called "ultimate concern." This dimension has generally been left to philosophers and theologians, but I believe that it must be part of a scientific psychology as well.

In the paradigm I have been using, then, there is a proximate dimension, which includes issues of connection versus separation, movement versus stasis, and integrity versus disintegra-

---

ing a life-death context, though placing it within the instinctual idiom of his time. In this sense I would like to view my use of the more contemporary symbolizing idiom (much influenced by the work of Ernst Cassirer and Susanne Langer) as a form of continuity with Freud.[1]

tion. Each of these dualities proceeds from the physiological (on the issue of connection-separation, for instance, the newborn's innate tendency to seek out the mother) to image formation (the infant's developing capacity to recognize the mother) to increasingly elaborate symbolization (of love for, and attachment and loyalty to, various people and to ideas and principles). Similarly, earliest separation from the mother creates the basis in image and feeling for the idea of death, which begins to take shape, however primitively, during the second or third year of life.

There is also an ultimate dimension, involving the individual's broader human ties. I refer to a *sense* of immortality as part of the universal inner quest for continuous symbolic relationship to what has gone before and what will continue after our finite individual lives. This symbolization of immortality is by no means mere denial of death, though denial and numbing are rarely absent. Rather it is an appropriate symbolization of our biological and historical connectedness. And it draws on a psychoanalytic tradition more associated with Otto Rank than with Freud.

The sense of immortality can be expressed in five general modes. There is the biological (or biosocial) mode, the sense of living on through or *in* one's sons and daughters and their sons and daughters in an endless chain of biological attachment that can come to include group, tribe, organization, people, nation, or even species. A second mode is the theological, the idea of transcending death through spiritual attainment, whether or not it includes specific imagery about life after death. The third mode is the creative, the sense of living on in one's work or "works," whether notable artistic or scientific creations or more humble human influences. A fourth mode involves living on in nature itself, as part of the theme of "eternal nature" emphasized in all cultural traditions.

A Way of Seeing

A fifth mode, of a somewhat different order, depends solely on a psychic state, that of "experiential transcendence." It is a state so intense that time and death disappear. We recognize it as the classic state of the mystics, involving principles of ecstasy or "losing oneself," and can occur also in song, dance, battle, sexual love, childbirth, athletic effort, mechanical flight, or in the contemplation of artistic beauty of intellectual elegance. This state turns out to be especially important, because it is the means by which we experience our relationship to the other four states. Wildly or gently, one must psychologically travel outside oneself in order to feel one's participation in a larger human process. Here the ecstatic message may be no more than a momentary sense of inner unity or pleasure in wholeness, but it is nonetheless our source of awareness of larger connection.

All this has to do with what has been called "the ecology of infinity." And it is this larger psychic ecology, no less than immediate psychological struggles, that is threatened by imagery of extinction.

CHAPTER 8

A Break in the Human Chain

We now have a way of asking about the impact of imagery of extinction. Our question is this: In what way does this imagery affect our symbolization of larger connectedness—our *sense* of immortality? We are asking here about strains or breaks in the "great chain of being." That chain is, as we know, symbolic and psychic—its power for us is a function of our imagination. And in terms of our imagination, we are faced with nothing less than a *potentially terminal revolution.*

That is what Secretary of War Henry Stimson meant when he said (on May 31, 1945) that "this project [the making of the atomic bomb] should not be considered simply in terms of military weapons, but as a new relationship of man to the universe." And it is what Margaret Mead meant when, drawing upon a metaphor of Norbert Weiner's, she said: "The whole of human civilization can be compared to a vast explosive device, and almost any country or any segment of the population can trigger event sequences with spreading and disastrous consequences."[1] Mead articulates our deepending uneasiness about the purpose and future of human existence.

This psychological and symbolic predicament can be approached by means of the modes of larger human connectedness, or symbolic immortality, mentioned before, beginning with the biological mode. For if we anticipate the possibility of nuclear weapons being used—as I believe everyone in our society from about the age of five or six in some measure does—we can hardly be certain of descendants in whom to live on. From the standpoint of psychic impact, it does not matter much whether we imagine the end of *all* or merely *most* human life. Either way, we can no longer feel certain of biological posterity. We are in doubt about the future of *any* group—of one's family, geographical or ethnic confreres, people, or nation. The image is that of human history and human culture simply terminating. The idea of *any* human future becomes a matter of profound doubt. In that image we or perhaps our children are the last human beings. There is no one after us to leave anything to. We become cut off, collectively self-enclosed, something on the order of a vast remnant. The general human narrative would come to an end, and nothing in that narrative can justify to us or explain the reasons for that end.

This sense of radical futurelessness (to return to my original assumption about nuclear weapons impact) does not *in itself* cause any of our mental conflicts or aberrations but at the same time influences all of them and colors all that we experience.

The image of biological severance has ramifications in all directions. If we lose our future we question our past. That questioning may take the form of exaggerated, even desperate, hunger for roots or the seemingly opposite (but closely related) tendency to flee entirely from one's past in the equally desperate attempt to imagine a believable future. The fact is that we do not yet know how to evaluate the psychological consequences of this extraordinary image of biological extinction. But we must assume that every relationship along the great chain of being is in some degree affected. This specifically includes generational relationships, already existing and imagined, between parents and children, grandparents and grandchildren, and great-grandparents and great-grandchildren. But it also includes relationships between husbands and wives, lovers, and friends. Consider the radical new situation between parent and child. Undermined now in that relationship is the fundamental parental responsibility: that of "family security," seeing the child safely into some form of functional adulthood. The parent must now doubt his or her capability of doing just that. And the child must also sense, early on, the parental doubt and associate it with the overall inability of the adult world to guarantee the safety of children. (Indeed, we are already familiar with precisely those feelings as expressed in the Beardslee and Mack reports and in my own workshops with adolescents.) We have, then, beginning evidence of significant impairment to the overall parent-child bond and its balance between protection and love on the one hand and not just compliance but inner acceptance of authority on the other. With nuclear subversion of that authority, the ambivalence from both sides, always present in any case, can be expected to intensify and perhaps subvert feelings of love.

The marital relationship itself may well be threatened in another way. The long-term, indeed virtually permanent, committment traditionally associated with marriage becomes much harder to make in the face of uncertain biological continuity. The permanence of any relationship is thrown into question, and even more so the central function of marriage of providing a reliable institution for the rearing of children. As a result there could be greater reluctance to marry, increasing ambivalence among married people about the institution and what one gives up in its name, or an increasing need to maintain love relationships outside of marriage. It is possible, moreover, that these strains could be greatest in the United States, where expectations of marriage (around exclusive romantic love, companionship, and general togetherness) are highest. Imagery of extinction, then, could well contribute significantly to recent increases in such phenomena as divorce, experimental substitutes for marriage (people living together in different ways for varying lengths of time), modified marital arrangements and practices involving extramarital relationships, and the decision on the part of married couples not to have children.

These influences are likely to be subtle and indirect. We need not be in the habit of consciously connecting imagery of biological extinction with these various relationships, but that imagery may nonetheless hover around and within those relationships, so that all of them are perceived as tenuous, sometimes precious, but always vulnerable links on the human chain. A variety of already-existing conflicts may become further polarized. Decisions about family and future can take the negative direction already mentioned (why have children who are likely to be victims in a world facing destruction; better to pursue our own personal goals and pleasures) or one of exaggerated, uneasy "affirmation" (we need lots of children in order to try to insure the survival of *someone* in our family line). Or future parents may crave the benefits of genetic engineering— improving the genes of their offspring—in the hope, however irrational, that such an improvement will render progeny more able to survive the extinction that threatens.

The quest for new frontiers becomes a search for biosocial territory. Thus we plan "space colonies" and imagine them to be sanctuaries for our species after we have destroyed our own planet. While the original projection of the *idea* of space colonies may have had little to do with the threat we speak of, the colonies nonetheless become associated with our struggles to imagine life beyond nuclear holocaust.

Concerning the nuclear impact on the theological mode, I can draw upon a certain amount of experience with Hiroshima survivors. Many tried to invoke Buddhist principles, and others Shinto, Christian, or various spiritual combinations as evolved in postwar sects. But they consistently found that such religious imagery, conventional or otherwise, helped relatively little in their psychological struggles as survivors and rarely enabled them to give form or meaning to the experience. The magnitude of the experience seemed to defy the religious precepts that were accessible to them.

The general principle operating for them—and now for us— may well be that as death imagery comes to take the shape of total annihilation or extinction, religious symbolism becomes both more sought after and more inadequate. Certainly the issue of nuclear extermination has profoundly affected recent theological attitudes. One thinks of Paul Tillich's insistence that "the courage to be is rooted in the god who appears when God has disappeared in the anxiety of doubt"[2] And also of widespread imagery of the "death of God" and of spiritual crises of similar dimensions. Again, none of these developments can by any means be attributed only to the nuclear threat; and in none is the nuclear threat without great significance. (Nietzsche proclaimed the "death of God" during the late nineteenth century, but with post—World War II imagery of extinction the deity has been threatened with a new, more pervasive death—so much so that the wave of "religious revival" we encounter often takes the compensatory, fundamentalist direction we shall discuss in chapter 10.)

Since Hiroshima, religion has been faced with the perhaps

irresolvable contradiction of promising spiritual continuity beyond individual death in an imagined world with no one (or virtually no one) among the biologically living. In that contradiction—including the absurdity of spiritual claims in the face of absurd human extinction—lies the essence of the spiritual corrosion bound up with the existence of nuclear weapons. Once more the weapons tarnish and taint; spiritually they destroy and kill, even without being used.

Even more directly affected is the mode of work and works. The possibility of nuclear holocaust makes us doubt that anything we do or make will last. This is the new ephemeralism we have already mentioned. One could say that sensitive human beings have always viewed man's works as essentially ephemeral because they are destined to decay or be destroyed or be forgotten. But the new ephemeralism derives from an image of an active destructive force that, within moments, can annihilate *everything* along with everyone. To speak of the destruction of all of our works is to contemplate nothing less than the elimination of the substrate of what we call human culture.

That is, these physical elements of culture represent in our minds culture itself, the entire constellation of human works passed along from generation to generation. Hence what we anticipate is on the order of a reversal of the evolutionary process—a loss of our status as the only "cultural animal." We sense that survivors, should they exist, will be, by accepted evolutionary criteria, no longer human. Once more we are hard put to describe the exact consequences because the nature of the perceived threat outstrips our psychological imagination.

But we may look for these consequences in various realms of cultural creation. In the visual arts, for instance, we find increasing acceleration in shifts in styles and movements—from the radically nonrepresentational to the periodic return of the human figure, from action painting to pop art, to hard-edged art, to pattern and decoration, to kinetic art, to minimalism, to conceptual art, to photorealism. But more than that, some of the artists involved ask very specific, if poignant and sometimes desperate, questions about destruction and disappearance on the one hand and lasting impact on the other. The most literally relevant example here is that of the kinetic artist Jean Tingley's machine whose function was its own self-destruction—as displayed to a distinguished audience at the prestigious Museum of Modern Art in New York City. Here is the artistic rendition of man's general machine-age—and ultimately nuclear-weapons—dilemma.

In a related spirit is the work of some conceptual artists, their products specifically designed for their own gradual decomposition. An example here is Peter Hutchinson's placing his work under water and creating it of materials that will gradually be dissolved.

One might also mention Christa's wrapping of huge natural areas—including a segment of the Australian coast—with miles of cloth and canvas material. The material was eventually removed while the artistic events are recorded in photographs and books.

There are of course many influences that go into these tendencies—the struggle with historical change; financial manipulations on the part of dealers, artists, and art consumers; and much else. And the tendency toward shifting ways of seeing and painting had begun well before the appearance of nuclear weapons. But we may strongly suspect that the overall pattern has been radically accelerated by perceived threats to the very existence of human culture. Similarly, artistic questions about the ephemeral and the enduring are influenced by many things, including an impulse to subvert the commercial and materialistic cultural structures into which American art so readily enters. But once more we sense the importance of imagery of extinction. Thus one conceptual artist, Charles Simonds, creates "dwellings" for migratory "Little People" (perhaps the elf-leprechaun societies of the world), described by a leading art critic as "Tiny, quasi-primitive structures made of unfired clay bricks so small that they can be put in place only by using metal tweezers. Paint is then applied to these clay surfaces, and the look that is obviously aimed for is that of a ruin, or survival, of a lost, or at least a threatened, primitive civilization."[3]

Indeed one may recognize related uneasiness in attitudes toward work in general. I have in mind here the shifts from what was called the "hippie ethos" of the 1960s and early 1970s, in which most work was to be avoided as meaningless and unpleasurable, to the seemingly opposite attitude during the late 1970s and early 1980s of embracing the safest and best-paying jobs in society (a considerable run on the legal and medical professions, for instance). In both attitudes—and they are clearly related—there is a struggle around the psychic inroads of the new ephemeralism and a quest for either work or cultural substitutes for work that can suggest meaning, pleasure, lastingness.

Nature as the ultimate life source becomes equally problematic, and also in ways we have hardly learned to address. Consider Loren Eiseley's angry anticipation of "the evil man may do" as "not merely the evil of one tribe seeking to exterminate another . . . [but] the thought-out willingness to make the air unbreathable to neighboring innocent nations, and to poison in one's death throes, the very springs of life itself."[4] Eiseley here echoes the kind of image that was contained in the Hiroshima rumor mentioned earlier that vegetation would never again appear in that city and nature would dry up all together. But nature did not dry up; the continuing growth of wild "railroad grass" during the immediate postbomb days provided a source of food for some and an image of strength for others.

And the later spring buds, especially those of the March cherry blossoms, evoked what the mayor of the city called "a new feeling of relief and hope." A few survivors, in that spirit, quoted to me an ancient Japanese (originally Chinese) saying: "The state may collapse but the mountains and rivers remain."

Yet what Eiseley suggests—and what we must fear—is that the next nuclear bombs will make that Hiroshima rumor an actuality. In a very real sense, nature *would* dry up—would be extinguished along with its human species or would deny its life-giving nutriment so desperately sought by a band of human survivors rendered both pathetic and brutal.

Indeed, Lewis Mumford, noting how in the late 1960s many of the young were fleeing the cities and going back to the land, growing their food from it and reducing their existence to maximum simplicity and self-sufficiency, remarked that they seemed to be behaving as if the bomb had already been dropped.

As in other spheres, the bomb here further confounds an already problematic human struggle. We may say that, among animals, only man removes himself from nature in the way he lives while drawing upon nature not only for material but fundamental psychic needs. As the "cultural animal" and the "symbolizing animal," we struggle to assert *in our minds* our sense of continuing connection with what we know to be our source as a species. When the source itself is threatened with extinction, we react with intensity, though by no means always in the same fashion. On the one hand there are the young returning to the land and forming communes—not only because they may be anticipating the bomb's use (as Mumford claims) but because bomb imagery aggravates an already existing sense of pained separation from nature's *symbolic* fount, from crucial images of eternal nature. Yet at the same time (as of the end of 1981), an activist Secretary of the Interior brings literally devastating determination to dismantling the natural resources of the United States, to providing large blocks of formerly protected lands for exploitation by oil and gas companies. There is evidence, moreover, that his project is related to an apocalyptic sense, within the idiom of fundamentalist religion, that the world may soon end and that until that time his mission is to contribute as much as possible to maximum development of the resources of the United States. He too may well be impelled by a fear of the extinction of nature, leading in turn to a desperate race against time in drawing upon nature's life-giving elements.

And all the while the sustained destruction of nature by our poisonous industrial substances takes place before our eyes as a kind of prefiguring of a final, natural Armageddon.

We can understand the invoking of a powerful philosophical tradition—such as the one insisting that "the mountains and rivers remain"—to deny that threat, to assert nature's ultimate hegemony over nuclear weapons themselves. Mao Tse-tung did just that in a famous interview with Edgar Snow in 1965, describing how he went to the trouble of reading reports of an investigation of the effects of the hydrogen bomb tests conducted over the Bikini Islands in the South Pacific in 1953. Mao became nothing short of lyrical in describing how research workers in 1959 found "mice scampering about and fish swimming in the streams . . . foliage . . . flourishing, and birds . . . twittering in the trees" and the vegetation so thick they had to "cut paths through the undergrowth." While things might have been problematic for a year or two, Mao claimed, "nature had gone on."[5] But Mao was wrong. Nature had not quite gone on. Subsequent studies have revealed significant radiation effects among some of the people of the islands and lingering dangers from radiation still affecting the habitat. Mao here philosophically compounded the illusory findings of the original American investigators, so that he could conclude that "the atomic bomb was a paper tiger." But the truth that increasingly penetrates our consciousness is that everything else—including even nature—is a "paper tiger" in the jungle of nuclear destructiveness.

Destroying most or all of human life is, to say the least, an extreme transgression. But to destroy nature itself in the process is a still further transgression around which we experience a quality of dread, hidden guilt, and nothingness—these emotions frequently amorphous and beyond our grasp, but on the order of ultimate deadly sin.

The effect of imagery of extinction the fifth mode, that of the experience of transcendence, is bound to be of a somewhat different order. For as a state of mind per se, it does not depend on imagining the destruction of specific elements associated with the other modes (endless generations, creative influences, spiritual truth, nature itself). We find a tendency to seek this mode with special intensity when, during times of crisis, the other modes are threatened. And this is especially true when the threat is so extreme.

Hence the cultural hunger for "high states"—whether through rock music, literature, drugs, or meditation and other disciplines of the mind. To be sure, this is partly in response to the general unavailability—even suppression—of these states in advanced industrial culture. And there are of course great traditions from which today's experiential radicals can draw upon—from Abraham to Saul of Tarsus to St. John of the Cross, and from William Blake to Baudelaire to D. H. Lawrence to Wilhelm Reich. But the post-Hiroshima development, at least in the United States, takes on a new urgency and pervasiveness: in music (rock groups constantly upping the experiential ante), and in literary developments such as Norman Mailer's "hipster" of the 1950s (which he directly attributed to something close to imagery of extinction), the tones of the "beat generation," and the novels of Gunther Grass, Kurt Vonnegut, Thomas Pynchon, and William Burroughs (in which we find various combinations of high states and their muted opposites, the ethos of the survivor, and interplanetary visions). And in recent psychological work one may mention Abraham Maslow's stress on "peak experiences" and a variety of individual and group therapies in which these are sought, along with still more radical utopian visions of the diffuse (polymorphously perverse) sexuality of the infant, the "vision" of the schizophrenic, or the auditory and tactile sensuality of the dolphin.

These quests have varying creative and intellectual merit, but they all seek an experience of transcendence as an *alternative* to extinction. In the shadows, however, there lies a totally unredeemable image, that of the nuclear explosion itself as the ultimate "high state." How far this image extends, how it affects our mental processes, is difficult to say. Its presence in Carey's interviews with young adults suggest that it is fairly extensive in our society. And the apocalyptic ending of the film *Dr. Strangelove*, in which man rides bomb to its target while utttering a wild Texas yodel, both exemplifies and serves as a warning against this nuclear high.

I suspect that the image continues to haunt us. We have descriptions of the sense of awe and transcendent power and even beauty experienced by witnesses of bomb tests and by both perpetrators and victims of the two atomic bombings of cities. These provide glimmerings of—for some, enticements toward—experiencing the unexperiencible. In psychological terms that could mean overcoming one's imagery of extinction and radical futurelessness by means of what may be perceived as the only form of transcendence worthy of the age, that provided by the weapon itself.

We shall return to related questions when we discuss questions of fundamentalism, including nuclear fundamentalism. Here we do well to recognize one of the many ways in which a need created, or at least intensified, by imagery of extinction can in turn make that actual process of extinction more likely. So "flexible" is the human mind that it can, in this way, contemplate annihilation as a joyous event, more joyous than living with the sense of being meaninglessly doomed, that is, with the various impairments to human continuity that have been described.

It would be psychologically naive to dismiss these impairments as trivial or to assume that they do not affect character formation or the emerging sense of self. From early life, relationships between self and world take on a fundamental insecurity, within a context of confusion around the threat of death (including the already-mentioned merging of "plain old death" with grotesque, absurd death). Every attitude and human tie becomes colored by a constellation of doom, which includes, in varying degrees, fear, expectation, and embrace of that fate. There is widespread resort to psychological maneuvers designed to diminish feeling, but underneath that numbing are struggles with anger and rage along with every other kind of suppressed passion. Deep confusion and absence of meaning bedevil both one's emerging self-definition and one's larger aspirations toward human connection.

And all of these struggles become in some measure tainted by suppressed (or numbed) guilt and shame stemming from one's sense of being part of the potential act of mass murder. For Americans in particular, there can be an uneasy, resisted sense of lost innocence or worse. And this kind of self-condemnation, however unconscious, can be experienced by Americans who oppose nuclear weapons policies (the mass murder could, after all, be done in their names) or even in citizens of countries that do not possess the weapons (who, however amorphously, feel tainted by potential actions of fellow human beings).

This numbed guilt not only affects one's life in general but one's attitudes toward nuclear weapons in particular. For the guilt may be static and immobilizing, part of the resigned or cynical stance of "waiting for the bomb" described earlier. Or, if confronted, it may become animating, a stimulus toward imagining the real and taking constructive action (as shall be discussed in chapter 1). When that happens, the self calls upon more constructive elements within it that live side by side with the nuclear impairments we have described.

But before we get to these more hopeful possibilities, we need to spend a bit more time in the nuclear shadows.

CHAPTER 9

Nuclear Fundamentalism

We have been talking about the most vicious of vicious circles—the nuclear entrapment. By impairing our imagination of the future, the bombs enter into all the crevices of our existence. And at every point they diminish us, thereby making it still more difficult for us to confront the extraordinary threat they pose. And that assault on our humanity includes, as we know, an illusory sequence of devastating consequence. We feel the pain of loss of security, credibility, and stability; we embark on the literally impossible quest to regain these by stockpiling the very nuclear devices (along with accompanying secrets) responsible for their loss; and we are left with a still greater sense of vulnerability and insecurity, along with further decline in credibility and integrity. Moreover, that bomb-induced futurelessness becomes a psychological breeding ground for further nuclear illusion, which in turn perpetuates and expands current arrangements including bomb-induced futurelessness and so on. We sense that the cycle cannot continue indefinitely. Either we will do something to interrupt it, or we are likely to exterminate ourselves. For *everything* is at stake.

Nuclear Fundamentalism

It is the kind of situation that is bound to invoke desperate attempts to preserve something fundamental and to carry us into the righteous quicksands of *fundamentalism*. The term derives from an early twentieth-century American Protestant movement seeking to stem the liberal theological tide and re-state what was considered to be the fundamental doctrines of the Christian faith—the virgin birth, the physical resurrection of Christ, the infallibility of the Scriptures, the substitutional atonement, and the physical second coming of Christ. But the quest for the fundamental readily lapsed into a belligerently narrow form of totalism, in which literal readings of the Scriptures were called forth as absolute truths for all persons in all times, and as the basis for an ideology of reductionistic moral-ism that could provide answers to (really replace) the various dilemmas of the modern era.

The process is more general. Faced with the loss of funda-mental structures one has depended on in the past—of a reli-able spiritual or physical universe—one important response can be an exaggerated restatement of those threatened "fundamen-tals" that can readily lapse into the narrowist of fundamental-isms.

What, then, is the nature of this psychological sequence from the fundamental to fundamental*ism?* To be secure about fundamentals is to live within an intact framework of larger human connectedness, or what I have called symbolic immor-tality. In that state one believes in—or at least has no reason to question—the value and everlastingness of one's relation to the chain of generations, to work and works, to higher spiritual principles, to eternal nature, and to experiences of transcen-dence that directly affirm the intactness of one's psychological universe. When these ultimate—that is, fundamental—connections are profoundly threatened, confidence in the over-all continuity of life gives way to widespread death imagery, even to a collective sense of being inundated by death and nothingness.

There are many possible reactions to that state of death-dominated historical (or psychohistorical) dislocation, including the embrace of all-or-none idea systems and institutional structures (what I have called ideological totalism), in which there is a collective effort to reassert the endless life of a group (the "Thousand-Year Reich," for instance). Totalistic (or, in political terms, totalitarian) movements may then require victims to whom they can psychologically assign a death taint, that is, designate as lacking and being unworthy of the larger— fundamental—human connections of which we have spoken. That death taint serves to contrast and enhance the dominant group's own claim to symbolic immortality and to life power in general. This *dispensing of existence* may take the form of merely dishonoring those considered unworthy of it, but in more active forms of totalism it leads to mass murder.

Fundamentalism is a form of totalism with a very specific response to the loss of larger human connections. It is a doctrinal restatement of those connections in which literal, immutable words (rather than the original flow of vital images) are rendered sacred and made the center of a quest for collective revitalization.

Fundamentalist movements tend to be expansive in their projection of a promised future. American Protestant fundamentalism stems from millenarian movements of the nineteenth century—groups committing themselves to the "millennium" or thousand years of peace immediately following the bodily advent of Christ. The conviction stems from a biblical reading (Revelation, especially Chapter 20) that is not only literal but also dubious (as it leaves out the biblical qualification that only those who have been "beheaded for the testimony of Jesus" are to live in such a period).[1] Thus Nazi imagery of the Thousand-Year-Reich undoubtedly has Christian origins. In regard to the Chinese Communist slogan "May the Revolutionary Regime stay Red for ten thousand generations," there are sufficient millenial images in traditional Chinese writings, though Christian imagery could also have played a part. In any case, these thousand-year units serve primarily to project a sense of the eternal, of the doctrine's absolute permanence. (The Chinese image specifically suggests the biological mode—the ten thousand *generations*—which has had extraordinary emphasis in their traditional culture.)

Fundamentalist doctrine tends to invoke ancient images, to call forth a past (or past visions) of perfect harmony that never was. And even in the case of revolutionary fundamentalism—for instance, tendencies within Chinese communism or the still more radical communism of certain Japanese student and splinter groups—imagery of such a past plays a prominent, relatively unacknowledged role. (This has been pointed out by a number of writers on revolution, and I found it confirmed psychologically in interviews I conducted some time ago with Japanese student members of a purist communist group. In dreams and fantasies, nostalgic images of a beautifully harmonious past fused with those of a projected communist future.)

In the 1970s and 1980s we have witnessed nothing less than a worldwide outbreak of fundamentalism, some of it religious, some political, much of it both. In the United States we encounter extremist cults, or "new religions," which in many cases combine doctrinal fundamentalism (the doctrine mainly Christian, but sometimes mixed with Buddhist or Hindu elements); a charismatic leader who may claim messianic status; extreme manipulativeness from above together with genuine spiritual search from below, resulting in various forms of exploitation (often economic and sometimes sexual) of members; intense indoctrination procedures that can be applied deceptively and can have most of the characteristics of "coercive persuasion" or "thought reform" (or what is popularly but confusingly called "brainwashing"); and various forms of fanatical adherence to doctrine and practice, the most lethal of which was the mass suicide-murder of about 950 members of the "People's Temple" in Guyana in 1978.[2] Also prominent in this country are fundamentalist Christian groups that remain within established religious structures—mostly Protestant, but also Catholic and Jewish. And the fundamentalist religious impulse made bold entry into the political arena in the form of the Moral Majority, which, whatever the exaggeration inherent in its name, has found ways to channel fundamentalist religious impulses into radical-right politics by means of brilliant organizational use of computer-mailing technology. There are parallel movements in Europe and Asia, and in the Middle East we encounter the resurgence of fundamentalist religious and political mixtures in Arab countries, Iran, and Israel. In that area of the world we become particularly aware of the dangers posed by fundamentalist literality and absolutism, whether in the form of Moslem revival (including the Khomeini movement in Iran) or of Jewish "biblical politics."

When we look for causes of this epidemic, we must first point to the widespread experience of loss of fundamentals as a necessary prelude to their doctrinal embrace. Here we must postulate broad patterns of dislocation accompanying social change or pressures toward change, with enormous confusion surrounding basic symbolizations of religion, authority, education, and the rituals of the life process.*

*It is important to keep in mind that fundamentalism can be very varied in its form and style. American fundamentalists, as a close observer tells us, could be "backward looking and reactionary," "imaginative innovators," "militant and devisive," "warm and irenic," "ready to forsake the whole world over to a point of doctrine," "heedless of tradition in their zeal to win converts," "optimistic patriots," or "prophets shaking from their feet the dust of a doomed civilization."[3] Fundamentalism is one aspect of what I call the mode of restoration. Restorationists can be all of the above.

Nuclear Fundamentalism

The nuclear threat brings its apocalyptic aura to that confusion. Fundamental convictions, like everything else, are threatened with annihilation. And fundamentalism can be seen as an attempt to reverse that process in its own literalizing fashion. It is, among other things, an extreme response to the threat to the theological mode of symbolic immortality.

One reason for the greater success of fundamentalism, as compared to other responses, is the "high state" so often associated with it. Fundamentalist movements tend to offer the direct *experience* of transcendence, the moment of conversion to the true path as well as subsequent extensions and reenactments of that moment. Indeed, many young people have come to these movements directly from experiments with drugs or other forms of altered states of consciousness. That experience, moreover, is very much shared, and there are few more powerful emotions than those around the shared experience of transcendence.

Fundamentalist religious movements can go still further in integrating their doctrine, however crudely, with the apocalyptic nuclear event. They may do this by invoking Old Testament imagery of Armageddon and view nuclear extinction as God's punishment of humankind for its sins. The nuclear event may then even be welcomed as necessary or even cleansing. Or by means of another reading of Armageddon, these groups may claim that their followers alone represent the camp of the

---

They can at times use their invocation of an idealized personal and collective past to try to stop or reverse the flow of history; but they can also employ the same imagery in combination with new historical influences as a means of absorbing the latter and enhancing historical change. The Meiji Restoration in late nineteenth-century Japan was both a genuine restoration (of ancient emperor-centered images and values) and a means of achieving something close to a revolution (the absorption of overwhelmingly powerful and painful Western influences).

"good" and will therefore be the sole survivors in the destruction of "evil."*

In the United States in particular, fundamentalist cults have formed specifically around the anticipated nuclear event, which provides them with a concrete focus for their millenarian impulses. And we can also classify as fundamentalist various nonreligious "survivalists," groups whose main function is to provide "training" for that event, training that will ostensibly enable members to survive. Much of their activity revolves around collecting and mastering guns and other weapons, as if to form a circle of power and violence to counter the greater power and violence expected.

In these various fundamentalist patterns we encounter a failure to distinguish between mind and its material products. Technological (nuclear) devices threaten, and mental states are called forth. Mental activities are devoted to subsuming the threat to a more or less removed or solopsistic thought structure, rather than to countering the threat in some fashion. I call this tendency *psychism,* by which I mean the one-sided focus upon intrapsychic purity at the expense of extrapsychic reality.[4] The psychism may be directly related to nuclear weapons in ways just mentioned, or it may follow the more general fundamentalist pattern of substituting biblical images for actual scientific observations. A case in point is the extraordinary reappearance in the United States of the biblical version of the creation of the world as an antagonist to Darwinian principles

*Fundamentalist end-of-the-world imagery has been attributed by some to our approaching the year 2000: that is, to a "millennium" of our Christian historical calendar. It is pointed out that there was a parallel outbreak of millenarian fever at the time of the year 1000, with the appearance of many end-of-the-world cults and doctrines. Given the mind's ingenuity in combining images, it is quite possible that this millennial threshold of the year 2000 contributes additional impetus to the tendency we are discussing. But the context for any such influence is the already existing technology-related imagery of extinction with which we are familiar. *That* is the psychological baseline upon which images from this significant historical transition must operate.

of evolution. Here one of the most fundamental of all human questions is answered by fundamentalist doctrine that flies in the face of an overwhelming array of scientific evidence. And now, in the 1980s, that doctrine elevates itself to the claim of a "creationist science" demanding equal time in our schools with "evolutionary science." That last maneuver can be called political (a way of getting around the American principle of separation of church and state), but it is essentially ideological. And it is, of course, an ultimate form of psychism, whose appearance now is part of the nuclear-related apocalyptic atmosphere I have been describing.

Yet precisely because they depend on this pattern of psychism, fundamentalisms in our time are likely to be tenuous. They are prone to waves of intensity followed by decline and dishonor. For they maintain a fragile equilibrium between their intense mental states and the transcendent psychological satisfaction of those states on the one hand, and the claims of historical actuality on the other. But if they recede, they do not disappear. If they are tenuous, they are also recurrent, since the historical conditions producing them may diminish but do not disappear. And in an age of potential nuclear genocide, we may expect these waves of fundamentalism to become relatively permanent manifestations of our collective experience.

But we are in grave difficulty if that is also true of the most corrupt and dangerous of all fundamentalisms, that focused on the nuclear devices themselves. I have in mind here the condition of *nuclearism*: the embrace of the bomb as a new "fundamental," as a source of "salvation" and a way of restoring our lost sense of immortality.

However appalling, perhaps the phenomenon should not surprise us. Consider a description of the first atomic bomb text explosion:

Thirty seconds after the explosion came, first, the air blast pressing hard against the people and things, to be followed almost immediately by the strong, sustained, awesome roar which warned of doomsday and made us feel that we puny things were blasphemous to dare tamper with the forces heretofore reserved to The Almighty. Words are inadequate tools for the job of acquainting those not present with the physical, mental and psychological effects. It had to be witnessed to be realized.

Undoubtedly the chaplain speaking, one assumes. But these were in fact the words of a tough brigadier general and engineer, Thomas F. Farrell.[5] A regular army officer who had been Chief Engineer of the State of New York, Farrell was the deputy of General Leslie R. Groves, who commanded the Manhattan Project from which the bomb emerged. (Nor did his reaction signify opposition to the bomb's use. As coordinator of military arrangements on the Pacific island of Tinian, where the airplanes carrying the bombs were based, Farrell refused to delay the second atomic bomb mission—to Nagasaki, it turned out—despite the fact that the plane carrying the bomb was discovered to have a defective fuel pump and had to take off with a combination of less than a full fuel supply and extra fuel weight.) Rather Farrell quite naturally associated to biblical imagery of "doomsday" and "blasphemy" that he was undoubtedly exposed to from childhood. "Doomsday," we recall, is the moment of the "Last Judgment" (or "Judgment Day") accompanying Christ's Second Coming—precisely the millennarian imagery so central to the development of Christian fundamentalism.

What Farrell said in the same passage, just before the portion already quoted, is also instructive:

The effects could well be called unprecedented, magnificent, beautiful, stupendous and terrifying. No man-made phenomenon of such tremendous power had ever occurred before. The lighting effects beggared description. The whole country was lighted by a searing light with the intensity many times that of the midday sun. It was golden, purple, violet, gray and blue. It lighted every peak, crevasse and ridge of the nearby mountain range with a clarity and beauty that cannot be described but must be seen to be imagined. It was that beauty the great poets dream about but describe most poorly and inadequately.

Here is an experience of absolute awe—of an event of indescribable beauty and of a dimension that was staggering. Scientists present at the same test had similar sentiments: "The sun can't hold a candle to it!" "This was the nearest thing to doomsday one can possibly imagine," and Oppenehimer's famous association to the words of the Bhagavad-Gita, "If the radiance of a thousand suns/Were to burst at once into the sky/That would be like the splendor of the Mighty-One . . ./I am become Death/The shatterer of worlds." These expressions of apocalyptic witness, of end-of-the-world imagery, resembled William James's descriptions of religious conversion. James spoke of the "fear of the universe" as experienced by the "sick soul" as part of his religious conversion. And James's quotation from Tolstoy—"I felt . . . that something had broken within me on which my life had always rested, that I had nothing left to hold onto, and that morally my life had stopped"[6] is reminiscent of the post-Hiroshima comment in the *New York Herald Tribune* quoted earlier describing the new force as "weird, incredible and somehow disturbing" so that "one forgets the effect on Japan or on the course of the war as one senses the foundations of one's own universe trembling."

Men experiencing such an awesome event were likely to convert to *something*, to take on a survivor mission of some kind. And many did—either the mission of warning the world about the danger of this extraordinary new power, or the opposite mission of embracing that new power as something close to a deity.

An extreme expression of nuclearism was that of William Lawrence, one of the most prominent science writers of his day. Long interested in atomic questions, Lawrence was the man chosen to be the official early spokesman on bomb matters and official journalistic eyewitness on the Nagasaki mission. His descriptions of the Alamogordo test included such phrases as "mighty thunder," "great silence," as well as repeated images of rebirth: "One felt as though he had been privileged to witness the Birth of the World" and "the first cry of a newborn world." And in response to the reaction of the scientist George Kistiakowsky to the effect that "in the last millisecond of the earth's existence—the last man will see something very similar to what we have," Lawrence suggested the alternative possibility that "If the first man could have been present at the moment of Creation when God said, 'Let there be Light,' he might have seen something very similar to what we have seen." We sense Lawrence to be a man who has experienced nothing less than a "conversion in the desert".

And in a later sequence describing the test explosion of an airborn hydrogen bomb in the northern Pacific in 1956, Lawrence's nuclearism becomes full blown: There is a sequence from awesome beauty associated with annihilation, including the annihilation of one's own cities ("I was momentarily staggered by the thought of what the fireball and mushroom I was then watching would do to any of the world's great cities— New York, Washington, Chicago, Paris, London, Rome or Moscow"), to total security ("the dawn of a new era in which any sizeable war had become impossible. . . . this world-covering, protective umbrella . . . shielding us everywhere. . . . an effective substitute for war"), to salvation (". . . mankind . . . harnessing the vast power of the hydrogen in the world's oceans to bring in an era of prosperity such as the world has never dared dream about").[7] The deity is awesome in its destructiveness but is also the savior of humankind—a deity to be embraced and worshipped. Indeed, one comes to depend on the nuclear deity not only to keep safe and prosperous but to keep the world going.

Edward Teller is a still more extreme exemplar of nuclearism. With Teller we may speak of a nuclearistic constellation of attitudes, each blending with the others and part of the whole. There is the insistence that we must be prepared for nuclear war; that we can fight and win a nuclear war and "save perhaps 90% of our people." There is the assumption (in the illusory scenarios mentioned earlier) that nuclear weapons, properly employed (within limits), can help us to win small wars, stop Communist revolutions, and maintain beneficent American power and the American way of life. There is, therefore, strong advocacy of a very extensive shelter-building program and of other means of "preparing" for nuclear war. There is the association with the heroic history of scientific search for truth, so that Teller can equate any restraint on work on the hydrogen bomb as being "unfaithful to the tradition of Western civilization," and insist that "my *scientific duty* demanded exploration of . . . [the] possibility" of making it. There is a combination of polarized imagery of American virtue and Soviet evil with commitment to maintaining the ever-destabilizing absurdities of the arms race (Teller himself calls it "an Alice-in-Wonderland world") *ad infinitum.*

Above all, there must be no *restrictions* on the deity: "We cannot and must not try to limit the use of weapons." There is then recourse to extraordinary psychologizing, referring to fears of nuclear annihilation as "a monstrous anxiety" (by which Teller means inappropriate and extremely harmful, though it is possible that at some unconscious level he also recognizes the "monstrousness" of the source and experience of the anxiety). Teller similarly equates reservations about nuclear weapons with "fears of improbable and fantastic calamities," departures from "rational behavior" and "courage," "seek[ing] refuge in a make-believe world," and "the eclipse of the American dream." (These are among the most extreme examples we encounter anywhere of equating appropriate psychological responses, especially the warning signals of anxiety and fear, with irrationality; and of the advocating measures that actually increase dangers as a means of overcoming that anxiety and fear.) Even more remarkable is his denial, against all evidence, of fallout danger. He speaks contemputously of the "fallout scare" and goes on to make quite a remarkable statement even when placed among the absurdities of the nuclear weapons literature in general:

Radiation from test fallout is very small. Its effect on human beings is so little that if it exists at all, it cannot be measured. Radiation from test fallout might be slightly harmful to humans. It might be slightly beneficial. It might have no effect at all.

And finally there is the inevitable nuclearistic deliverance—lyrical descriptions of a utopian future, under such chapter headings as "The Renaissance of Alchemy," "The Lure of Infinity," and "The Seeds of Tomorrow."[8]

Teller's nuclearism has been unusually intense and, unfortunately, influential. And his identification with a weapon, the hydrogen bomb, has been uniquely personal—so much so that he has frequently been referred to as its "father," and sometimes by his colleagues (with perhaps greater psychological accuracy than they realized) as its "apostle." But he is still only one example of a far-reaching and highly malignant problem.

Robert Oppenheimer, who suffered for his opposition to the

development of the "Super," or a large hydrogen bomb, also underwent an earlier stage of nuclearism. He too developed a personal identification with the weapon, in his case the early atomic bomb; so much so that he discouraged circulation at Los Alamos of an early scientists' petition (initiated in Chicago) asking that the president hold back use of the atomic bomb on a populated city. After the war he continued to take an active consultant's role in weapons development at a time when many of his colleagues were embarking on a mission of warning their countrymen about the dangers of precisely such an arms race. In applying his extraordinary intellectual and personal gifts to coordinating the entire Los Alamos project, Oppenheimer, according to one biographer, "always believed he had a higher purpose than to beat the Germans," and that the bomb would "shake mankind free from parochialism and war."[9] But when he emerged from nuclearism (in confronting another man's bomb) he became a brilliant critic of precisely that cast of mind. He wrote "What concerns me is really not the technical problem . . . but that we become committed to it as the way to save the country and the peace appears to me full of danger."[10]

Even Leo Szilard, one of the few authentic scientist-heroes of the antibomb movement, was not free of nuclearism. We know him as the man who initiated American interest in the making of the bomb (fearing with good reason that the Germans might do so first) and who, from the time of the first scientists' petition, was a leading voice in opposing it. But recently it has become known that in 1944 he became impatient with the slow progress in producing the bomb, because he feared that unless bombs were used in the war and their destructive power demonstrated, the American public would not be ready to make the sacrifices (including rigid control of all uranium and thorium deposits) necessary to keep the peace.[11]

And nuclearism has been all too extensive in diplomacy, often taking the form of seeking direct negotiating achievements, mostly with the Soviet Union, around possession of the bomb. (I choose American examples because they are well documented, but they certainly exist for other countries as well.) James Byrnes (American Secretary of State during the latter part of the war and afterward) considered the weapon as one that "might well put us in a position to dictate our own terms at the end of the war" and disturbed one of his colleagues by the "attitude that the atomic bomb assured ultimate success in negotiations." For Byrnes and other high-ranking American statesmen (including President Harry Truman and Secretary of War Henry Stimson) as well as for leading scientists and science administrators involved in making the bomb:

not only the conclusion of the war but the organization of an acceptable peace seemed to depend . . . on the success of the atomic attack against Japan. Secret development of this terrible weapon, during the war fought for total victory, created a logic of its own: a quest for a total solution to a set of related problems that appeared incapable of being resolved incrementally.[12]

That tendency has continued to this day. It reached a certain apotheosis under the Eisenhower-Dulles policy of "massive retaliation." According to that policy, should the Soviets cross a certain line anywhere in the world, but particularly in the form of an incursion into Western Europe, the United States would immediately initiate a full nuclear attack. In this form of nuclearism, or "nuclear diplomacy," there was an important double dimension: its *economic* appeal (the nuclear weapons requried, expensive as they were, cost much less than alternative conventional military preparations in the form of a large and well-equipped standing army) and the *moral-psychological* juxtaposition of "total power" (American) to attack "total evil" (Soviet communism). Subsequent nuclear weapons policies, while sometimes less candid, have maintained the fundamental illusion of diplomatic-military nuclearism: that we could depend upon the weapons—the deities—to prevent the nuclear war we deeply fear, to enable us to win that war and thrive as a moral society, or in the absence of war to gain political and military goals that otherwise elude us.

Nuclearism, then, is the ultimate fundamentalism of our time. The "fundamentals" sacrilized are perverse products of technicism and scientism—the worship of technique and science in ways that preclude their human use and block their true intellectual reach. Those all too understandable but no less dangerous tendencies were reflected in Robert Oppenheimer's comment that "It is my judgment in these things that when you see something that is technically sweet, you go ahead and do it, and you argue about what to do about it only after you have had your technical success"[13] More than that, we seek in the dazzling performances of technology and science a replacement for something missing in our individual and collective lives. We invoke the illusions of the "bomber gap" or "missile gap" in order to fill the meaning gap. In what may be the ultimate human irony, we seek in a technology of annihilation a source of vitality, of sustained human connectedness or symbolic immortality. At the heart of this illusory structure is our struggle for a sense of power, which in the end turns out to be power over that ultimate adversary. The conquest of death—the restoring of youth to the aged—is after all a central goal of premodern alchemy. And that vision of conquest has never disappeared from the human mind. We are not surprised to find William Lawrence evoking the large principle within which nuclearism operates, as expressed in the words of a doctor-pharmacologist: "Medicine today is accomplishing greater

miracles than, for example, atomic-energy developments . . .
because . . . we have conscientiously evolved a technique and
a scientific philosophy that finally enables us to wrestle with
death itself, and on increasingly even terms."[14]

There is one more important point to be made about the
fundamentalist religion of nuclearism. It has to do with the
way men, at or near retirement, renounce precisely the nuclearistic structure so central to their entire professional lives.
A striking recent example was Admiral Hyman B. Rickover,
generally characterized as "the father of America's nuclear
navy," who when forced to retire in early 1982 at the age of
eighty-one declared that both nuclear weapons and nuclear
power should be outlawed. He further declared that these
weapons would probably be used in a future war because history showed that nations employ whatever weapons are at
hand; that "I think we'll probably destroy ourselves"; and that
"I'm not proud of the part I played."[15]

We immediately think back to President Eisenhower's celebrated Farewell Address of 1961, in which he warned against
"the acquisition of unwarranted influence . . . by the military-
industrial complex" and "the potential for the disastrous rise
of misplaced power."[16] Eisenhower feared that this "misplaced power" would lead to exaggerated weapons building and
greater danger of nuclear war. Yet it was under the Eisenhower
Administration that the military-industrial complex took on its
menacing shape, that hydrogen bomb–centered nuclear weapons systems were vastly expanded around a doctrine of dominant air power and extreme nuclearism ("massive retaliation").

It turns out that on leaving the presidency not only Eisenhower but others, notably Jimmy Carter, expressed similar
warnings against the danger of nuclear war. Yet it was during

the Carter Administration that the doctrine of limited nuclear war became official.

We think also of Oppenheimer's turnabout from his insistence that "his" atomic bomb be used to his later opposition to the larger or "Super" hydrogen bombs of the next nuclear weapons generation, for which not he but Edward Teller was primarily responsible. And William Lawrence, the science writer who waxed so poetically about both of the first two generations of weapons, not only opposed but was appalled by what was perceived as a third generation in the form of the neutron bomb. During early discussions of that development, Lawrence called the propsoed new weapon both "highly inefficient" and "a highly immoral weapon, a poison gas abhorrent to civilized humanity, a monster that rather than kill would, in the current nuclear jargon, 'juice its victims' " so that many would "linger on to a horrible death after days, weeks, or months of infernal torture." And he spoke of the need for "spiritual regeneration . . . . Not 'juicing'."[17]

Finally, there is the example of the man most responsible for the original decision to drop the bomb, then Secretary of War Henry Stimson. A man with a sensitive conscience who referred privately to the weapon as "the dreadful," "the awful," and "the diabolical," Stimson arranged to have available to him a subordinate whose task was mainly to listen to his pained concerns about the weapon. Yet Stimson never waivered in his determination that the bomb be used, and he arranged committee deliberations in a way that this was a foregone conclusion. Among his last acts before leaving office, however, was a memorandum about the bomb in which he described it as "merely a first step in a control by man over the forces of nature too revolutionary and dangerous to fit into the old concepts," spoke of "the race between man's growing technical power for destructiveness and his psychological power for self-control and group control—his moral power," and urged that we "enter an arrangement with the Russians, the general purpose of which would be to control and limit the use of the atomic bomb as an instrument of war . . ."[18]

All of these are examples of what I call "nuclear backsliding"—a retreat from, and often a condemnation of, that contemporary religion of power that had so held one in thrall. In the past I have explained this process in relation to the release of death guilt to which one had previously remained numbed, and that indeed is a central component. But now I would stress the release from a whole constellation of man-weapon nuclearistic emotions with which those closely involved with the bombs become bound. These emotions include consuming dependency on the weapons for carrying out what one perceives to be one's duty in maintaining national power, and eventually for one's more personal sense of life power as well. Provided with a measure of distance, either because the new weapons system is primarily the responsibility of someone else or one is close to retirement from public office, one can extricate oneself from relying on the weapon for one's own vitality and larger connectedness or symbolic immortality. And one then can convey, often with eloquence and passion, truths about the weapons learned from the inside. But we no longer have time for the sequence ending in this nuclear backsliding or "nuclear retirement syndrome". And indeed, what we learn from it helps us to confront more directly the original disease, that of nuclearism.

An immediate lesson here is that the possession of nuclear weapons tends to create a pattern of nuclearism that pervades a country's overall bureaucratic structure. One need not be a Teller or a Kahn or pre-retirement Rickover to live and act within nuclearistic assumptions; merely being part of a ranking military or political group tends to entrap one within that man-weapons constellation. One's nuclearism, moreover, may be passionate (like Teller's) or expressed more quietly in the language of the technocrat. In either case nuclearism becomes combined with psychic numbing, with diminished feeling toward others. And it is to that general impediment that we must now turn.

CHAPTER 10

On Numbing and Feeling

We are always much less than we could be. We have moments of high intellect or of passionate emotion, but seem limited in our capacity to sustain optimal combinations of the two.

Diminished feeling, in one sense, begins with the structure and function of the human brain. Neurophysiologists make clear that the brain serves as much to keep out stimuli as it does to receive them. In other words, our brain is so constructed as to limit what we can eventually feel, lest it be so overwhelmed as to lose its capacity to organize or to respond at all.

For as human beings we must do considerable psychic work in connection with anything we take in. That is, we perceive nothing nakedly but must re-create anything we encounter by means of our marvelous and vulnerable cerebral cortex. If we can speak of anything as *human* nature, it is this symbolizing principle as such. Hence I speak of a "formative process," the constant creation and re-creation of images and forms that constitutes human mentation. Much of this process takes place outside of awareness, or is what we call "unconscious." But it is the existence of this formative-symbolizing tendency that makes possible the wonders of our imagination on the one hand, and our psychological disturbances and destructive impulses on the other.

Here too psychic and physical survival require a balance between feeling and not feeling. And that balance can readily go out of kilter, causing us to feel either too much or too little. Indeed, our contemporary nuclear threat not only contributes to upsetting that balance but raises questions about just what kind of balance between feeling and numbing is desirable or possible.

In Hiroshima, people I interviewed told me how, when the bomb fell, they were aware of people dying around them in horrible ways but that, within minutes or even seconds, they simply ceased to feel. They said such things as "I simply became insensitive to human death," or referred to a "paralysis of the mind." I came to call this general process psychic numbing and, in its most acute form, psychic closing-off. For survivors it was a necessary defense mechanism, since they could not have experienced full emotions in response to such scenes and remained sane. The numbing entailed derealization of what was actually happening along such inner psychological sequences as: "If I feel nothing, then death is not taking place," or "then I cannot be threatened by the death all around me," or "then I am not responsible for you or your death."

As useful to them as it was at the time, the numbing process did not necessarily end when the immediate danger was over. It would continue over weeks, months, or even years, and become associated with apathy, withdrawal, depression, despair, or a kind of survivor half-life with highly diminished

101

capacity for pleasure, joy, or intense feelings in general.

Observing victims, I began to wonder about the numbing that must take place in those who make, test, or anticipate the use of nuclear weapons. For potential perpetrators simply cannot afford to imagine what really happens to people at the other end of the weapon.

This was true of American scientists constructing the first atomic bombs at Los Alamos in New Mexico. Responding to the call to win the race against an evil enemy to construct a decisive weapon, then after the defeat of Germany still seeing themselves as contributing to their country's wartime military struggle and intent upon succeeding in what had been an extraordinarily dedicated collective effort and on confirming that the thing would really *work*, "they were frantically busy and extremely security conscious and . . . there was even some half-conscious closing of the mind to anything but the fact that they were trying desperately to produce a device which would end the war . . ."[1] And so powerful was their scientific leadership that almost everyone else at Los Alamos "let Oppenheimer take protective custody of their emotions."

Moral questions were raised only by a few scientists from the Chicago group when they had essentially completed their work on the project. But their reflections were informed precisely by a beginning capacity to imagine and feel what might occur at the other end of the weapon. Eugene Rabinowitch, five years later, recalled how "In the summer of 1945, some of us walked the streets of Chicago vividly imagining the sky suddenly lit by a giant fireball, the steel skeletons of skyscrapers bending into grotesque shapes and their masonry raining into the streets below, until a great cloud of dust arose and settled over the crumbling city."[2] And he goes on to say that "From this vision arose the weak and inadequate attempts that groups of scientists made to stop the hands of the clock before it struck the first hour of the atomic age."

Nuclear scientists had experienced such images long before that.

Standing around the first nuclear fire lit under the West Stands of the athletic field of the University of Chicago in December 1942 and, two-and-a-half years later in July 1945, watching the flash of the first atomic bomb explosion at Alamogordo, the scientists had a vision of terrible clarity. They saw the cities of the world, including their own, going up in flames and falling into dust.

But once they embarked on making the bomb, once the numbing had set in, that kind of vision was in most cases suppressed. And subsequently, over decades, there was the psychological process of "learning to live with the bomb," which scientists came to share with political and military leaders along with the rest of us; specific forms of numbing evolved that blocked out what happened at the other end of nuclear weapons and enabled one to get on with things.

What I am calling psychic numbing includes a number of classical psychoanalytic defense mechanisms: repression, suppression, isolation, denial, undoing, reaction formation, and projection, among others. But these defense mechanisms overlap greatly around the issue of feeling and not feeling. With that issue so central to our time, we do well to devote to it a single overall category, which we can observe operating in different ways and under different conditions in virtually any individual mind.

Psychic numbing has to do with exclusion, most specifically exclusion of feeling. That exclusion can occur in two ways. There is first the blocking of images, or of feelings associated with certain images, because they are too painful or unacceptable. The second is absence of images, the lack of prior experience in relation to an event. We have difficulty imagining nuclear holocaust or responding with feeling to the idea of it happening, because we have virtually no prior images that readily connect with it. In either case—and the two patterns are likely to coexist—the formative process is affected. Indeed, just as the defense mechanisms are part of Freud's model of instinct and defense, so may we view the concept of psychic numbing as a part of the model of symbolization of life and death. When numbing occurs, the symbolizing process—the flow and re-creation of images and forms—is interrupted. And in its extreme varieties, numbing itself becomes a symbolic death: One freezes in the manner of certain animals facing danger, becomes as if dead in order to prevent actual physical or psychic death. But all too frequently the inner death of numbing has dubious value to the organism. And it may itself become a source of grave danger.

We may thus speak, very generally, of three levels of numbing: the numbing of massive death immersion; the numbing of enhancement; and the numbing of everyday life. The first, the numbing of massive death immersion, is epitomized by Hiroshima and Nagasaki. The "paralysis of the mind" already mentioned involves a radical dissociation of the mind from its own earlier modes of response—from constellations of pain and pleasure, love and loss, and general capacity for fellow feeling built up over a human lifetime. We may, indeed, speak of the mind being severed from its own forms. When that happens, psychic action—mental process in general—more or less shuts down. There are in-between states in which limited forms of planning and action (flight or rescue of family members) can occur, even though feelings are largely blunted.

The numbing of enhancement is of the opposite variety. Here feeling is diminished in some spheres of the mind in order to make possible more accomplished behavior or more intense feeling in other spheres. One can point to the selective professional numbing of the surgeon, who cannot afford to feel the consequences of failure. Or to that of the painter or musician, who block out a great variety of influences in order to enhance and intensify the image or the musical phrase.

Finally, there is the problematic category of the numbing of everyday life. Here we may say that the ordinary brain function of keeping out stimuli becomes strained by the image overload characteristic of our time. Apart from nuclear weapons, the mass-media revolution creates the unique situation in which virtually any image from anywhere on the globe, and indeed from any point in our historical or cultural past, becomes available to any individual at any moment. This historically new situation contributes to a contemporary psychological style of perpetual experimentation and increasing capacity for shifts from one kind of involvement (with people, ideas, ways of living) to another. I speak of this as the Protean style, after the talented but unsteady Greek sea god who was a notorious shape-shifter and could readily change into virtually any natural, animal, or human form, but who had great difficulty holding on to a functional form of his own.

Our current image overload, moreover, comes at a time of considerable loss of confidence in traditional symbols and forms as discussed in chapter 9 in connection with a sense of historical dislocation. That sense also contributes importantly to the pain and possibilities of the Protean style. It deprives us of the channels of feeling that had existed around earlier rituals and symbols. We then grasp at the extraordinary array of images available to us, seeking to recover significant forms of feeling. But our successes are spasmodic, and we run the risk of diffusion and unconnectedness, potential sources of further numbing.

These tendencies, moreover, are furthered by other sources of social distancing: various forms of high technology (which keep us from more direct experience); large-scale bureaucratic hierarchies (which confuse and defuse questiosn of responsibility and blame, and certainly of feeling and not feeling); ideological assumptions (about the American way of life or Soviet communism, about friends and enemies); racial or other kinds of human variation (one is less sensitive to the needs of people who are distinct and separate from oneself); and, of course, any threats emanating from a society prone to violence (such as our own) or to terror and suppression on the part of the state (such as the Soviet Union).

Nuclear numbing arrives, so to speak, on this psychological soil. And when people are deeply uneasy about what and how much to feel, the specific call to feel what happens on the other end of a nuclear weapon is not a very inviting one. A more compelling call to feel may be experienced around the sense of power and allegedly increased security offered in connection with more advanced and sophisticated (both bigger and smaller) nuclear weapons. Further, we *domesticate* these weapons in our language and attitudes. Rather than feel their malignant actuality, we render them benign. In calling them "nukes," for instance, we render them small and "cute," something on the order of a household pet. That tendency was explicit in the naming of the two atomic bombs dropped on Japanese cities—the first "Little Boy" suggesting a newborn baby or small child, the second "Fat Man" after Winston Churchill. (So universal is the bomb-related impulse toward numbing that even Japanese survivors domesticated their bomb by referring to it with the not-unpleasant-sounding term *pikadon*, or "flash-boom.")

Many have commented on the anesthetizing quality of the language of nuclear weapons, sometimes referred to as "nukespeak." What are we to make of terms like "nuclear exchange," "escalation," "nuclear yield," "counterforce," "megatons," or of "window of vulnerability" or (ostensibly much better) "window of opportunity." Quite simply, *these words provide a way of talking about nuclear weapons without really talking about them.* In them we find nothing about billions of human beings incinerated or literally melted, nothing about millions of corpses. Rather, the weapons come to seem ordinary and manageable or even mildly pleasant (a "nuclear exchange" sounds something like mutual gift-giving).

Now, much of this domesticated language is intentionally orchestrated by military or political bomb managers who are concerned that we stay numbed in relation to the weapons. But it is a process in which others collude, so that we may speak of a more or less spontaneous conspiracy of linguistic detoxification that contributes to the comfort of just about everyone. Part of the linguistic conspiracy involves technical distancing—an American Secretary of State, for instance, avoiding painful issues by referring to the existence of "quantitative and qualitative questions" and to "an exceedingly complex process."

This pattern of numbing via technicization has extensive cultural roots. But the "nuclear experts" serve a special function here, something on the order of hired anesthetists. They contribute to the numbing by further technicizing everything, by excluding human victims from their scenarios, and by conveying the sense that nuclear matters are completely under control because they are in the hands of experts. Not only are the rest of us excluded from matters presumably beyond our technical capacities, but we tend to collude in our own exclusion as a way of retreating to the resignation-cynicism-waiting-for-the-bomb-axis.

The truth is that we have found no language, and perhaps there is none, to express the destructiveness, evil, and absurdity of the nuclear devices. The problem existed for Hiroshima and especially for survivors of that first bomb. One wrote: "There exist no words in any human language which can comfort guinea pigs who do not know the cause of their death."[3] Here the writer refers both to the dead and to other survivors who (as nuclear "guinea pigs") fear ambiguous but deadly symptoms of radiation effects or "A-bomb disease." A few survivors emphasized the term "nothingness" as coming closest to what was needed. One suggested that the atomic bomb be commemorated by leaving a completely empty area around the place where the bomb struck Hiroshima, a representation of "nothingness at the hypocenter—because that is what there was" and because "Such a weapon has the power to make everything into nothing." In a similar spirit, a colleague recently suggested to me that we speak no longer of nuclear war but only of the "nuclear end" or "ending."[4] Even when determined to imagine and feel as strongly as possible images of past and potential atrocity, we experience barriers in doing so. There is a real question about how much ultimate atrocity the human mind is capable of taking in and absorbing—to which our tentative answer must be: much less than the full narrative, but considerably more than we have.

We may speak, then, of a historical or even evolutionary paradox: The degree of numbing of everyday life necessary for individual comfort is at odds with the degree of tension, or even anxiety, that must accompany the nuclear awareness necessary for collective survival.

We have many reasons, then, for avoiding a holier-than-thou

On Numbing and Feeling

(or more feeling-than-thou) attitude toward psychic numbing. For one thing, no one, psychologically speaking, can live in the realm of nuclear weapons all the time. Even those who are preoccupied with the problem find themselves slipping in and out of it, and for the most part they are relieved (though sometimes they feel guilty) about that being the case. And however great one's involvement with these matters, there are moments in which one suddenly realizes that one has been blocking out important nuclear truths that others have confronted more directly.

More personally, I referred earlier to my discovery in Hiroshima that, seventeen years after the event, no one had studied its general human effects, but I must note here my own previous resistance to the city. Although I had first gone to Japan in 1952 (as an air force psychiatrist in response to the medical draft of that time) and had spent more than two-and-one-half years in Japan (about half in the military and half in connection with a study of Japanese youth), it was not until my second long stay was drawing to a close in 1962 that I first visited Hiroshima. And I did so then because I thought I should take a look at the city, having begun to be concerned about nuclear dangers through participating in the early academic peace movement at Harvard during the late 1950s. (I suspect now that a part of me anticipated the possibility of doing a psychological study there, but even then I seemed to have to complete the other, less threatening work first.) When I began to talk to various people in Hiroshima about working there, I felt encouraged by their responses and enthusiastic about proceeding. But from the first moment I began to conduct actual interviews with survivors, everything was different. Now the bomb seemed right there with us, virtually in the room. I felt myself overwhelmed and frightened by the detailed, grotesque descriptions of specific atomic bomb experiences, by the very descriptions I sought from the people I talked to. I was staying in a Japanese inn alone at the time, my wife and infant son not having yet joined me from Kyoto where we had been living. For a few days I felt anxious, and at night slept fitfully and had disturbing dreams. I began to ask myself whether I should abandon the study and leave Hiroshima.

But then, quite suddenly, my anxiety seemed to recede as I found myself listening carefully during the interviews for psychological patterns in survivors' descriptions. In other words, I had begun to carry out my professional task, with the aid of the selective professional numbing I have mentioned in connection with surgeons. Without some such numbing I would have been incapable of doing the work. And it is also true that I hardly ceased to feel the pain altogether in what I was hearing. Nonetheless, it was a form of numbing, and I go back to that experience whenever I try to sort out the never fully resolvable struggles of professionals and others around how much to feel. Since then I have frequently become aware of situations in which I used various psychological maneuvers to distance myself from precisely the nuclear weapons threat with which I have been so consistently concerned.

In response to nuclear weapons, numbing is all too easy, widespread, and "natural" for just about everyone. But in saying that, and in depicting these various forms of numbing— indeed, in exploring our mind's dilemmas around nuclear weapons—we are doing something that only human beings can do. We are reflecting on ourselves and our situation in the service of greater awareness. And in that awareness, even just its beginning, lies our hope.

CHAPTER 11

Imagining the Real

"What story are we in?" asks John Dunne, the contemporary theologian. Our story is our personal and historical destiny. It is "what happens to us and what we become." Do we have any choices concerning the narrative and its outcome?

Our story, to be sure, concerns death and the continuity of life—the plea, echoed by Yeats: "O Lord, let something remain!" But even more than that, it is a story of the human imagination.

People frequently ask me whether I think a nuclear war will actually occur, whether we have a chance of averting such a catastrophe. My answer is always that the issue is undecided. It depends on what we human beings do. The odds are probably against us. But the weapons are a product of human imagination, and human imagination is capable of getting rid of them. At the heart of the matter than is our struggle for awareness. But what would that awareness consist of? The original meaning of the word has to do with vigilance, with being watchful, prepared for danger. Here awareness is related to words like wary, beware, and guard. But in current usage, awareness tends to be associated with perception, sensation and sensibility, with knowledge, consciousness, and realization. It may also suggest the most advanced capacity, in psychological terms, for understanding and insight; or in spiritual terms, for illumination. Awareness, then, involves the full work and play of the imagination. It means imagining danger that is real, but also imagining possibilities beyond that danger, forms of thought and action beyond immediate assumptions.

The kind of awareness we are discussing applies directly to these nuclear weapons issues but is inevitably concerned with the rest of psychological experience as well at both immediate and ultimate levels. One becomes aware (from the standpoint of the model we have been using) of experiences (and anticipated possibilities) of connection, movement, and integrity, no less than those of separation, stasis, and disintegration. One is also aware of one's relationship to the endless continuity of human life and to the products of collective imagination we speak of as human culture. We include here *self-*awareness as well as *shared* awareness, and these become associated with feelings of vitality and of larger connectedness and transcendence. Understood this way, awareness is an ideal state claiming the full human organism in maximum effort and realization. We know (from the discussion of everyday numbing, for instance) that we are limited in our capacity for sustaining a state of awareness. Our goal, then, is a matter of degree, a closer approach to achieving and sustaining that state. The goal is extremely demanding, plausible, and in fact newly visible.

Nuclear awareness has certain specific requirements. It means breaking out of the illusory system we have described, renouncing the illusions of limit and control, of the benefits of foreknowledge, of preparation, protection, stoic behavior of survivors, and recovery. It also means extricating ourselves from our deadly dependence on and worship of the weapons, extricating ourselves from nuclearism. The process is psychologically difficult in the extreme because our relationship to both nuclear illusions and nuclearism has had the quality of an addiction. Addiction is always a life-death pattern. That is, one's emotions become so invested in one's relationship (or "connection") to a particular object that all vitality and attachment— one's existence itself—are at stake in that relationship. In the language of addiction, nuclearism and nuclear illusions are the "nuclear connection." Never has that connection been more malignant; nor has it ever been more under critical scrutiny. While one can feel the attraction of a "cold turkey" (immediate, total cessation of the use of the "drug") cure, a more gradual, incremental approach is undoubtedly more practical.

The key to nuclear "withdrawal" is a radical revision of our concept of security. Once identified as deficient, the thermostat has to be set right. The psychological sense of security must be made consonant with our physical-historical situation. That sense of individual safety is ultimately inseparable from the actuality of human security. And our resulting image of security reverses prior assumptions. We can *feel* and *be* safe only when the weapons are decreased rather than increased; security requires not nuclearization but *de*nuclearization, and in the end not militarization but *de*militarization. The reversal is radical, and yet we are close to precisely that awareness.*

The process I am describing does not require fundamental

---

*Part of the awareness must include anticipation of possible responses from those in power. They too would be subject to a change in consciousness, and that possibility must be ardently pursued. But they could also react with a resurgence of nuclearism all the more primitive because of its gnawing disbelief in itself. They could then take steps to repress the new awareness, whether by attempting to dishonor, threaten, or otherwise undermine those who become associated with it, or by further control of information and manipulation of media. In this way our society could become dangerously divided into antagonistic camps embracing and rejecting precisely this awareness. For that reason its dissemination needs to be as broad and encompassing as we can make it, so that rather than further divide, the awareness can serve to unify disparate groups within our society.

change in our psychological makeup, in what we call "human nature." An increase in awareness does not eliminate fundamental conflicts, whether one understands these to take place around instinct and defense (as Freud did) or around symbolization and meaning (as suggested in our paradigm). In either case, there are irreducible struggles over the course of the life cycle involving dependency and autonomy, identity and sexuality, death and death equivalents; with experience of guilt, shame, and anxiety; and with anger, rage, and violence. Nor will one, even with increased awareness, automatically become a completely moral human being. This gain in awareness is feasible precisely because it is no more than a *partial* personal change. Our symbolizing model enables us to understand that kind of change as both psychologically limited and profoundly significant.

An example of that kind of highly significant partial personal change was the experience of many Vietnam veterans. Upon returning from Vietnam, over a period of months or even weeks, some of them underwent dramatic transformations in their attitude toward the war, in their general worldview, in their immediate relationships and feelings around maleness, and in their sense of personal and collective future. They clearly retained much of their original character structure, but they nevertheless underwent profound and lasting change.[1] Crucial to that change were a confrontation with unacceptable forms of death and a vision of alternative possibility. In our present imbroglio with nuclear weapons, we are confronted with the first and summoned by the second.

There is a very compelling basis for nuclear awareness. Put most simply, it is that of *shared fate.* At the most primal individual level—involving especially Americans and Soviets—the message could not be more primal: *If I die, you die; if you survive, I survive.* And equally, if you are destroyed as a nation, so are we; if our country survives, so does yours. The psychology is not unlike that of terrorist and hostage, with the major nuclear powers playing both roles and the rest of the world merely the role of the hostage. In cases of airplane hijacking or other forms of hostage taking, observors have been surprised by the extent to which hostages have identified with their captors. One important reason for this is the sense of shared fate inherent in such situations. Hostages and terrorists live, at least for a while, in a kind of limbo, recognizing that a frontal assault from the outside would probably result in everyone's death, and that as long as that assault is not forthcoming and hostages are not killed by terrorists, everyone survives. I am suggesting that everyone on earth is now in some measure subject to the logic of the hostage and the aura of nuclear terror.

But unlike ordinary hostage taking, nuclear terror encompasses everyone. Precisely for that reason it throws us back on our *collective* humanity. In calling into question the idea of a human future, it raises equally ultimate questions about our evolutionary equipment for shaping that threatened future. Here I would stress three interrelated characteristics of our evolutionary emergence as human beings: our knowledge that we die, our symbolizing nature (we have no other way to function mentally as adults), and our status as the "cultural animal" (the animal who must create culture in order to live). Each of those attributes takes on special importance now.

Knowing that we die means knowing that we can kill others or ourselves, that we are capable of murder and suicide. This knowledge has been made use of repeatedly for both, and at every level from individual acts of self-destruction or murder to their grotesque combination in the mass exercises of killing and dying we call modern war. Yet contained in the knowledge that we die is the imaginative possibility of reclaiming "plain old death" and distinguishing it from grotesque nuclear universal murder-suicide. To do that we require two imaginative acts: deepening our acceptance of individual death and picturing the "dead universe" of nuclear war.*Recognizing that we have confused the two is a first step toward reestablishing the distinction. There is in fact a widespread movement in consciousness toward a realization that, yes, we each must die, but we need not die in an absurd nuclear "end."

Being inveterate symbolizers is also a source of special possibility. It means that we constantly create and re-create images and meanings, and press toward new or modified interpretations of the world. We therefore need not be bound by our nuclear illusions and addictions, need not maintain our malignantly deceptive constellation of "security." Above all, as symbolizers we have a psychobiological impulse toward imagining the future. As Lionel Tiger has put it, "It would indeed not be unreasonable to suppose that the origin of 'mind' is coincident with and related to the origin of the future as a phenomenon.[2]" In that sense nuclear weapons threaten the mind's symbolizing process at its biological core. But the mind presses for release from that impairment, seeking to reestablish its crucial future-imagining function. In struggling to imagine a nonnuclear future we sense that the *immediate* existence of the mind is at stake. And that same symbolizing function enables us to bring endless combinations of ideas and images to that task. The abnormal phase has been the sustained numbing that has interfered with that symbolizing function, and we are beginning to see evidence of its reappearance—evidence of our imaginative power in confronting the threat.

That power is inherently collective. Imagination is bound up with cultural sharing. Indeed, as Clifford Geertz tells us, "The human nervous system relies, inescapably, on the accessi-

*The appendix , "The Effects of Nuclear War on the Mind" is offered as a specific contribution to imagining that "dead universe."

bility of public symbolic structures to build up its own autonomous, ongoing pattern of activity." And this imaginative sharing in culture is fundamental to being human: "Culture, rather than being added on, so to speak, to a finished or virtually finished animal, was ingredient, and centrally ingredient, in the production of that animal"[3] namely man. The search for the necessary "public symbolic structures" for our emergence from nuclearism is again inherent in our evolutionary organism.

There can be little doubt about our evolutionary impasse: We will either come close to ending the whole process or else make the necessary forward-moving adaptations to keep it going. We may see ourselves as a bit like early *Homo sapiens*, struggling to find ritual and to express in crudely profound cave drawings our fears about individual and collective death as well as our efforts to become part of something eternal. But as in the case of those forebears, we have extraordinary mental equipment for the task, equipment we are only beginning to mobilize on behalf of the partial but significant individual and collective change required for survival.

The change is well underway. We have reached the point of at least *fragmentary awareness,* based mainly upon increasing consciousness of actual danger, of the possibility of extinction. The movement is toward what we might call *formed awareness,* awareness that *in* forms our sense of self and world, that affects our actions and our lives and is part of and evolving pattern of illumination and commitment. People ask, Why now? Why is this movement toward awareness suddenly so strong? The question is an important one and not entirely answerable. The usual reasons given include the fear generated by increasing talk of nuclear war by our leaders, the heating up of political confrontations between the United States and the Soviet Union, the influence of the European antinuclear weapons movement, and the increasing skepticism about government policies and claims as a result of the Vietnam and Watergate experiences.

All of these factors seem to me significant, but I suspect that underlying them is something still more fundamental. Here one must turn the question around and ask, Why has this beginning awareness taken so long? Why has it taken more than thirty-five years since the appearance of the weapons in the world for us to begin to develop a widely shared awareness of their danger and of possibilities for doing something about them? Perhaps the answer has to do with the minds' eventual rebellion against distorting processes to which it has been subjected. As the weapons systems have proliferated and people sense that we closely approach a "doomsday machine" (the fact that a single submarine from either of the nuclear superpowers can destroy the other as a functional power comes close enough), the numbing, the illusory mental structures, and the nuclearism no longer suffice to keep out the fearful truth. And at that point the other influences (loose talk of limited nuclear war, political confrontations, and skepticism about official claims) have increasing impact. If this explanation has any merit, we may assume that the process is not easily reversible. We are in the midst of a phenomenon of release from psychological bondage, and whatever its ebbs and flows, there is unlikely to be a full reinstatement of numbing and illusion.

We are talking about crossing threshholds, and the principle applies to individual transformations one can already observe. In order to relinquish a stance of immobilization—or the various combinations of resignation, cynicism, and waiting for the bomb described earlier—each person seems to have to cross a certain line, on the other side of which is some degree of commitment in one's life toward combatting the nuclear threat. There are many ways to cross that line, but it is worth mentioning a few of the psychological elements involved.

In many cases there appears to be an extraordinary impact made upon people simply by new information—for instance, the clear statement by physicians of the full medical consequences of nuclear war. What actually happens is that this seemingly new information makes contact with amorphous, menacing fears that had been suppressed by the numbing process. Now these fears are named, and images that have the ring of truth are presented forthrightly; however grim the images, the effect is liberating. The menace one has known but kept hidden comes, so to speak, out of the closet and into the open. And there is a beginning sense that one might just possibly be able to do something about it.

As always in matters of collective change, the process is enhanced by models and leaders. They provide an important source of identification: the sense that he or she, in the face of the same overwhelming threat, has found not just a means of countering that threat but an honorable way of living. Leaders and models perhaps always display a certain amount of human vulnerability, but in this case the leader's vulnerability is a particularly intense part of the equation. The leader embraces nuclear weapons vulnerability as a way of emphasizing its universality, as well as conveying the possibility of both accepting and transcending that vulnerability.

In these ways the person crossing the antinuclear threshhold experiences very quickly a new sense of shared power—a vision, almost inchoate at first, of the possibility that, by joining together in a struggle, people can alter the situation and gain control over their deaths and their lives. And here the message is the traditional one that leaders and heroes have shared with their followers—a message of death and rebirth, of distinguishing between necessary and unacceptable forms of death and thereby reasserting and illuminating the immortal chain of human life.

We begin to sense why, for many, there are moments of exultation in this movement toward awareness. That exultation has to do with a new sense of integrity—or of the possibility of integrity—in one's relationship between self and world. No longer bound by nuclear distortions only half believed, one's world seems to open out into new personal options. One may experience a rush of energy toward connecting with like-minded people, assimilating the new perspective, and in one way or another acting upon it. In the process one may shed several forms of self-condemnation bordering on guilt and shame. One need no longer struggle against self-critical feelings around complete inactivity in response to nuclear threat. Rather one takes on an animating relationship to that self-condemnation, as one moves from amorphous guilt or shame toward responsibility.

One renounces the role of the victim, perhaps most characteristically described by images around that humble laboratory animal, the guinea pig. In Hiroshima people invoked this image again and again, and always with anger. Most immediately they felt themselves made into guinea pigs by being asked to participate in an elaborate research project, conducted by doctors from the country that had dropped the bomb, investigating the possible long-range medical effects of their having been exposed to that bomb. But more fundamentally that guinea-pig image had to do with their sense (mentioned earlier) that an extraordinary weapon whose effects had been unknown was "tried out" on them. That sense seemed understandable in the face of their ordeal. But years later that nuclear guinea-pig image was to appear closer to home. In the late 1970s it was used by people who had been exposed to radiation dangers in the area of the first large-scale American nuclear-energy accident at Three Mile Island, and also by people in Nevada and Utah who had been exposed to nuclear weapons tests during the 1950s and were learning of increased incidence of leukemia and cancer among them. A woman whose son had died of leukemia invoked that imagery with telling bitterness: "We were forgotten guinea pigs. At least real guinea pigs are checked." And European antinuclear demonstrators have carried signs declaring their refusal to be American or Soviet "guinea pigs," in the sense of being the "theater" for an "experimental" conflict between the nuclear superpowers.

Psychologically, the image suggests not only being treated as an expendable subhuman—a laboratory animal—but being exposed to an invisible poison by experimenters who are both powerful and ignorant of the consequences of their experiments. The image includes being passive and helpless in the extreme, and devoid of human worth (not even worth hating, since one is a victim of detached technical inquiry as a form of numbed violence). Moreover, something of the image is experienced by *everyone* as soon as he or she begins to acknowledge nuclear actualities. One can only cease to feel oneself a passive guinea-pig victim by rejecting the global experimental death-trap of the nuclear weapons system. One is again an active human being, a creature of worth who rejects deadly experiment, however uncertain the outcome of one's antinuclear efforts.

One also renounces any association with perpetrators of nuclear death. Here too there is release from amorphous discomfort bordering on self-condemnation, having to do with the bombs being built and possibly used by one's countrymen, and in one's name. In the case of Americans, this discomfort could also connect with residual uneasiness (again bordering on guilt) around our being the first and so far the only country to use the weapons on human populations.

We see, then, that the exultation we speak of in association with crossing the line to antinuclear commitment has to do with extricating oneself from massive nuclear versions of the two roles Camus warned us never to assume, those of victim and executioner, as well as from the role of the immobilized bystander who, in this nuclear context, takes on aspects of both.

Now allied to life-enhancing projects, one's sense of self-worth improves. And in beginning to imagine a world free of nuclear weapons, one can more readily imagine a human future. One may feel oneself suffused with that most valuable of spiritual commodities, a sense of hope.

To be sure, that initial exultation can quickly recede. It can even give way, as one faces the difficulties of the antinuclear task, to emotions of anger, depression, and despair—to what is sometimes spoken of an antinuclear "burnout." In any case one can hardly expect the exultation to be sustained. But the general sense of joining an honorable antinuclear community *is* sustained, as is the sense of the enrichment of one's own life.

In all this we must avoid static models and anticipate the possibility of continuing collective change. Moreover, there is much to suggest that certain kinds of shifts in cultural consciousness can occur more rapidly than is generally assumed. For instance, Edmund Leach, in discussing the relationship between individual symbols and the "public symbols" of a culture, points out that recent developments in certain cultures "owe their emergence to the innovative acts of individuals rather than to the unanalysed processes of historical accident or cultural diffusion, which are commonly held to account for cultural change."[4]

In fact we are in considerable ignorance about how significant changes in human consciousness come about. We see many examples of prolonged gaps in awareness, of human groups all too slow to recognize what they need to do to extricate themselves from a threatening predicament. But we also know that relatively sudden shifts in collective awareness are possible, as initiated by prophetic individuals or relatively small groups of people. Indeed that may be the case right now in regard to the nuclear weapons threat. At this point we can speak of something on the order of a turn toward awareness, much as we recently spoke, during the latter phases of the Vietnam War, of a turn toward peace. But this general turn toward awareness is by no means decisive as yet. Nor is it anything on the order of an automatic "greening" process. Rather it requires, and will continue to require, painful struggle on all levels of existence.

In all this our historical and evolutionary adaptation become virtually inseparable from ethical achievement. Surviving equates with behaving well—at least on a collective level. This recognition in itself can contribute to the always-tenuous human capacity for collective decency—at least sufficiently to overcome numbed genocidal indecency. Thomas Merton, in a discussion of collective Danish commitment to their own humanity in saving Jews from Nazi mass murder, concludes: "Such action becomes possible when fundamental truths are taken seriously."[5] For us those fundamental truths converge in what I have been calling imagining the real. To do that, as many are, means accepting the pain of actuality—since, as Merton also states, "the worst insanity is to be totally without anxiety, totally 'sane.' "

Something like this combination of pragmatic need and shared pain on behalf of decency has probably always accompanied significant ethical advances. Slavery could be abandoned by most societies over the course of the latter part of the eighteenth and first half of the nineteenth centuries because it had become increasingly unprofitable (with industrialization) and in various ways harmful and problematic to the society—*and* because of an increasingly shared moral aversion to it accompanying an awareness of what it did to actual human beings. These pragmatic and moral elements were inseparable, each contributing to and helping to articulate awareness of the other. And similar combinations probably have prevailed in less decisive advances, such as the end of traditional forms of nineteenth- and twentieth-century European imperialism; and, in the matter of weapons, the general restraint, since World War I, on the use of poison gas. In suggesting these developments, I make no claim of a quantum leap in human virtue. The point is quite the reverse—namely that a reasonable mix of necessity and virtue is within the demonstrated capability of human beings on something approaching a universal level. In the case of nuclear weapons, that would be enough.

One senses now a worldwide hunger for nuclear truth. One senses that hunger, for instance, in response to the doctors' movement—now strong not only in the United States but throughout Western Europe, the Soviet Union, and part of Eastern Europe. Certainly in this country one becomes aware of the eagerness of audiences to be told, accurately and systematically, the bad news about nuclear weapons—along with the good news that one can become part of a worldwide struggle to get rid of the weapons. Indeed one can sense that hunger in people everywhere—in students at universities and secondary schools, and in their elders throughout our society. In psychological terms also, pragmatic considerations enhance potential decency: Numbing ceases to work, more people become emboldened to articulate and receive the painful message and to reflect on the morality of extinguishing ourselves as a civilization, as a species. And those reflections take intense form at a time of unprecedented worldwide communication. Any constructive nuclear idea—any movement forward in awareness, slight or dramatic—is immediately available everywhere. And everywhere the quest is for real, not bogus, security; for life, not massive murder-suicide.

And we are beginning to suspect that the struggle to get rid of the weapons ties in with the most profound collective values. If we address these problems seriously, with reasoned thought and appropriate passion, we find ourselves recovering certain qualities we had very nearly lost. Physicians become more genuine healers; universities become true centers of learning, inhabited by genuine teachers and students. We become more genuine professionals, more genuine working people, attuned to the central dilemma of our time.

And strangely enough—or perhaps not so strangely—other things happen to us as well. While confronting massive death is irreducibly grim, we find ourselves more in touch with what we care most about in life—with love, sensuality, creative realization, and the capacity for life projects that have meaning and satisfaction for us. We find ourselves in no way on a death trip, but rather responding to a call for personal and professional actions and commitments on behalf of that wondrous and fragile entity we know as human life.

Section II

Political Anatomy of Nuclearism

Richard Falk

CHAPTER 12

Taking Stands

To write about nuclear weapons is inevitably to adopt a cause. It is partly a matter of urgency. More than rhetoric is implied when we speak about a mounting condition of emergency: either we lift the curse of nuclearism in the next decade or the human prospect is likely to be decisively shattered.

It is also a matter of integrity. To pretend dispassion is to mask a commitment at some level of consciousness to a continued reliance on these infernal weapons of mass destruction. At the very least, to adopt a tone of rationality is to gloss over the quintessentially absurd reality of contemplating the use of apocalyptic weaponry for the sake of the secular state based upon a rushed decision by poorly qualified politicians and generals. In an encounter with absurdity there is an elemental necessity to acknowledge this core reality as honestly as possible. Our proper enterprise as "thinkers" is to mount a struggle against the nuclear menace, not a mindless struggle but a struggle where our contemplative understanding is enlivened and guided by a passionate commitment to the hard work of securing the full set of conditions for our survival as a people, as a species, and as mental and mortal participants in an embracing sacred and natural order of life.

In the end we may even come to understand that our specialized ways of producing "knowledge," abstracted ideas leading to deadly applications, gave us not only the bomb but the entire entrapping mind-set, a world map based on a capacity for mastery over everything except the conditions of our survival and well-being.

We need to acquire and nurture feelings for the concreteness of fallible leaders and social arrangements to grasp how fragile our world has become in these early decades of the nuclear age. We require a concrete sense of how nuclear war might begin, not only based on plausible scenarios but also taking into account the crazed emotions, faulty perceptions, scrambled computer programs, and misleading beliefs that could, especially under the pressure of crisis, produce that most definitive of all imaginable human irrationalities—recourse to nuclear war.

One day back in the fall of 1970 I received a letter from the Secretary of the Air Force inviting me to go on a one-day whirlwind tour of some leading defense facilities in the United States in the company of twenty or so others, a few academics like myself with international interests, several former high-level Defense Department officials recently returned to civilian life as leading lawyers and bankers, and a sprinkling of corporate executives with wider civic interests. We visited the sprawling, cavernous NORAD defense arrangements dug into the center of Cheyenne Mountain in Colorado in the first part of the day and SAC headquarters at Offutt Air Force Base outside Omaha, Nebraska, in the afternoon and evening. It was an instructive experience for me, although, I am sure, not in the manner intended by the Pentagon public relations people who dream up such junkets to build support.

The part of the experience that I remember best occurred at SAC headquarters, where we were given an elaborate tour. The main idea was to impress us with the ingenious quality of the electronics then available to monitor events everywhere in the world enabling devastating American military responses, as necessary, in a matter of minutes to security challenges. The essence of the enterprise was, of course, associated with the defense of the United States and its allies against Soviet military moves and, above all, a nuclear surprise attack. I understood as never before what a strain it was on this central command facility to stay ready day after day to fight a war of ultimate survival on a few minutes' notice. And I glimpsed how morale for such a mission was sustained over time. The SAC commander was a four-star general. As did most of the higher ranking officers we met, he also exhibited an extreme preoccupation with the malicious designs and great capabilities of the Russian bear. In other words, being an ideological fanatic helped a military leader with this sort of strategic role to keep his forces tensed for action over a prolonged period. I was also impressed at the time by the junior personnel we encountered. They seemed to be virtual extensions of the computer terminals they were seated at, as close to robots as I have ever seen. Some years later I read some classified studies of "human reliability" that helped explain this impression. The personnel chosen to operate sensitive equipment associated with nuclear weapons were supposed to be selected, in part, on the basis of their *absence* of moral scruple. The express idea was that individuals with an active conscience might hesitate in a crisis to follow orders leading to nuclear war, that such soldiers would, in this decisive military sense, be unreliable.

After the tour we received a briefing from the SAC commander. He told us how glad he was that prominent Americans could be reassured firsthand about our readiness to defend "the free world" against nuclear attack. He was eloquent in his description of SAC morale and of the essential need for more public support. Then he said something I have never forgotten. He said he wished that during the Cuban Missile Crisis of 1962 the Soviet Union had attacked Florida because then we could have "wipe[d] them off the face of the earth" and that this would have "finally pull[ed] this country together!" (My visit occurred during a peak time of Vietnam-related domestic unrest.)

As far as I could tell, none of my distinguished companions were especially disturbed by the SAC general's "performance." It did strike me as a rather bizarre assertion but not, I admit, in any very profound way. I slept well that night, told friends about my tour of SAC headquarters mainly in the spirit of entertainment and exposé. Only in recent years, looking back, have I succeeded in genuinely scaring myself by the extent to which virtually all of us accept such extremism without flinching. We have been conditioned by so many social and political forces to accept as normal the deranged wisdom of nuclear logic!

Even if the current command structure presiding over the array of nuclear weaponry is less prone to such grandiose impulses, the prevailing attitudes remain essentially oriented toward the initiation of nuclear war in "suitable" circumstances, that is, whenever authorized by the president and, most particularly, in response to or even in anticipation of a nuclear attack. Actually we know very little about the procedures governing recourse to nuclear weapons. We know even less about the Soviet setup for nuclear weapons use, but it is probably reasonable to assume a roughly similar state of readiness and willingness. The actual workings of nuclearist arrangements are guarded as a prime state secret, and we, their supposed beneficiaries, are also treated with suspicion as soon as we express doubts or raise questions, for to do so is to encroach on the sacred and profoundly fragile preserve of this new phenomenon—the permanent nuclear national security state.

What makes this routine anecdote about life at SAC headquarters of more than passing interest, I think, is its vivid reminder that what passes for peace in the nuclear age is entrusted to human beings who are certainly fallible and may quite possibly be clinically disturbed but who are shielded from the scrutiny of citizens by unchallengeable bureaucratic arrangements. We, the general public, rarely get even a glimpse how of these arrangements actually work. Instead our understanding lies buried beneath a pile of abstractions and technical arguments with the effect, if not the intention, of keeping us, above all, quiet, or if aroused, of limiting our challenge to marginal matters. It is as if a patient in terminal condition asks about his health and is told, in response, a list of Latin words that identify some medications that have been prescribed to dull the pain and incidentally, or not so incidentally, to dull at the same time all possible forms of self-awareness of his dying condition.

The context is very much dominated by the eruption of an antinuclear movement of worldwide scope. It started in Europe during 1978, spread through North America and Japan in late 1980, and now flourishes wherever in the modern world free political life takes place. There are even stirrings in Eastern Europe that display anxiety about the nuclear arms race, including a large demonstration in Rumania, unprecedented church-centered protest activity in East Germany, and strong links of support between the peace movement in Western Europe and the struggle of Solidarity in Poland. This popular movement is creating a new climate for discussion of nuclear issues. It is also putting pressure on political leaders to respond, and it may allow new leaders with antinuclear platforms to get a hearing and mount electoral challenges.

Yet we must not be too encouraged. The entrenched forces that stand behind nuclearism are powerful, wily, and, if necessary, ruthless. Popular movements are notoriously easy to coopt, divert, infiltrate, bore, and outlast. For the antinuclear movement to succeed, it desperately needs "a politics," that is, a clear understanding of what must be changed and how to do it. This understanding must also include an alternative idea of security. The antinuclear ranks are not composed of idealists who believe that peace on earth, goodwill to men and women is an idea whose time has come. Overwhelmingly they are acting out of fear of the nuclear menace, increasingly deciding that this fear takes precedence over their more traditional concerns about national defense and preserving a way of life. But in the end this movement will not succeed unless it combines a negation of nuclearism with the persuasive creation of new ways to protect the independence and territorial integrity of the states that make up world society. At this time, then, it is crucial to initiate discussions of the politics of antinuclearism. My hope is that this book is read primarily as a contribution to this work.

Leaders, too, are remarkably remote from the actuality of nuclear war. In a revealing passage in the second volume of his memoirs, *Years of Upheaval*, Henry Kissinger tells briefly of his one and only visit to a missile site. Even then, as Kissinger acknowledges, his "principal reason" for the visit is revealingly incidental to helping out an important senator in the midst of an election campaign in North Dakota. Kissinger writes that the view "flying over the fields of missiles" was "an awesome sight." He is immediately conscious of the central reality that "a single decision by an individual of normal fallibility, whatever the safeguards" could end up "destroying humanity."

Kissinger backs off at once from such a line of reflection and dwells instead on the strategic uncertainties that flow from the fact that these missiles have never been tested under genuine battle conditions. He notes that despite the dependence of our strategy on "multiple launches in an extremity," the missiles might not work in battle conditions. He then goes on to worry that political leaders in the country, with their scant strategic sophistication, might not resist over time what is for him the dread enemy, namely "the simplifiers—mindless pacifism on the left and on the right the equally mindless insistence on treating the new technology as conventional." This leads Kissinger directly back to an embrace of the nuclear status quo, which he somehow, reassuringly, associates with moderation: "Will we, I wondered, forever maintain the sense of proportion that does not stake the fate of mankind on a single judgment—and the fortitude to shun the pacifist temptation that will abandon the world to the most ruthless?"

Kissinger goes on to praise "the professionalism and dedication of the personnel" and expresses his appreciative sense that the weapons setup was a "technical marvel." He ends the anecdote on a characteristically fatalistic note: ". . . the survival of our civilization must be entrusted to a technology so out of scale with our experience and with our capacity to grasp its implications."[1]

This digression occurs while Kissinger is en route to see Nixon at San Clemente, traveling in the company of Hans-Dietrich Genscher, the German Foreign Minister. It is important testimony, I think, because it expresses in a relatively unguarded way the prevailing mood of resignation in the face even of a fairly clear-sighted insight into the absurd reality constituted by nuclear weaponry. Kissinger grasps fully the tragic circumstances of our current situation, yet note how lamely he responds. In the first place, Kissinger suggests that our present reliance on nuclear weapons is the only alternative to the greater threats posed by mindless simplifiers on the left and right, placing the existing pattern of reliance in the middle region of reasonableness. Then to make the case for sustaining the nuclear arsenal more compelling, he portrays "the mindless left" as consisting of "pacificists." We are left, then, with the choice of either maintaining the nuclear arms race or abandoning the future to the whims of foreign tyrants. Of course, to associate the left with pacifism is ridiculous. Also, to refuse to entertain even the possibility of some way out by means of mutual disarmament is virtually to throw the key out the window before the lock has been tried.

Kissinger's views are very characteristic of official thinking on these issues. Their various elements help explain how we have ended up where we are and why so pathetically little energy and attention has been devoted over the nuclear years to finding ways out. Underneath the fatalism is a power structure that has become entwined with the dynamics of militarism, technological innovation, and bureaucratic privilege. Anyone who seriously challenged the premises of this structure, or even doubted their viability, could not gain access to or exercise power in this country. The nuclearists exercise a veto over personnel choices for higher echelon posts in government. It is notable that what dissent from nuclear orthodoxy we have observed—precious little until the recent upsurge of popular concern—has all been the work of ex-officials with little hope of a return to government. George Kennan has been consistent over the last decade in warning us about the menace of nuclear war, but such men as Robert McNamara, McGeorge Bundy, and Gerald Smith, now proposing a no-first-use policy for the West in Europe, are welcome latecomers who are acting in a supportive climate partly created by a broad popular protest movement.[2] Their call can also be seen as part of a broader effort to defuse the more radical demands of the antinuclear movement as well as to accommodate its minimum call.

As yet none of these officials has faced clearly the political crux of nuclearism: either transform the power structure or remain yoked to policies tending toward Armageddon. Of course, some forms of nuclearism are more reckless than others, and we should support wholeheartedly measures designed to reduce immediate risks and costs associated with particular weapons systems, procurement programs, doctrines of use and militarist leadership. And yet such campaigns for prudent management are mounted, if at all, firmly *within* the boundaries of nuclearism. What kind of political movement could shift the struggle to center upon the viability of the nuclearist boundaries? What kind of alternative security could be substituted for nuclearism without exposing our destiny to the evil proclivities of others (realizing, of course, that it is already overexposed!)?

If a modern society is to grapple with such complex and fundamental questions, then it will require the full vitality of its democratic process, which includes the creative influence of religious and cultural perspectives. The challenges posed by nuclearism are overwhelmingly questions of values, belief systems, and underlying imagery of human destiny; specialized rational discourse contributes little to the resolution of such questions. And yet since the outset of the nuclear age, the basic policy has been set in secret by politicians and generals, reinforced in their biases by a vast corps of intellectual mercenaries ("the experts"). As a result, the drift toward nuclearism has gone virtually unchallenged in the inner counsels of government. Those few experts who did not share the nuclearist consensus were kept out of the corridors of power, and since 1945 specialized discussion has focused almost exclusively on the proper size of the defense budget and on how best to spend dollars available for military purposes.

There is a further dimension involving legitimacy. A democratic political process rests on consent, which presupposes active participation and general approval of governing policies by the citizenry and representative institutions. Yet at the root of the dependence on nuclear weapons lies the unspeakable. The entire willingness to visit such devastation on a people has been shrouded in shame from the outset. The general anti-Japanese sentiment prevailing in 1945 led Americans (and most others) to accept the Hiroshima and Nagasaki bombs as mere demonstrations of American military superiority, but even then there was a strong impulse to hide the reality at horrifying levels of particularity. The United States Government at the time seized and suppressed films and other evidence of atomic horrors. Even more revealingly, families of several American citizens who were in Hiroshima and killed by the bomb were never told about the place or circumstances of death. Even back in 1945 it was difficult for a democratic government to acknowledge the reality of what was "achieved," but by refusing to acknowledge what had occurred to its own citizens, it was at the outset of the nuclear age entering into an adversary relationship with the public on the most crucial issue of policy facing the nation and thereby undermining the democratic relationship.

More dispassionately, from either a moral or international law perspective, it is virtually impossible to vindicate reliance on nuclear weaponry. Of course, moralists and legalists can be found who endorse nuclearism, but their positions are so tortuous or their identities so bound up with state interests as to be unconvincing. The issue of political legitimacy is a time bomb bound up closely with reliance by our leaders on weaponry whose proposed use strains to the breaking point notions of constitutional and humane governance. Inevitably, in these circumstances a profound dilemma exists for political leaders. Either they peer deeply into the moral and legal status of nuclear weapons, thereby undermining the legitimacy of nuclearism, or they refuse to acknowledge such difficulties and undermine the legitimacy of their leadership by failing to face this most basic challenge. The path chosen has clearly been the latter one, and its success has depended on an acquiescent Congress and public opinion. An aroused citizenry, unless it can be confined to specific substantive demands, will sooner or later insist on their prerogatives to set the broad outer limits on what can be done at home and abroad in their name beneath the banner of national security.

Of course, some confusions have been sown, partly deliberately, partly unwittingly. At least since the Soviet Union became a nuclear power in August 1949 it has been possible to emphasize in public the deterrent role of weapons of mass destruction, but it is clear to any student of nuclear strategy that the actual role contemplated for nuclear weapons is broader than their announced deterrent role. Besides, moral and legal objections to nuclear weapons are not resolved by deterrence. Even aside from the effect on the rights of peoples living elsewhere in the world or on those as yet unborn, it remains morally and legally dubious, to say the least, to claim the discretion to inflict indiscriminate and possibly irreversible destruction on the entire population and industrial base of an enemy society.

In central respects, then, the reliance on nuclear weapons to uphold national security interests has severely compromised the legitimacy of political power in our country. This condition of tarnished legitimacy is linked to the passion for secrecy, the official control and management of news, and the easy readiness to identify morally concerned citizens as fools, at best, or if they persist so as to obtain a hearing, as enemies of the state.

The dependence on nuclear weaponry over these decades has sapped the strength of our democratic institutions. As a result, one of the hidden costs of nuclearism has been an impairment of the quality of democratic political life, and yet we find ourselves more dependent than ever before in our history as a nation on the capacity of the citizenry to mount and sustain a struggle against entrenched interests.

Ever since Hiroshima, a whole set of antidemocratic political arrangements have emerged and become permanent features of the governing process in the name of national security. The early insistence on secrecy culminated in sending Julius and Ethel Rosenberg to the electric chair in the first instance of capital punishment for espionage in the history of the United States. Protecting atomic secrets made eminent sense when the consequences could, in the public mind, lead directly and ultimately to a Soviet-engineered nuclear Pearl Harbor. From this premise has evoked the buildup of a huge intelligence and secret police establishment, the insistence on a classification system so rigid that on occasions an author has lost access to his own work because of clearance difficulties, and a permanent "enemies list" that has been used to justify surveillance and domestic spying as routine exercises of governmental authority has evolved.

Underneath this superstructure that gradually extended its repressive reach out from Washington was a pretext for permanent emergency. The red scare was the superficial justification, but far more profound was the structural effects of nuclear weaponry and war planning. Only in peacetime can the relationship envisioned by democratic theory and constitutional order be seriously enacted. Wartime conditions inevitably concentrate power in the presidency and exclude normal kinds of accountability between government and citizenry. The longer a war lasts, the more atrophied become the separation of powers, checks and balances, and citizen's rights that are the essence of Western democracy. Also during a war the military sector gains in influence and stature, and its leaders move close to the very center of power. It was not surprising that such prominent military figures as George C. Marshall and Dwight D. Eisenhower moved easily into civilian leadership roles in the decade after 1945, or that after the Korean War Douglas MacArthur returned to the United States as a deposed war hero who was looked upon as a natural aspirant to the presidency by those of rightist persuasion. That is, even the prime commitment to civilian control of the governing process erodes in a wartime atmosphere.

Nuclear weapons have reshaped our political lives over the years in ways that have not been generally noticed. The state of readiness required to fight a war of ultimate survival on a few minutes' notice has resulted in a permanent pre-war posture. One casualty of this reality has been meaningful congressional participation in war making. Any reading of our constitutional history would uncover the concern of the founders about depriving the president of exclusive authority in the war/peace area. In fact, this deprivation was one way a president was to be fundamentally different from a king. This difference was formalized in the constitutional provision requiring a declaration of war prior to entry into war. Many social forces have conspired through the decades to make our presidents into kings when it comes to war making, although Congress made a half hearted effort in the aftermath of the Vietnam experience to reverse the trend by enacting the War Powers Act. Underneath the procedural guidelines lie the felt necessities of the nuclear age that are thought to require the president's (aided as he sees fit by a handful of like-minded advisors) sole discretion over committing the nation (and world) to nuclear war. Wartime also becomes the institutional norm, with emer-

Taking Stands

gency prerogatives taken for granted as routine and reasonable. Year after year the relevant sectors of the government bureaucracy have grown ever stronger, reinforced further by mutual links of economic and professional interest with key sectors of the economy as well as with the scientific and foreign policy academic establishment.

What is important to realize at the outset is that the decay of democracy has itself impaired our capacity for response. Nuclear weapons are integrally related to this process of decay, although other forces are also partly responsible, including the general buildup in business and government of super-scale organizations that operate on an authoritarian basis and the gradual expansion of the global role of the United States at a time of geopolitical rivalry to the point where even in peace and even without the advent of nuclear weapons, there would be a call for a high level of military mobilization that would lead to strong antidemocratic effects on the governing process.

Of course, nuclear weapons policy has been bound up with the debate about national security ever since 1945. We started off the nuclear age with a decisive advantage, and that has made our government particularly reluctant to consider seriously objections to nuclearism. Also, soon after World War II we were in the midst of a severe rivalry with the Soviet Union for a global influence. In that struggle U.S. nuclear superiority was consistently presented as the only way to offset Soviet manpower and geographic advantages, especially in Europe. In a sense, ever since Hiroshima the implicit slogan of our foreign policy has been "Better nuclear than Soviet primacy." This outlook has been reinforced by a strong ideological campaign based on a struggle of good (us) against evil (them), presented for years as "the free world" against "godless, totalitarian communism."

More and more people sense that the old ways to uphold

141

the social order are losing ground, and yet there is little understanding of what else might be done. This loss of confidence leads to a weakening of morale in all sectors of society and to a need by leaders to insist ever more stridently that everything remains under their control. As a result, the failures of the old ways are disguised by claiming that what is needed now is an even tighter embrace of habitual methods, that old models of solving problems are not themselves defective but rather it is the niggardly nature of our investment in their success that is lagging. It is not surprising that in these circumstances the politics of nostalgia strikes a responsive chord, many people craving, at the very least, a coherent response to the problems of the day. The fatal flaw of nostalgia, of course, is that the yearning for the past distorts current reality in a manner that leads to deformed policy. These general comments apply to the kind of leadership offered by all those who still bestow confidence on military prowess when it comes to maintaining security in world affairs.

There is now evident a widespread public anxiety about the prospects of nuclear war, while at the same time strong support persists for increasing our arsenal of nuclear weaponry at breakneck speed even while we cut vital social services to the bone. Recent public opinion polls show that a large majority of our citizenry expect a nuclear war to occur (according to one poll 47 percent of Americans expect a nuclear war in the next five years) and are doubtful about their personal chances of survival, or about whether it would be worth surviving in a postnuclear setting. This anxious expectancy is itself a severe deterioration of security. In the past most people, especially in the United States, with its insular location, felt reasonably safe during periods of international peace.

The context, then, is being shaped by contradictory forces: an unprecedented surge of doubt about the viability of nuclearism as a foundation for national security and an intensified commitment of resources to the nuclear arms race in the hope of somehow regaining the geopolitical upper hand. The question confronting the opponents of nuclearism is how to proceed, considering three main elements: the power structure in this country, the harsh realities of the game of nations, and the crude behavior of the Soviet government at home and abroad.

A direct awareness of the nuclear war danger is the indispensable first step in any process of reducing or removing the danger. This awareness has to include some sense of anguish about the current state of our security, an awareness unmitigated by bureaucratic painkillers. One of the high costs of modern nationalism is a decline in the willingness, perhaps the capacity, of leaders, especially of powerful countries, to speak the truth to their citizens.

This deterioration of public discourse is especially dangerous where citizens generally trust the government. In Soviet society citizens know how to read the morning edition of *Pravda*. They often get hints from what is not said or about how official policy is celebrated, but they have few illusions about the completeness or reliability of what they are told. We in a democratic society are less on guard, partly of course because we enjoy the benefits of freedom and because the media nurture our trust in their independence and objectivity.

CHAPTER 13

Nuclearizing Security

Nuclear weapons were absorbed by political leaders into a pre-existing world map that had grown up around the war system. Three ingredients of prenuclear political wisdom helped pave the way for an acceptance of nuclear weapons: (1) never renounce any important potential military advantage; (2) stand ready in a conflict to use whatever tactics and means are helpful in the pursuit of victory; (3) realize that relative security is largely a reflection of relative strength, which can be measured by capacity to destroy, numbers of weapons, and other quantitative guides.

It is especially important to realize that these traditional imperatives of military power are couched in unconditional or absolute form. The magnitude of destruction or the growing vulnerability of American society to similar thinking by enemy states is not properly taken into account by nuclear planners except within the framework of this traditional logic of military power. Of course, this refusal to acknowledge the revolutionary character of this weaponry also reflects the strength of various social, economic, and psychological forces that provide domestic reinforcement for nuclearism.

At the heart of the antinuclear position is an insistence that these three assertions are dreadful guides for policy in the nuclear age. The risks of seeking military advantage by reliance on nuclear weapons are far too great to make sense any longer. If war is likely to produce mutual destruction, the pursuit of victory becomes grotesque. And to count missiles, warheads, and the like, given the current enormity of nuclear stockpiles on both sides, is to draw conclusions about superiority and inferiority that are divorced from real-world circumstances. As matters stand, whether one side has more or less hardly matters once the rather low threshold of unacceptable retaliatory capability has been reached. Ever since the 1960s both the United States and the Soviet Union have made huge investments in excessive destructive capabilities ("overkill"); it is now time to create pressures for disinvestment.

The depth and special quality of American nuclearism is closely associated with a special relationship to the weaponry based on prior acquisition, that is, arising from a proprietory sense of achieving the scientific and technological breakthroughs that produced the first atomic bomb. This relationship will be explored more fully later in this chapter.

Much of the recent discussion of the "decline" of American power rests upon an alleged loss of strategic superiority to the Soviet Union. Such "gaps" in relative capabilities have been a periodic feature of the nuclear arms race. There was the so-called "bomber gap" in the 1950s, the "missile gap" in the 1960s, and now "the window of vulnerability." In each instance, the professed fear of falling behind hides the drive to stay ahead. This fear has been used as a pretext to ratchet up the arms race a further notch and to solidify the pseudo reality of American strategic superiority in the continually altered technological environment of newly emerging weapons systems.

Scare tactics are used, highly dependent for their persuasiveness on arousing public fears of a Soviet nuclear attack (the Soviets use similar tactics to justify their enormous military effort). As such, the moments of official anxiety about "falling behind" necessarily coincide with orchestrated efforts to inflame Cold War tensions. The American public must be convinced on these occasions to devote peacetime tax dollars to an increased commitment of resources to the military sector. Here we witness another distortion of the political process arising from the requirement that major policies of a democratic government require popular backing. That is, additional to the abridgments of democracy that the nuclear age has produced by blurring the distinction between peace and war are pressures on leaders to convince the public that their leaders know best. Perhaps no clearer instance exists than the response of Western leaders to the peace movement that has emerged in the last few years. Ronald Reagan, for instance, while opposing the call for a freeze on nuclear weapons production that gained such momentum early in 1982, offered characteristic words of reassurance:

I have to be heart and soul in sympathy with the people that are talking about the horrors of nuclear war and the fact that we should do everything we could to prevent such a war from happening . . . I would hope that some of these people, however, who are insisting on some of these things would realize that I'm with them as to the need to do something to lessen the possibilities, *but I would ask them to consider that no matter how sincere and well intentioned, only in this position do you have all the facts necessary to base decisions upon action, and therefore I would ask then trust and confidence that feeling as sincerely as I do, that they would allow us to take the actions that we think are necessary to lessen this threat.* (emphasis added)[1]

In effect, after some patronizing words of pro-peace sentiment, the citizens are told to lay off as only the president "reads the cables" and, hence, knows enough to act prudently to defend vital interests, including the avoidance of nuclear war. Leaving it to Reagan or any other mainstream president has meant, of course, going along with massive arms buildups and a quickening arms race, which are the very tendencies that led the popular movement of opposition to grow so rapidly in the first place. Indeed it is mainly to stem this rising tide of public distrust that leaders of the state have displayed concern with the danger and horror of nuclear war, belatedly attempting to reassure us that they share our worries while pleading for a renewal of trust in *their* efforts to secure nuclear peace.

A growing tension has developed between the dependence of a democracy on the consent of citizens and the antidemocratic tenor of official policies on nuclear war and peace. Occasionally we get glimpses of a vicious type of nuclear-age paternalism in which the state discloses its resolve to act as it deems appropriate regardless of what the citizenry may deem desirable. In an influential study published under the auspices of the Council on Foreign Relations we find a passage that vividly expresses this new cynicism about the relationship between state and society:

If, over time, the need of governments to field expensive deterrent forces is not appreciated by citizens who no longer sense a real nuclear threat, popular support for the maintenance of forces could fade —*and governments might feel themselves compelled to provide for deterrence without the consent of the governed.* (emphasis added).[2]

The abstraction "governments might feel themselves compelled" avoids the concrete process by which particular individuals claim a capacity to determine on their own the requirements of the public good without any explicit constitutional mandate. In effect, what is involved here is a blatant usurpation of popular sovereignty that takes the form of subordinating the citizenry to nonaccountable decisions made by bureaucrats, generals, corporate executives, and politicians. This process of usurpation has taken place more or less invisibly, generally obscured by official claims over the years of "emergency" and "necessity." The invisibility makes this threat to democracy no less real. In fact, making the invisible visible is the first step in a long process of reviving the democratic process in relation to nuclear weapons policy. The Soviet leadership has no need to whip up hostile propaganda because it is almost oblivious to the opinions of its citizens.

In the background of the nuclear arms race is a psychological need "to stay ahead" reinforced by a completely misleading official anxiety about what it might mean "to fall behind." Ever since the Soviet Union achieved the capability to deliver nuclear weapons on the United States in the late 1950s, an essential condition of mutual deterrence has existed. Only a crazed politician or lemming fanatic would test the willingness of the other side to retaliate if attacked. The idea of superiority and inferiority does not mean anything relevant to the course of conflict in the world since mutual deterrence. The volume of megatonnage available for delivery could disclose relative levels of potential destruction, but for more than two decades both sides could substantially destroy the other with a fraction of available megatonnage. It is a sign of cultural and moral decadence that our war thinkers continue to vindicate relative force levels by arguing about the effects of civil defense programs, relative dispersion of population and industry, and comparative times to recover from nuclear attack. To suppose that *any* political result could possibly be worth relying on such an "advantage" is to treat an extreme absurdity as if it were a rational basis for government policy. Indeed it is the very rationality of the discourse that masks and marks the craziness of the thought!

On one level of discourse and behavior leaders generally understand the extraordinary inhibitions of mutual deterrence and generally refrain from testing each other. But on the level of military spending, strategic posturing, and public debate the old illusions persist and are fostered by the political leadership. In these wheelings and dealings hundreds of billions are expended, illustrious careers and fortunes are made, as excessive weaponry becomes treated as a matter of national security necessity.

Underneath this dreadful mythology of superiority and inferiority is the initial set of unequal relationships to nuclear weaponry. Additional to the vested interests that have grown up around an arms race in both superpowers is the belief that the United States needs to retain its terribly real nuclear advantage established initially at the Almagordo test site and revealed a few weeks later by the atomic bombings of Hiroshima and Nagasaki that quickly produced Japan's surrender. American security has been associated ever since with keeping that nuclear lead, although there has been, as I have said, no tolerable meaning to such imagery of superiority in the context of mutual strategic capabilities.

The Soviet position is the obverse. Having experienced genuine nuclear inferiority in the period before some sort of mutuality was achieved, the Soviets have persisted in acquiring nuclear weapons capability in a relentless drive "to catch up." Since their leaders can never be sure what we might be doing and since their capabilities are developed in light of their particular technological strengths and weaknesses, which are different from ours, any effort to catch up is necessarily ambiguous. It can easily be seen on our part as striving to get ahead, thereby reinforcing the temperament on the other side that a race is underway. Each side, then, observes the other acting as if superiority was important and is encouraged thereby to embrace the fiction. This "as if" process of action and interaction yields a shared set of illusions that are deeply ingrained in political consciousness. How can we cut through these illusions? This seemingly psychological question is also, at once, profoundly political. We need to explore the power base of these illusions and how we as citizens can act effectively to challenge and transform them.

We must remember at all times that the arms race is without sane substance. Even if they are ahead, what then? So long as the other side has some reasonable prospect of retaliating with ten or more weapons of mass destruction, it is hard to imagine what might prompt even a rather desperate enemy leadership to invite national disaster on such an unprecedented scale by initiating a nuclear attack.

Pretending that superiority still counts imposes additional heavy costs. By basing weapons procurements and doctrine on ideas of relative capabilities, there is a gradual, subtle subversion of the essential insight—namely that a nuclear war between states with highly unequal strategic arsenals would be the greatest imaginable tragedy for the stronger side, and in the most fundamental sense, indistinguishable from the tragedy inflicted on the weaker side. What has happened through time is that arguments made primarily to keep the arms race going and the military-industrial complex growing have become confusingly close to guidelines for actual policy, as shown in targeting plans, war-fighting scenarios, postattack planning, and the like. Thus both superpowers, by their behavior and by the kind of consciousness deemed appropriate for their leaders, have largely abandoned the most genuine element of rationality incorporated in the doctrine of mutual deterrence; this rationality, if embodied in policy, would confine existing nuclear weapons to minimum numbers and capability, while creating high credibility for their retaliatory capacity under all circumstances. Each side would have an incentive to reinforce the credibility of its enemy's retaliatory capability, thereby creating maximum stability with respect to the avoidance of nuclear war. In effect, by believing in the illusions of nuclear superiority an especially dangerous circumstance is credited. It would be far safer if each side acted cynically to satisfy various cravings for influence and profits on the basis of illusion for illusion's sake. But no, the governing process is not yet *that* corrupt or cynical. Ironically, this degree of integrity heightens the danger as credible leaders are recruited from among those who believe in the illusions of winnable nuclear wars and the like, and who might act on such beliefs if pushed in a crisis.

It is never entirely clear whether our leaders or their leaders think superiority really matters. Therefore we engage in an expensive, dangerous path because their leaders might otherwise be tempted to act in a crazy way (relying on their superiority), but the pursuit of superiority is itself crazy! How can a normal person be expected to respond to such an arcane tangle that is at once falsehood and seemingly the ground of operative policy?

Yet might not this reasoning be wrong? Is it not preferable to have insurance against the temptation of an enemy to think it could use its nuclear advantage? We can confidently say no to both questions. Of course, we cannot exclude this possibility altogether. All we can say is that the clarity of mutual deterrence at minimum levels is the best protection we can hope to have this side of utopia against the temptation to rely on a nuclear advantage. Any messing around with that clarity by action or words on either side introduces ambiguity and rejects the essential insight that such weaponry is not rationally usable.

Relying on a nuclear advantage also evades the moral challenge. To the extent that "security" is associated with a discretionary option to threaten or even to use nuclear weapons, a government embraces a policy of terror on the largest imaginable scale. It seems hardly an accident that the widespread outbreak of political terrorism should coincide in time with the full embrace of nuclear terrorism, and not only as a weaponry of last resort but rather as a legitimate choice available to leaders in periods of national crisis. Much of our political life is shaped by the combined force of terrorism from above and terrorism from blow. Decent individuals are caught in the crossfire and rendered helpless and impotent. In this crucial respect the process of claiming a nuclear advantage, even if no firm resolve to use these weapons exists, has serious demobilizing effects on political life, discouraging the very questioning and alternative thinking needed to release us from the tightening trap of the arms race. Of course, it should be realized that removing the burdens and menace of the arms race would not entirely end the danger arising from the possession of nuclear weapons. Proposals such as "the freeze," deep cuts, and no first use are all efforts to live with the existence of the bomb. Put differently, such proposals are made with the awareness that at this stage any wider effort to destroy nuclear stockpiles altogether would seemingly create an acute vulnerability to nuclear blackmail by any government or terrorist group that possessed (or even acted as if it possessed) some nuclear weapons. Thus retention of a small, secure stockpile operates as a minimum hedge against blackmail for the foreseeable future.

By relying on nuclear weapons, governments undermine the fragile authority of international law, drawing into serious question the long struggle to bring measures of restraint and accountability into the conduct of warfare. Quite obviously if nuclear weapons are treated as permissible weapons, then it becomes politically unconvincing, and even morally questionable, to insist on the prohibition of various practices relating to war. If the most powerful states insist on their discretion to inflict ultimate barbarism, then any moral or legal objections directed at those with lesser capabilities are much eroded. Indeed the decline of international law during the last several decades is, in part, a reflection of unbridled nuclearism by the leaders of world society. If law is being reconciled with discretion by government to use nuclear weapons as it sees fit, then it seems accurate to conclude that the most excessive image of the Hegelian absolute state now exists as a reality of everyday life.

Getting there first, using nuclear weapons first, developing the hydrogen bomb first, introducing multiple independently targeted vehicles (MIRVs) first are among the stages in this race to stay ahead. Over the long cycle of the nuclear arms race, the United States initiates, the Soviet Union responds.

There is no reason to suppose that other states would have displayed greater restraint than the United States had they found themselves similarly situated in relation to nuclear technology. In fact, the moralism inherent in American political culture probably disposed the United States more than it would have most other states to feel uncomfortable about its nuclear advantage and, hence, to contemplate some kind of unilateral gesture of renunciation. Certainly the Baruch plan put forward by the United States after World War II for the international control of all nuclear weaponry and technology can be conceived of in this light. Whether the gesture was seriously intended to be the basis of a genuine policy of renunciation will remain forever shrouded in mystery. There are reasons to be skeptical about how seriously they were meant. The proposals inevitably issued forth as a compromise within the

American bureaucracy at the time that definitely preserved an element of national advantage while claiming to eliminate the nuclear danger from the scene. If such an international regime for the control over nuclear capabilities had actually been established, it would probably have produced either a different American strategy for staying ahead (the announced Soviet apprehension) or it would have succumbed at some point to stiff domestic opposition from overtly militarist forces assembling in the wings and ready to strike in the event the proposals had been accepted by Moscow. Surely the Soviet Union, with its well-confirmed distrust of "the outside world," including international institutions, had it achieved the bomb first, would never have seriously considered handing over its nuclear advantages to some custodial arrangement beyond its sovereign reach.

More revealing, I think, is the overall United States adjustment to the rejection of the initial offer to internationalize control over atomic energy. The offer was never again repeated or recast in an alternative form. To be sure, some proposals for general and complete disarmament surfaced in the early 1960s but in a halfhearted, ho-hum spirit. They were, at the time, internally discounted by leaders in the Kennedy Administration as intended only to deprive the Soviet Union of a propaganda edge deriving from their earlier similar grandstanding proposals.

In the 1970s a position of substantive parity at the strategic level was achieved and generally acknowledged. Such parity did not necessarily mean equality of weapons arsenals or symmetry of weapons systems. It meant that such inequalities that existed could not be brought to bear in any meaningful fashion in the context of international conflict. Whether that parity can be superceded by new American weapons procurements seems doubtful, although there are those who talk increasingly in such a bold vein. Herman Kahn, war strategist and head of the Hudson Institute think tank, talks ebulliently these days about the United States requiring "a not incredible first strike" capability. The pursuit of such a hare is what the current phase of the arms race is mainly about.

The Soviet Union's later arrival on the nuclear scene has naturally shaped Soviet attitudes toward nuclear weaponry. For one thing, it meant in the first decade after 1945 dealing with a situation of utter vulnerability to the uncertain designs of an increasingly hostile and suspicious adversary. For another, it created an enormous incentive to neutralize the intimidating features of nuclear weaponry by challenging its acceptability on all possible grounds. In effect, Soviet nuclear inferiority during the early years after 1945 led Moscow to dwell on the moral issue. In this regard the Soviets mounted a global campaign against the legitimacy of nuclear weaponry, trying to summon the energies of world public opinion around the proposition that recourse to nuclear weaponry was nothing less than a crime against humanity. It does not pass judgment on Soviet motivations, which might have been relatively sincere, to suggest that stressing the moral issue under these circumstances was itself a way of catching up. The existence of pragmatic benefits, however, does not dispose of the moral issue, or make it any less pressing to address. Presumably, had the United States started the nuclear arms race in a distant second-place position, our leaders would have screamed foul when it came to the propriety of using the weaponry.

As time passed the interaction of the two superpowers based on this initial sequence of acquisition has hardened into a pattern. To this day American strategic thinking reacts angrily to peace crusades, discounting whatever position is taken as a result of Soviet sponsorship. It regards anyone who succumbs to such appeals as quite literally a dupe of Moscow, and, in fact, support by an American for the Stockholm Peace Petition of the early 1950s, quite a laudable document if taken at face value, was actually regarded in the McCarthy Era, because of links to Soviet propaganda efforts against nuclear weaponry, as an important indicator of questionable loyalty. Somehow, probably unwittingly, but with media cooperation, being strongly opposed to nuclear weapons has until recently been merged in public consciousness with being anti-American. Such a sinister confusion is breaking down as increasingly respected figures are speaking clearly about dangers and moral concerns. However, the earlier red-baiting tactics persist. President Reagan and top United States officials have frequently tried to discredit the European peace movement by contending that it has various illicit ties to Moscow. In a slightly more civil tone, American leaders and the media habitually dismiss antinuclear positions as "pacifist" or "neutralist," ways of stigmatizing positions as irrelevant in a hardball world of geopolitics. In the European movement only a tiny minority among antinuclear militants can be classified in these ways; the movement's character and politics is overwhelmingly what it purports to be—an insistence that security be based as little as possible on the threat to use nuclear weapons first, especially when such a threat creates temptations by the other side to attack preemptively, thereby increasing the prospect that a devastating "theater" war might break out unintentionally at a time of crisis and heightened East/West tension. Many Europeans have reacted strongly to statements by American leaders in the last several years that seem to reflect the conviction that the nuclear advantage still belongs to the West in the event that warfare breaks out in Europe.

Using the nuclear advantage of the United States rests on a broad notion of deterrence. If we are inhibited by our scruples, then the inferior nuclear power is likely to become bolder in pursuing opportunities for expansion. Advocates of "the nuclear option" are infatuated with the idea that a greater willingness to use nuclear weapons can make the Soviet Union more cautious, and if it did not, then a limited application of nuclear firepower (of course, far from our shores) might be worthwhile to persuade Moscow not to act provocatively beyond Soviet borders. Somehow, if American leaders keep a finger on the nuclear trigger, Moscow and its friends will grow cautious overseas; calling the nuclear bluff will never seem like a decent risk to Soviet leaders, even should they grow convinced that Washington is bluffing. Further, it need not be a bluff if we convince ourselves that nuclear weapons can be used in a "theater" of conflict without setting off a global war that even most professional nuclearists agree would be a mutual disaster. One of the elements of the current debate is the breakdown of even this nodule of sanity, a willingness "to think the unthinkable" and plan to fight and win a nuclear war on a grand scale (that is, in the more than 1000-megaton range) should deterrence fail. Underneath these quite demented schemes, put forward in the name of security, is a psychological war of nerves about human destiny reminiscent of the most involuted logic in the best Catch-22 tradition. If we can get ourselves psyched up to use nuclear weapons more readily, then the Soviet Union must assume that we will do it and moderate its behavior to avoid unleashing a chain of events that culminates in its destruction.

Historical memories are short, especially when defense contracts are large and the struggle for public influence intense. Our current generation of analysts forget, or act as if they do, that we "freed" ourselves of our nuclear inhibition during the Eisenhower years with the adoption of the doctrine of massive retaliation. Behind the scenes a National Security Council document (NSC 162/2) set forth in 1953 guidelines that oriented American military forces around a relatively routine reliance on nuclear weapons. In John Foster Dulles's famous words addressed to the Council on Foreign Relations on January 12, 1954, we must now be prepared to respond to Soviet provocations with "a great capacity to retaliate, instantly, by means and at places of our choosing." Such a doctrine coming at the end of a debilitating war in Korea where various pressures within the United States Government to use nuclear weapons on the battlefield or against China, had been mounted unsuccessfully. The nuclear temptation had been resisted, in large part, because advocates of nuclear weapons use were unable at the time to develop a persuasive case for military decisiveness without greatly expanding the arena of combat to include China. The Eisenhower/Dulles approach was significantly stimulated by budgetary considerations (nuclear weapons seemed to be the only fiscally viable way to service the United States' farflung global commitments). As one specialist on the evolution of nuclear strategy observed, Eisenhower "attached overriding importance to the goal of keeping military spending in check."[3] The cost advantages of substituting nuclear weaponry has been a surprisingly important factor over the years and is certainly part of "the nuclear advantage." Nuclear weapons, in the jargon of Washington bureaucrats, were definitely seen as "cost-effective," and to this day arguments for their role in defense planning rest heavily on economic considerations (that is, the cost of equivalent nonnuclear capabilities). Massive retaliation was announced at a time of clear nuclear preponderance—the United States could effectively devastate the Soviet Union and could not be significantly attacked in return. Still, this lowering of the nuclear threshold did not seem to work; at least it did not seem that way to the next group of political leaders in the United States.

At best, massive retaliation rested on wildly implausible assumptions of Moscow's control over the world revolutionary process and its willingness to govern its actions by our text, however unreasonable it might be expected to seem to the Soviets. Remember that after Korea threats to Western interests mainly came in ambiguous settings of Third World countries racked by civil strife. The cold warrior leadership insisted then, as they do now, that these threats were decisively magnified, if not caused, by Moscow's evil meddling and armaments. Then, as now, there were attempts by Washington to justify expanding the area of combat by charging our enemies with "indirect aggression" that made it proper and necessary to attack the danger at its source. Despite their posturing, American leaders increasingly in the late 1950s realized that internal struggles for political control were being shaped by the domestic realities of national revolution. This threatening to attack the source could not prevent the challenge to Western interests, and failing to fulfill the threat would damage credibility while carrying it out could unleash a general war. Even during the period of American nuclear predominance, fortunately, our leaders, once they realized the dilemma, sought to decouple intervention in Third World conflicts from the use of strategic nuclear weaponry. It was at the time of John Kennedy's arrival in Washington that this realization prompted the creation of counterinsurgency doctrine and capabilities (e.g., the Green Berets) to fight so-called "brushfire wars." These low-level conflicts were given great significance in the global struggle with the Soviet bloc as affecting the overall balance of power. It was also argued by foreign policy officials from the Eisenhower era until the present that the outcome of a given struggle was linked to the political destiny of the region (the so-called domino theory). The early justification for the American involvement in Vietnam rested heavily on such a rationale, as does the current involvement in El Salvador. Often, as in Central America, similar revolutionary conditions pertain in a given region and therefore it is quite likely that there is a relatedness of the various struggles against the status quo, but it is not a mechanical relatedness of the sort implied by the image of a row of falling dominoes. The decoupling response does reduce the risk of escalation, but it is unstable, as when defeat looms; at that time a recoupling or linkage is likely to occur so as to account for the failure of interventionary policy.

Of course, there were some wild voices in the early period who, with the memories of Hitler still fresh, repeatedly invoked the Munich analogy to warn that backing down anywhere was "appeasement" that could only end in making the aggressor ever bolder. Others, emphasizing the monolithic nature of the Communist bloc (especially prior to the mid-1960s when the Sino-Soviet split became manifest) and its revolutionary ideology, believed that general war was at some stage inevitable and that time was on their side. Hence it was argued that a readiness to fight in the favorable context of Western nuclear superiority meant that a notion of massive retaliation, even if not responsive to the actual confrontations in the Third World, would give the United States Government an acceptable pretext for eliminating once and for all the mounting Soviet challenge. Remember that the peculiar form of "legalism" that has operated throughout the entire cold war has always based claims to escalate the scale of conflict on some kind of justification, alleging the provocation of the adversary as "the cause" and thereby claiming that a response, however massive, was "defensive" in character. During the period of nuclear preponderance there were those behind the scenes who believed that while we had the nuclear advantage we should use it, seizing a pretext, or creating one, if necessary.

Such voices were kept in the background by a number of considerations. It was not clear that the Soviet Union could be made to surrender quickly by an all-out nuclear attack. Even if it did, the prospect of occupying and reconstructing such a huge country devastated by nuclear weaponry was, to put it mildly, not an attractive one, even to hawkish war planners. More than this, Soviet reactions to an attack were always assumed to include, at minimum, a willingness to exercise its capability to destroy or occupy Western Europe. And, then, some moral scruples were at work. Eisenhower was not a warmonger. In fact, his experiences in World War II made him wary of militarist approaches to foreign policy, and it was Eisenhower's Farewell Address in 1961 that contained the first serious warning that our own "military-industrial complex" might be as dangerous to American national security as were increasing Soviet armaments.

My concern here is not with the evolution of American nuclear strategy, but with the uneasy adjustment of the United States to the position of getting there first and our current reluctance to accept the psychopolitical consequences of nuclear parity.

Ever since the Soviet development of ICBMs (intercontinental ballistic missiles) and missile-firing submarines in the late 1950s, no sane meaning can be attached to the notion of nuclear advantage. Indeed the political sickness of our time may center on this desperado official effort to be misled and to mislead on this crucial point, an effort that may go on in Moscow as well as Washington, for all we know. The point is that the peoples of both countries and of the world are being held hostage to this madness. To maintain that heavier or more numerous missiles create "vulnerability" is to overlook the underlying radical reality that maximum vulnerability is with us from the moment an adversary has nuclear warheads that could reliably be delivered on prime targets. To carry on politics in the dark shadow of this vulnerability—the unthinkable enterprises of the think tanks—is to foster the grand illusion that normal ends of collective existence can be pursued in such a postattack context. And that illusion, above all others, must be sustained if we are to continue with this strategic game of preserving, regaining, using our nuclear advantage or suffering adverse consequence from its loss, which is, after all, the basic mythology that has kept arms races going throughout the history of international relations.

There were other options of strategic policy available to the United States after Hiroshima, after the rejection of the Baruch Plan, after it was evident (no later than the early 1960s) that the Soviet Union could catch up in the crucial respect of surviving any first strike sufficiently to deliver its own crushing retaliatory blow. We could have approached the issue of nuclear "legitimacy" in a much different spirit with possibly quite profound effects on the whole course and pace of the nuclear arms race. We could have easily and persuasively adopted the view that nuclear weapons can never be used first in a combat situation. Most readings of international law and morality would lend support to this conclusion. A no-first-use position could have reconciled the genocidal characteristics of the weaponry with a geopolitical prudence that refuses to trust altogether the goodwill of others.[4] We could effectively have done this (and might yet do it—see proposal to this effect in chapter 18) even while continuing to stockpile and develop some additional weapons as protection against a possible Soviet nuclear threat. Most states, including the Soviet Union, indicated their support for such a move to delegitimize nuclear weapons altogether. This support was not a reflection of the greater civic virtue of foreign states, but rather an expression of their far greater freedom from the illusion of nuclear advantage. Without that illusion, confining the role of nuclear weapons seems like the most natural of all imaginable expressions of self-interest, that is, a political embodiment of mental health.

No inspection apparatus is necessary to implement no-first-use moves. In all probability the nuclear arms competition would have proceeded, but in a much less threatening and expensive fashion. If the weapons had not entered into diplomacy in the form of "options," threats, and forward deployments, then the salience of this weaponry of mass destruction would have been greatly reduced, the absolute priority to stay ahead at astronomical force levels would not have been easily financed, and nonnuclear states would not have been nearly as tantalized by the symbolic and substantive status associated with membership in the nuclear weapons club.

I acknowledge that such an international security regime of reduced nuclear dependence might itself not have been politically sustainable, given the other forces at work in the world. It would always have been susceptible to the claim, now being made at a higher level of absurdity, that Western or American decline in the world is somehow associated with strategic weakness, and that this weakness is centrally connected to the scale and quality of the nuclear arsenal, as well as with the willingness to use these and other military capabilities to pursue goals of foreign policy. We must assume that the Kissingers and Brzezinskis would have convinced us at some point that our woes in the world came from this refusal, allegedly unprecedented in the annals of Great Powers, to use whatever military capabilities are at our disposal, including especially nuclear weapons. Without more fundamental shifts in political consciousness and socioeconomic structure, the unconditional ends of state policy might not long have remained containable, especially if geopolitical defeats were being sustained, as they would be, given the persistence of revolutionary nationalism in the Third World. And so I would have to say that, given the political play of forces in this country, over the course of the last thirty-five years or so an argument to seize the nuclear advantage would very likely have prevailed, and that a no-first use policy would probably have been scrapped at some point.

Even granting this probability, the question remains why such a dampening of the nuclear fire was not attempted or even seriously considered. My assessment is as follows. The dominant view in the United States from the moment of that first test explosion was heavily weighted on the side of acquiring and then preserving the strategic advantages implicit in the possession of nuclear weaponry. This view, to be sure, never triumphed altogether. In fact, the post-Hiroshima emphasis on the nuclear firebreak was a sort of concession to the no-first-use approach, that is, the appreciation that crossing the nuclear threshold again would be a serious precedent with dangerous implications even if it didn't produce an immediate escalation to general war. Nuclear weapons have not actually been exploded in combat since Nagasaki, even though strong advocacy of their combat value in a specific setting has been presented to American leaders from time to time, and their possible use has been on occasion threatened diplomatically by every president up to Jimmy Carter. These threats are discussed and enumerated on p. 179.

The result, of course, has been a story of deep ambivalence and confusion. We have neither renounced the nuclear option nor pressed its possible advantage to the maximum. At times firebreak thinking has been strong; at others, nuclear option thinking has grown more attractive. In the background, is the abiding concern about whether conventional weapons can satisfy existing commitments at acceptable dollar costs; there has been a consistent reliance on the nuclear option created by the orthodox view that the defense of Western Europe depends on a willingness to threaten and use nuclear weapons so as to offset Soviet conventional superiority. Recent studies by such English defense specialists as Mary Kaldor or Dan Smith argue that Europe is currently quite capable of defending itself at present levels of expenditure without reliance on nuclear weaponry, a position drastically at odds with the views of the most liberal pundits in the United States, who generally concede overwhelming Soviet conventional superiority in Europe and the Persian Gulf.[5] If this is conceded and if the need to safeguard these regions against the contingency of a Soviet attack, however remote, is a presumed requirement of national security, then reliance on the nuclear option (that is, a first or initiating use of nuclear weapons) follows as clearly as night follows day. What makes the current period particularly frightening is that Soviet nuclear deployments now seem to deny the United States/NATO the availability of a "theater" option by which is meant a sufficient advantage in the region so as to require the Soviet government to escalate to all-out war in order to avoid defeat in Europe. This apparent shift in the burden of escalation combined with the myth of conventional inferiority is what produces the American pressure to deploy those 572 Pershing II missiles on European soil during the 1980s, missiles with a capability of devastating the western centers of Soviet population and industry. Here the fiction of U.S. strategists is that credibility is restored to the nuclear option in Europe by putting a significant slice of the Soviet Union within the European theater, thereby supposedly relocating the burden of escalation back in Moscow. The whole process, for obvious reasons, frightens the European public (and quite likely, the Soviet leadership). For one thing, the deployments themselves become targets for a Soviet preemptive strike at a time of crisis. For another, the American strategy—if it works!—that is, if the boundaries of the theater are respected, results in the assured destruction of most of Europe, with or without the destruction of a sector of Soviet society. Finally, the expectation that the theater will not be expanded, in such circumstances, to include the United States is rejected vigorously by Soviet leaders, as it would certainly be by American officials sitting in their place. Drawing boundaries on the orbit of nuclear devastation that excludes the American homeland is the work of Pentagon regulars who have programmed too many war games. To argue in such a vein is not meant to exonerate Soviet buildups in missile strength targeted on Europe over the last decade. This buildup helps lend plausibility to an arms race response, thereby weakening protection on both sides against the outbreak of nuclear war.

Similarly, but more understandably, in the Persian Gulf region. Here again the central argument is that Western dependence on oil requires a military presence that includes the nuclear option. The argument has been most carefully put forth by Robert W. Tucker in his book *The Purposes of American Power* as the only way out of critical Western weakness and vulnerability. Again, the possibility of a Soviet military challenge is taken seriously. Retention of Western control over the Gulf oil is regarded as absolutely essential for the independence of Europe and Japan. Once more the significance of conventional inferiority is stressed: "Given the conventional forces the Soviet Union can presently deploy on very short notice in the Gulf, there is no apparent way by which these forces could be repelled by conventional American military response. On this point there is virtual unanimity of judgment among military analysts"[6] Hence recourse to the nuclear option. To his credit, Tucker seeks to find an approach, in his terms, to redress the perceived imbalance at the conventional level, mainly by introducing a permanent American military presence in the region by stationing forces and acquiring basing rights, thus imitating the approach taken over the years to the defense of Western Europe. At the same time he insists that an adequate American approach to Gulf security "raise the meaningful prospect of nuclear escalation, a prospect we can—and should—no more attempt to disavow in the Persian Gulf than in Europe.[7] Let me emphasize, Tucker's formulation is the moderate approach to the nuclear option in the current context, a highly sophisticated defensive strategy for the United States to consider in a deteriorating world political situation.

And yet there is no doubt in Tucker's mind that we, as rational actors in the Machiavellian struggle perpetually being waged by sovereign states, should press our military advantages whatever they may be, including a willingness to initiate, if need be, nuclear war. Indeed it is this willingness that is critical, as it is expected to intimidate, to induce caution, to make risks unpalatable that otherwise might seem attractive to our chief adversary, thereby relieving us of the horrible task of following through in the event deterrence fails. If it is possible to make Moscow believe that if the Gulf is threatened Washington would have no choice but to use nuclear weapons, then Moscow will presumably avoid posing the threat.

It is reasoning of this sort that has dominated our strategic posture since Hiroshima. At each stage we were not prepared to give up, once and for all, the nuclear advantage. Now, decades later, our leaders find themselves more dependent than ever on creating this advantage, extending its immediate role to regions of contention beyond the European heartland, regions where inherent instability is easily confused with outside aggression.

And let us keep in mind, if we can, that the whole notion of nuclear advantage against a nuclear adversary is political fanaticism of the worst kind. It is the sort of terroristic politics that holds women and children at gunpoint until the well-armed opponent drops his weapons and submits or resorts to torture to gain valuable information. And remember also that the target of the terror may have little control over adverse developments that cannot be controlled at the local level. Underneath the revival of the nuclear option is an overall frustration with military power, an inability to translate superiority in weaponry into victories in either diplomacy or war. This frustration, however, is not registered as a loss of control. The imperial outlook existing in both Washington and Moscow seems incapable of acknowledging a lack of control over adverse events. The imperial reflex is to blame defeat totally on the machinations of the other side, on an unwillingness to go all out for victory, or on the wrong strategy of combat. One desperate reflection of this process is to associate decline and defeat with unwarranted nuclear self-denial.

As illustrative of where we might be going, consider an argument put forward with robust goodwill by Laurence W. Beilenson, former Reagan advisor, and Samuel T. Cohen, a nuclear scientist who is called "the father of the neutron bomb" in the pages of *The New York Times Magazine* early in 1982. They argue that the United States is "on the wrong road" because it is not "fully exploiting the military consequences of the nuclear revolution . . ." They concede that current security arrangements are catastrophe-prone: "No other conclusion is possible from the nature of nations and the human beings who compose them." One might have expected authors with such an awareness to advance a case for nuclear renunciation, but no, their "adjustment" is quite the reverse. Beilenson and Cohen insist that the biggest mistake of current United States foreign policy is "our well-intentioned but misconceived readiness to fight wars with conventional weapons all over the world." Their phrasing ("well-intentioned") makes it hard to resist the temptation to digress, but it is important to get at the core of the argument. Their real emphasis, exhibiting a capitalist affinity with the mission of the neutron bomb, is on costs: "Either we restore our nuclear armed might so as to deter nuclear war or we keep playing catch-up in conventional arms, with no hope of reaching parity."[8] Their answer is to shift our defense spending priorities in the direction of an additional emphasis on nuclear weaponry, embark on a costly civil defense program to reduce casualties, encourage our main allies to do the same, and withdraw from overseas deployments into a nuclear fortress America. That is, pure nuclearism—an extreme example of lunging from the frying pan into the fire! But their vision, however macabre, is indeed the logical fulfillment of pressing to the utmost the illusion of nuclear advantage (reinforced, in this instance, by contending that it is the only possible basis for a successful U.S. foreign policy. The extremity of such a position helps us, I think, grasp the absurdity of supposing that the Machiavellian world picture retains its validity in the nuclear age. In my view unconditional renunciation of the nuclear advantage (in essence, the realization that there can be no such advantage) is indispensable if we are to retreat from the realms of terror and catastrophe. Such a retreat alone might revive the possibility of limited means for limited ends as the framework for political action. Denying this framework of limitations, despite all the abstractions of the strategists and politicians, involves an ugly embrace of barbarism. The overarching concern for citizens, then, is how to create a political climate that enables leaders to renounce the nuclear advantage, a concern I will investigate more directly in chapter 19.

In effect, nuclearizing security breeds acute insecurity among nations and their population. To move toward genuine security will require us to find intelligent and effective ways to denuclearize security.

CHAPTER 14

Nuclear Intentions

The framing of nuclear intentions involves the actual policy governing the use of the weapons. These intentions have deliberately been kept cloudy. Until very recently the main effort has been to reassure citizens while frightening the enemy. These goals are obviously somewhat inconsistent, and include various kinds of deceptions, especially in relation to one's own public. Again, the quality of democracy suffers. The political leadership feels compelled to keep citizens misinformed.

As the nuclear advantage dissolved in the 1970s, there was increasing pressure on American leaders to resort to more overt means to frighten their Soviet counterparts. Earlier the structure of the relative stockpiles established a definite preponderance in favor of the United States. These "facts" were reinforced by secret American threats in crisis contexts. Nuclear weapons were being "used" by the United States as a prime diplomatic instrument of intimidation.

As the Soviet Union increased the scale and quality of its own nuclear arsenal, it became more difficult for the United States to rely on its nuclear advantage. The difficulty was aggravated by certain developments adverse to the United States' position in international relations: the defeat in Vietnam, the Indian nuclear explosion (1974), the rising oil price and the challenge posed by OPEC, and a growing rivalry among Western nations for export markets. Each of these dimensions was complicated, but it added up to a loss of control over the course of history. Such loss is always threatening to a global power.

This loss of control seemed to climax in 1978. During that year successful anti-American revolutions took place in Iran and Nicaragua, each a key country. A year later, while American hostages were held in Teheran, the Soviet Union invaded Afghanistan, having earlier intervened in several African countries in concert with Cuba. American leadership perceived these Soviet moves as violating the spirit of détente, which had earlier in the 1970s sought to moderate the superpower rivalry.

A principal effect of these international developments has been to make threats to engage in nuclear war more explicit. This explicitness seems associated with warning the Soviet Union that even without any context of nuclear superiority, the United States is prepared to act as if it possessed a nuclear advantage. At the same time the American public is warned that it risks being beneath the shadow of Soviet nuclear superiority unless it embarks on a rapid program of "rearmament." The new security posture, initiated by Jimmy Carter but carried to greater lengths by Ronald Reagan, has simultaneously produced intense bipartisan official support for increased defense spending and a burgeoning grassroots antinuclear movement. While politicians were fully convinced by the official arguments, the people were partly convinced (supporting higher military budget) and partly scared by the rising prospect of nuclear war. And in the background are evident Soviet fears of where this latest, most volatile round of the nuclear arms race may lead.

Until the last few years the basic image of the role of strategic nuclear weapons (weapons relevant to general conflict between the United States and Soviet Union) is their retaliatory function in the event of a Soviet surprise attack; that is, they had an essentially defensive role. Serious American discussions of these matters posit a level of Soviet casualties as sufficiently high to assure that any rational leader in Moscow will refrain from launching an attack on the United States or its principal allies. The scale of an adequate retaliatory response has itself been the subject of controversy, even among the armed services, with the air force setting a somewhat higher level of assured destruction.

The quantum of assured destruction has been nominally and variously established at 20 to 30 percent of the Soviet population and somewhere above 50 percent of its industrial capacity. Actually these figures, incredibly high by comparison to past wars, are gross understatements of the expected actual ones. The damage expected from a nuclear attack is calculated by government officials on a ridiculously conservative basis in which only expected deaths caused by direct (blast and heat) effects are counted. No account is taken at all of deaths caused by fire, fallout, famine, disease, and social and ecological dislocation, which could easily be twice again as much (e.g., one professional assessment of deaths from the explosion of a large nuclear bomb over Boston estimates 3 million deaths, 2.2 million of which would be from secondary effects). The assumed direct damage also occurs on the basis of "worst case" reasoning with respect to the attack and unconvincingly assumes that Soviet efforts to minimize damage by way of civil defense and evacuation capabilities will be successful. Any retaliatory strike would certainly be far worse than the figures, awesome enough, set forth by United States defense officials. These officials tend to inflate retaliatory requirements by exaggerating Soviet defense capabilities and the political willingness of the Soviet leadership to accept huge civilian and industrial casualties, thereby strengthening their arguments for the procurement of still more weaponry here.

Much of the public discussion pivots about this question of assured destruction and its central creed: "the only rational purpose of the United States' nuclear weapons is to deter, by threat of retaliation, an adversary's use of its nuclear weapons,"[1] to quote a typical misguided view of the actual role of nuclear weapons. Militarists periodically sound an alarm about the security of this retaliatory capability. Such anxieties are often used to promote whopping increases in defense spending and generally are accompanied by more militarist phases of foreign policy, justified to redress earlier failures to meet the Soviet challenge.

The United States' retaliatory force has for almost two decades been divided into three components: long-range bombers, submarines, and ground-launched missiles, the combination being known as the TRIAD. Each leg of the TRIAD could *alone* carry out the retaliatory mission implied by mutual assured destruction even if worst-case assumptions are made (that is, an effective Soviet surprise attack, some missiles malfunction, and the Soviet Union evacuates its cities). The prospect of any nuclear devastation of the Soviet homeland is probably enough to inhibit any Soviet use of nuclear weapons. Of course, the situation is not quite so simple. At a time of crisis and uncertainty, a government might be more likely to strike preemptively if it thought it could thereby either prevail in an inevitable struggle or limit its own damage dramatically as compared to what might ensue if it waited to be attacked. Nevertheless, the scale of retaliatory forces reasonably required is far, far smaller than the nuclear arsenal at the disposal of either superpower. Maintaining the TRIAD has acquired a quasi-mystical claim on our dollars, not least of all because each leg is entrusted to one of the three principal armed services that together make up the military establishment.

If technological developments and weapons deployments cast doubt on the survivability (that is, the capacity to survive surprise attack) of any leg of the TRIAD, then a situation of grave vulnerability is declared to exist and a vast public relations campaign is mounted to build public support for more defense spending. In the last several years such a campaign has developed in relation to the Minuteman force of ground-launched long-range missiles as a result of Soviet improvements in accuracy combined with their deployment of heavy missiles. Due to this so-called "window of vulnerability," it is alleged that by the middle of this decade the Soviets could destroy a substantial proportion of the United States' land-based missile force with a well-coordinated first strike. To close the window, Pentagon planners and politicians from both parties have proposed the construction of hugely expensive mobile missile systems that the Soviet Union could not reliably target, thereby restoring the land leg to the TRIAD. The notorious MX, originally conceived of as located on "racetracks" dug out of the ground, over which missiles would be shuttled from launch site to launch site, and spread out over a huge expanse of land in Utah and Nevada, was once the preferred "basing mode" (other plans included putting the missiles on small submarines and air patrols). Powerful public opposition in one of the most conservative regions of the United States, enlisting the Mormon Church, which has great influence in the region, led the government to abandon these basing plans for the present.

The MX debate illustrates the strange aura that has grown up around the TRIAD notion and its supposed link to assured destruction. Even worst-case thinkers concede that some Minuteman missiles as now sited would survive a well-timed Soviet attack, indeed enough to destroy the most prominent Soviet civilian/industrial centers. But, besides, there are in existence large numbers of invulnerable submarines and a considerable bomber fleet, part of which is in the sky at any given time. There is, in other words, abundant—indeed far more than abundant—retaliatory capability to deter any war planner in the Soviet Union who was not hell-bent on self-destruction, and if so hell-bent, then no opposing array of missiles, however formidable, could do more than act as a further enticement. Money is wasted, anxiety created, and a false consciousness shaped by accepting the essential thinking that underlies keeping the TRIAD (rather than the country) secure. The country could be more secure by moving away from the prospect of nuclear threats in periods of crisis, which would mean drastic reductions in arsenals and attitudes toward the role of nuclear weapons in global diplomacy. In this central respect the strategy of deterrence, as it has developed over the decades, is a prime instance of the disastrous path of our nuclear intentions.

Nuclear intentions are dangerous in other ways, as well. The public focus on the implausible scenario of deterring a Soviet first strike by threatening a second-strike onslaught diverts attention from the more sinister place of nuclear weaponry in the statecraft of our time. The pretense has been that our preoccupation with nuclear weapons is a defensive one, centering on deterring a nuclear Pearl Harbor or, at the very least, some massive instance of Soviet aggression. The actual nuclear weapons policy of the United States has always included various offense-minded ideas about how to translate its national nuclear advantage into beneficial political results in the context of rivalry with the Soviet Union.

As one defense analyst close to official sources expresses this hidden emphasis:

"This 'Assured Destruction' concept was attractive from the point of view of determining the size and characteristics of American strategic forces, since American planners could establish quantitative criteria to measure the effectiveness of these forces. *However, the actual plans for the use of American nuclear forces have been kept secret.* Most people assumed that the war plans simply incorporated the Assured Destruction criteria, but in fact, having relied on well-hedged planning assumptions when acquiring strategic forces, *the United States ended up with more weapons than it needed to carry out the Assured Destruction task. The actual war plans included large-scale attacks against enemy military targets (nuclear and conventional) as well as against military plus urban/industrial targets.*"[2] (emphasis added)

The secrecy of the real plans represents more than the standard protection of national security information. Here, at issue, is the manipulation of public beliefs among American citizens.

Normally strategic discourse is carried on in a technical vocabulary with little consideration of the human stakes involved. As a result there is no feeling of risk or danger generated. The prose is cool, abstract. Occasionally, of course, there is a revealing lapse, often almost as an aside, but it has been quickly covered up. For instance, the late Bernard Brodie, a leading RAND theorist on nuclear matters, made this acknowledgment: "The typical citizen does not believe that there is any chance of a total nuclear war occurring. In that respect he is plainly wrong."[3] Of course, as polls and interviews have shown, it is Brodie who has turned out to be plainly wrong as matters now stand. A great majority of citizens currently believe that a total nuclear war is quite likely to occur in the next several years. But Brodie's assertion remains important for what it implies, namely that leaders have felt it crucial to avoid setting off a citizen alarm about nuclear war dangers. Generally in this respect, over the years strategists and political figures have downplayed the danger, except in the narrow sense of urging increased defense spending to make ourselves more secure against the only acknowledged risk, that of Soviet aggression. The current anxiety among the public is a unique challenge and arises directly from the breakdown of citizen confidence in the capacity of the government to avoid nuclear war while it strains to stay ahead of the Soviets.

The gap between the stated emphasis of nuclear doctrine on assured destruction and the actual more expansive role assigned nuclear weapons in targeting plans reflects mainly an effort to avoid raising anxieties and, worse, objections and opposition at home. The United States Government has over the years sought a variety of ways to threaten the Soviet Union with limited nuclear attack to deter limited "provocations." It has *never* been American strategic policy to confine the nuclear option to a postattack setting. (Such a readiness to initiate the use of nuclear weapons against Soviet targets is to be distinguished from *tactical* or *theater* uses that have also been contemplated from time to time to achieve victory in geographically limited diplomatic or military encounters.) This basic notion of striking, or threatening to strike, at Soviet military targets while holding the main United States strategic force in reserve so as to deter the Soviet Union from responding with a general attack on American society is the essence of limited war thinking.

Such a weapons doctrine involves a lethal war of nerves, a reckless raising of the ante in a winner-take-all game of geopolitical poker. The central objective is to convince the Soviet leadership that we believe in this limited war scenario enough to embark upon it. If they believe in our recklessness, then it is always prudent for them to back down. No goal of foreign policy is worth inviting such a nuclear strike even if, as seems likely, the other side would hit back, in the event the threat was carried out, with at a minimum their own limited nuclear attack. Mutual assured destruction (MAD) doctrine is often contrasted with counterforce thinking, which most recently has been associated with the output of nuclear utilization theorists (NUTS).

It is significant that this broader targeting policy of nuclear weapons use has been kept secret until the last few years. Some deception has been perpetuated by every American president in the nuclear age. This reality alone tells us something about the effect of these weapons on the quality of our political life. Indeed the passion for secrecy, the persistent renewal of anxiety about "leaks," the harsh pursuit of alleged spies, and the elaborate apparatus of loyalty checks and clearance procedures are mainly a reflection of the insistence by American leaders to keep the American people confused, at arms' length, when it comes to the scary realities of nuclear policy.

I do not think this assessment is exaggerated or an expression of alienation. We get high-level acknowledgments of this actual situation from time to time. One of the most consistent advocates of militarist approaches to national security is Paul Nitze, a man who has exerted a great influence on the formation of strategic policy ever since 1950. He confirmed way back in 1956 that our actual policy was one of counterforce (that is, limited first-strike attacks on Soviet military targets, not so-called countervalue, second-strike attacks on Soviet cities and industry), but added to his admission that "what should ever be declared about it is more complex." More pointedly, Morton Halperin, a former Assistant Deputy Secretary of Defense, while discussing the counterforce role for nuclear weapons observed that ". . . all public officials have learned to talk in public only about deterrence and city attacks. No war-fighting; no city-sparing. Too many critics can make too much trouble (no-cities talk weakens deterrence, the argument goes), so public officials have run for cover. That included me when I was one of them."[4]

Therefore our leaders have always been closer to exercising the nuclear option against Soviet targets for limited ends than most of us have ever really understood. This reality is further magnified by the tactical/theater uses of nuclear threats over the years. We now possess strong documentation for the assertion that every president going back to Truman and up through Nixon has actually threatened, usually in a secret communication, the use of nuclear weapons so as to control the behavior of adversaries. A partial list of instances includes Truman's threats to use nuclear weapons in Iran (1946) and Korea (1950); Eisenhower's nuclear threats or preparations in Korea and China (1953), offering the French three atomic bombs for use in Indochina (1954), preparation and threats in relation to the landing of marines in Lebanon (1958), and the defense of the off-shore Chinese islands of Quemoy/Matsu (1958); Kennedy's consideration and threat of nuclear weapons in relation to Laos (1961), Berlin (1961), and Cuba (1962); Johnson's consideration at the time of the Khe Sanh seige in Vietnam (1968); and Nixon's repeated threats to Vietnamese negotiators (1969–1972). Some of these threats were more serious than others, but throughout this whole period, behind the backs of the American people, our leaders were secretly contemplating the use of nuclear weapons and, in each instance, for rather restricted foreign policy goals. The nuclear advantage was definitely being "used" as a weapon in the cold war.

This distinction between the public image and the operational reality of nuclear diplomacy is further confused by a controversy among defense intellectuals. All along, in public, there has been an attack on MAD by individuals with strong anti-Soviet and militarist credentials. This attack has, in varying ways, aptly stressed the immorality of holding the Soviet people hostage and the overall barbarism of a city-busting approach to core security. Take, for instance, Fred Charles Iklé, a specialist on military matters, now Reagan's influential Undersecretary of Defense, who plausibly warned the public years ago about the risks of war and the immorality of mainstream deterrence thinking: " 'Assured destruction,' " Mr. Iklé wrote, "fails to indicate what is to be destroyed; but then 'assured genocide' would reveal the truth too starkly. . . . keeping ready arsenals for instant and unrestrained slaughter of men, women and children is likely to impose a wrenching perspective on the officialdom of both nations" Iklé stressed the fallibility of human leadership, raising serious questions about the durability of the balance of terror, especially given the shrinking time available for response in light of the growing vulnerability of a portion of a superpower's retaliatory force. Iklé's grim tone is even suggested by his title, "Can Nuclear Deterrence Last Out the Century?"[5]

At this point in such reasoning, one might expect an abrupt retreat from nuclearism, but alas no, Iklé's proposed amendment of policy entails, of all things, a tighter embrace. What we need to do (actually what we have been, in any event, doing all along) is to concentrate our nuclear strategy on accuracy, sophisticated plans, and additional weaponry so that we can supposedly concentrate our nuclear firepower on Soviet military targets. Iklé, as is characteristic of this kind of "counterforce morality," urges a greater effort at civil defense, dispersal of industry, and the like so that we will be in a better position to fight and survive a nuclear war should it occur.

A double moral illusion envelops the notion of using nuclear weapons as instruments of discriminate destruction and of moderating to acceptable levels a Soviet nuclear attack. Attacks with nuclear weapons on missile sites, airfields, naval bases, command centers, and the like would cause collateral civilian damage in the millions without even taking into account any of the gruesome secondary effects on the human and natural environment. Civil defense and emergency war plans seem like a sham when it comes to offering genuine protection to the civilian population. But worse than this, there is an implicit implausible assumption that we can persuade the Soviet Union to play this game of killer diplomacy according to our rules, thereby allowing our leaders to make use of nuclear weapons to shape the outcome of specific encounters and, in accordance with limited war scenarios, that is according to rules that cash in unilaterally on threats and uses of nuclear weapons. As such, Iklé's kind of "moralism," which is atypical of the nuclear use theorists (the so-called NUTS versus the MAD men), puts people in a more nuclearist frame of mind by emphasizing the military mission of the weapons and their potentially nongenocidal function in a redesigned strategy. What is strange about this line of reasoning coming from insiders in the dialogue is that they argue *as if* they are contesting the actual policy. As I have explained, military-oriented targeting schemes have consistently incorporated the essence of Iklé's position, although his emphasis on civil defense and damage limitation has not been national policy in a serious way, partly because it is such an obvious sham as to worry people more than it reassures or protects them.

What really seems at stake here is the seduction of public opinion. Counterforce moralists like Iklé apparently believe that the actual targeting scenarios are less morally objectionable and more politically inhibiting than is the official doctrine. This runs against the experience of Robert McNamara, when as Secretary of Defense he retreated quickly from this type of counterforce thinking after his trial balloon sent aloft in a famous speech given at Ann Arbor, Michigan, in 1962 provoked a strong adverse reaction here and in Europe as a war-fighting program. A further reason for his retreat was that shelter programs and civil defense drills then underway were causing anxiety among citizens and allies, building an opposition to nuclearism. The whole damage-limitation emphasis can have the opposite effect to that intended to the extent it underscores defenselessness in the nuclear age; for to take civil defense seriously requires such grisly preparations as being ready with loaded guns to shoot neighbors who may try to enter one's shelter forcibly at the moment of crisis.

The overall situation is made more confusing because the liberal mainstream reacts strongly against counterforce thinking. They believe it makes nuclear war more likely because it tempts leaders to think that even a nuclear attack on the Soviet Union would not result in catastrophe and may be worth doing to prevail in a contest of wills. MAD adherents believe that the fear of mutual catastrophe is the critical element in keeping the peace between the superpowers in the nuclear age. Anything that weakens that fear is, in the prevailing discourse, "destabilizing." Technical byplay about what must be done to keep retaliatory capabilities secure and to convey to the other side the absence of any first-strike designs is a matter of continuous arcane debate among specialists. The underlying position is that it would be mad to erode MAD! "Improving the survivability of the U.S. strategic triad must continue to be an overriding goal of this country's defense posture" is a sensitive statement of this standard outlook.[6]

What is strange about this public debate is that it is cut off from the dynamics of actual policy. MAD has never been more than the option of last resort, the least likely nuclear scenario, as official policy has evolved over the years. The Soviet leadership has understood this essential feature, seeking on their side to convey their resolve to treat any limited nuclear strike as producing an irresistible upward pressure to escalate to all-out war. The Soviets are unwilling, of course, to play our game at the level of doctrine. Why should they? Soviet acknowledgement of limited war scenarios would mean conceding the results of our nuclear advantage, thereby subjecting themselves to nuclear blackmail. They have backed up their rejection of limited war options with deployments of strategic forces that complicate any effort by American strategists to plan "a disarming first strike."

How, then, can we explain this mysterious surfacing of limited war thinking in the post-1974 period? Secretaries of Defense James Schlesinger and Harold Brown implied in public statements a shift (that was not actually much of a change) to a limited nuclear war orientation. The basic rationale was the reasonable one that in a moment of national crisis a president needed options other than doing nothing or launching an all-out attack against the Soviet Union that would in all probability result in the destruction of both societies. But the president *always* possessed these flexible options, partly to make it possible to rely on our nuclear advantage. Yet when Secretary Brown announced that the "flexible response" doctrine had been incorporated in Presidential Directive (P.D.) 59 there was a dramatic flourish of response, somewhat similar to the reaction to McNamara's 1962 speech, as if something really new had happened. As Brown correctly explained in August of 1980:

The U.S. has never had a doctrine based simply and solely on reflexible, massive attacks on Soviet cities. Instead, we have always planned both more selectively (options limiting urban-industrial damage) and more comprehensively (a range of military targets). Previous administrations, going back well into the 1960s, recognized the inadequacy of a strategic doctrine that would give us too narrow a range of options.[7]

Why, suddenly, this public acknowledgment with its predictable stimulus to antiwar sentiments? No reasons have been given officially, but certain inferences seem convincing. The initial public assertions were made by Defense Secretary Schlesinger in Seoul, South Korea, shortly after the Vietnam defeat. The United States Government had grown anxious about the credibility of its farflung alliance commitments, especially as its old interventionary policy was discredited at home. This credibility crisis centered on letting Vietnam "go down the drain" *without using nuclear weapons.* Schlesinger seemed to imply by his statement that our allies could be reassured that we had learned *this* lesson, and that nuclear weapons would be available for use in the future, including in Korea if another war erupted there.

Similarly, the announcement of P.D. 59 occurred in the aftermath of the Iranian and Nicaraguan revolutions and the Soviet invasion of Afghanistan. The Carter Doctrine represented a more general diplomatic statement of national resolve to safeguard control over the Persian Gulf oil-producing region by a readiness to use *whatever* military means might prove necessary. Despite the prominence given to the Rapid Deployment Force as an instrument of effective intervention in Persian Gulf countries, it was evident that such a defense could not succeed in the face of a serious challenge. P.D. 59 and the Carter Doctrine seemed more expressions of diplomatic desperation than a shift in nuclear weapons policy. In any event, it is not evident how nuclear weapons might be used effectively if the challenge took the form of large-scale hostile national revolutions. Somehow the United States wanted to send a message that, rational or not, any further disturbance of the status quo in the region could easily get out of control and lead to general war.

The same kind of panic thinking was even more openly re-

184

lied on in Europe, occasioning agitated Soviet responses intending to show Europeans that extending "the theater" of Europe to embrace the Soviet Union (as proposed Pershing II deployments, with their 1200-mile range, would accomplish) was a virtual invitation to Armageddon. Furthermore, with such deployment patterns any crisis might produce a Soviet preemptive strike on missiles that, given European population densities, would by itself be catastrophic. The United States was trying to tell European leaders that these new deployments could show the Soviet Union that the defense of Europe could be undertaken in a limited way, hence would be more credible, as it would not depend on the willingness of the United States to commit suicide for the sake of the Europeans. The Soviet Union responded predictibly by sending one message to Washington (recourse to limited war would produce general war) and another to Europe (recourse to limited war would mean the end of Europe). Popular unrest posture has confirmed the reasons for earlier official inhibitions on discussing *actual* policy. The European peace movement has grown by leaps and bounds, and spurts forward whenever American leaders promote the limited war notion based on "theater" weaponry, neutron bombs, maintaining the United States as "sanctuary."

In concluding here I think it important to understand that the antidemocratic manner in which nuclear weapons policy has developed over the years makes it confusing for the general public to grasp the central issue—namely the continuous resolve of the United States Government to defend national interests by relying, as necessary, on nuclear weapons threats. As the quality of this reliance becomes more exposed, public anxiety and resistance has grown to such an extent that top leaders have retreated, offering new reassurances. Public anxiety is also heightened and the mood confused by the alleged need to run even harder to stay even with (or get ahead of) the Soviet

Union, which is running pretty fast itself, as well as by several war dangers in critical regions around the world, especially the Persian Gulf, and by tendencies of the weapons technology to cut down decision time in crises thereby risking escalation and tempting preemption. Confusion results because the domestic "audience" grows divided in several ways; sometimes the same individual experiences the contradictory pulls of being frightened by the danger of nuclearism and by the threat of Soviet militarism. Meeting the supposed Soviet threat has increased fear of nuclear war. How can American leaders pledged to augment military power calm the agitated nerves of the body politic?

But the situation is more serious than this. The basic retaliatory tenet of MAD is itself vulnerable in ways that have virtually nothing to do with the current measures of strategic strength: launchers, missiles, warheads, throwweight, accuracy. The entire capacity to respond depends on a secure command and control structure that could be effectively destroyed by a relatively small attack, possibly consisting of as few as (one to five) high-altitude nuclear explosions triggering ultra-electromagnetic pulses destructive of any modern communications system. John Steinbrunner, a defense specialist, has recently written a chilling article depicting this "command vulnerability," which he persuasively describes as "the most significant problem of modern strategic thought."[8] This feature of vulnerability has been understood by the Soviet Union and applies to them in reverse. So far few steps have been taken by either side to reduce this vulnerability. There is no prospect of a technical solution, although the situation can be improved, but only at great expense. Such expense would have some strategic significance in ways that adding to nuclear arsenals does not, but command and control technology does not evidently have the political constituencies needed to win large appropriations, nor does it attract big support from the separate military services, each of which has its shopping list headed by favorite weapons systems.

In other words, corruption of the deepest sort bears on the pursuit of security. Leaders do not even dare to seek defense appropriations that would make the deterrence system stable on its own terms! MAD is madder than we think, even taking the dubious view that this is the best of all possible nuclear worlds.

Because of this vulnerability there is now a great temptation to go all the way in any East–West encounter, lest the other side exercise its capacity to destroy the command system upon which coordinated response depends. In effect, strong bureaucratic pressures exist to ignore the kind of "flexible response" thinking incorporated in P.D. 59 or in the earlier targeting plans. But neither is this merely a reliance on mutual assured destruction. Rather, the situation now makes it more likely that policy could move in the direction of the SAC commander who had been eager for a pretext to wipe the Soviets off the face of the earth in the Cuban Missile Crisis. What Steinbrunner contends is that such extremists might well get their chance if such a crisis recurs in the future:

. . . command vulnerability has produced powerful incentives within the U.S. military planning system to conduct full-scale strategic operations at the outset of any serious crisis. . . . Once the use of as many as 10 or more nuclear weapons against the USSR is seriously contemplated, U.S. strategic commanders will likely insist on attacking the full array of Soviet military targets. . . . the existing U.S. command system is subject to strains powerful enough to trigger an unintended war.[9]

Notions of limited exchange could easily be swept aside by this logic of command vulnerability. The temptation in a crisis to strike first massively is powerful, and both sides might yield to this temptation. Further, Soviet awareness of these pressures could lead it to initiate a nuclear attack if it concludes that war is inevitable, which will encourage a rapid escalation of a military response on the U.S. part, and so forth. In other words, the mutual awareness of this profound structure of instability seriously aggravates an already dangerous reality.

As is so typical of strategic discourse, once the alarm is sounded there is no rational followthrough by way of an insistence that the framework be dismantled at the earliest possible moment. Steinbrunner apparently regards his audience as composed of those who cannot imagine a world without the bomb. His counsels of nuclear prudence fly directly in the face of a period of strategic assertiveness. Clearly it is utopian to suppose that the dynamic of the nuclear arms race can be transformed by one calm analyst talking to others. Something far more drastic is called for if we are to find our way back even to the setting of what has passed for safety earlier in the nuclear age.

Of course, there are even more deliberate assaults on the limited security afforded by the nuclear stalemate between the superpowers. A mixture of militarist criteria and technological momentum is producing a new generation of first-strike weapons systems and supportive doctrine. Here again the pressure for the other side to preempt is strong, as its own retaliatory capability (either silos, airfields, naval bases, or command facilities) could be destroyed if it waits to determine whether the other side really intends to attack. Such first-strike systems could produce an unintended war in which both sides misread signals, with little reaction time available, and decide under pressure that a launch of nuclear weapons is the lesser of evils. For instance, the Trident submarine can deliver its missiles on target in less than ten minutes if deployed near the Soviet coastline. These kinds of prospects encourage planners to work out war-fighting scenarios. Since deterrence is likely to fail at some point, it is vital to do the best we can at the next level of reality, with "best" still being defined by reigning strategists as "winning" in the sense of surviving catastrophe relatively more intact than the enemy. Such advocacy, in turn, does nurture a civil defense mentality (shelter building, postattack planning) not to save lives as much as to convey resolve to the other side and to provide one's own citizenry with some (false) assurance that the onset of nuclear war is not the end-point of personal and collective existence.

We are faced, I believe, with a situation of growing hazard, well epitomized by Jonathan Schell's stark acknowledgment: "Indeed, if we are honest with ourselves we have to admit that unless we rid ourselves of our nuclear arsenals a holocaust not only might occur but will occur—if not today, then tomorrow; if not this year, then next."[10] Being this honest with ourselves may be the critical next step, although by itself it leads nowhere. How can we act to undo what has been done in our name, yet not always with our understanding, much less our consent? Fighting to regain democracy, including a renewed insistence that the president is elected to serve the people and is accountable to them and their elected representatives, is one crucial way to resist the slide toward nuclear war. Without the spirit and substance of democracy it will be difficult to dislodge the nuclearist mind-set and support system. Challenging nuclear intentions will require, even at this stage, a repudiation of the right to initiate nuclear war. To mount this challenge involves going back in time and context to the Hiroshima bomb and our acceptance of its use against Japanese cities and civilians. Hiroshima provides the touchstone of legitimacy for the entire subsequent edifice of nuclearism.

CHAPTER 15

Emergent Nuclearism

When Pope John Paul II made his visit to the site of the first combat use of nuclear weapons, he declared: "To remember Hiroshima is to commit oneself to peace." Currently activists in the resurgent Japanese peace movement are demanding that their government include a visit to Hiroshima on the itinerary of any important public official from abroad. One recalls the Israeli insistence that Henry Kissinger visit the Museum of the Holocaust, Vad Yashem, as often as possible during his efforts to negotiate an Arab-Israeli settlement after the 1973 war.

On one crucial level starting with Hiroshima is not going back far enough. The rise of the modern state, its special claims to uphold state interests by *any* means, and the continuous expansion of the scope and destructiveness of war are part of the story. Even more central, perhaps, is the spirit of modernism, its emphasis on commodities and production, its depreciation of the sacred, and its association of happiness and progress with materialist norms. One expression of modernism has been the sidelining of religion and the reduction of the great healing profession of medicine to an assemblage of highly paid technocrats. It is notable, in this regard, that the first serious challenge to nuclearism has been so far led by clergymen and doctors, not by such traditional sources of protest as students, workers, radicals, or minorities.

Remembering Hiroshima is a crucial focus for grasping the totality of attitudes, institutions, and dangers we identify as nuclearism, but remembering the wider civilizational context that issued forth in history as Hiroshima is likewise crucial.

A natural first question is "Could it ever have been otherwise?" Was there a point back in the past when it might have been possible to say no? After all, at every stage human beings acted and decided on the assumption of choice. Given what we know now about the menace of nuclearism, realizations that could have been and were, in a real sense, anticipated ever since the early scientific work on the possibility of atomic explosions, could this drift toward cataclysm have been averted? What were the most opportune moments? Could these moments have been better used if the peace forces of the world had been more alert to their opportunities? Will such opportune moments occur again in the future or is it now, even if arguably it was not earlier, too late to do anything but wait, hope, and pray that somehow, despite all the malice and incompetence in the world, we shall somehow escape nuclear annihilation?

After sifting through numerous discussions of these issues by participants, especially scientists and political leaders, a basic conclusion emerges that the weight of influence at the highest levels of government has pushed forward the process of nuclearism at every critical stage. There were, of course, all along islets of resistance, sometimes larger, sometimes smaller, but always easily outmatched by the guardians of the state for whom the decision to say yes has always seemed easier and, in the end, necessary, even if not entirely satisfactory.

191

Let's begin with the development stage, the decision to develop a bomb in the first place. The context was dominated by the ongoing struggle against Hitler's Germany. Scientists, some of whom were refugees from Naziism, knew that the Germans were working to produce a bomb, believed that the German project was promising, and assumed that Hitler would have no compunctions about threatening to use or using it to gain victory. Therefore, developing an anti-Nazi bomb seemed, under the auspices of Manhattan Project, definitely validated by the overriding commitment in democratic countries to defeat Hitler's design for world conquest. The most humane voices, such as those of Albert Einstein and Leo Szilard, who would later crusade for nuclear disarmament, were early and influential advocates of developing the military applications of the new nuclear physics.

Most prominent among leading nuclear physicists, Niels Bohr of Denmark clearly foresaw at this developmental stage that long-range dangers posed by nuclear weaponry were likely to outweigh any short-term advantages. His prestige was such as to obtain wartime meetings with Winston Churchill and Franklin Roosevelt. His ideas were set forth in a July 1944 memorandum built around the central proposition "that the terrifying prospect of a future competition between nations about a weapon of such formidable character can only be avoided through a universal agreement in true confidence."[1] He warned of the consequences of postponing efforts to achieve "an adequate control arrangement" and of the importance of fostering cooperation by an early sharing of information. Despite his concern and prominence, Bohr made no impression even on such generally farsighted statesmen as Churchill and Roosevelt, apparently because they found his proposals "political" in character and out of keeping with the practical realities of the affairs of great powers.

Emergent Nuclearism

As soon as the test stage was reached, the focus shifted considerably. Germany had been defeated by the time of the Alamogordo explosion of July 16, 1945. The impetus to go forward came partly from the bureaucratic momentum associated with assembling, at high cost, such an elaborate project, the largest collective undertaking of its kind in human history, involving an investment one thousand times larger than the German effort. The participants, including those who like J. Robert Oppenheimer harbored some anxieties about longer range consequences, wanted to vindicate their enterprise by success, which meant a demonstration that the bomb really worked. There are those who celebrated the test explosion as an extraordinary vindication of the scientific enterprise, an achievement, however frightening in relation to social and political conflict, that was associated in fundamental respects with human fulfillment. The great French Jesuit philosopher-anthropologist Teilhard de Chardin greeted the test explosion in the New Mexico desert with wild enthusiasm because it "disclosed to human existence a supreme purpose: the purpose of pursuing ever further, to the very end, the forces of Life. In exploding the atom we took our first bite at the fruit of the great discovery, and this was enough for a taste to enter our mouths that can never be washed away: the taste for super-creativeness."[2]

Political leaders at the time were, of course, alert to the importance of a potential bomb for the relation of states, especially in the emerging postwar setting. Recent scholarship, especially Martin Sherwin's *A World Destroyed*, has demonstrated that Franklin Roosevelt, as much as Harry Truman, regarded the bomb as something to be guarded as a sovereign prerogative, shared only to some extent with Great Britain, then our closest ally. Not only the Soviet Union but even France was to be kept in the dark about the bomb as long as possible. At no point did the wartime atmosphere of alliance

193

extend to inviting French or Soviet scientists to take part in the Manhattan Project. From the moment Truman received word at Potsdam of the Alamogordo test explosion in 1945, its geopolitical importance became as obvious as the gold stocks at Fort Knox.[3]

Even in retrospect, there were no forces present on the scene that resisted carrying the Manhattan Project to completion. Hitler might truly have provided the initial justification for diverting the large quantities of money and talent, but once the project was underway it generated its own momentum, adopting a new rationale quite effortlessly. Even if World War II had not provided favorable circumstances for mobilizing talent and resources, it seems clear that some later context of world crisis would have prompted the effort to develop the bomb. Once the technological project of a bomb seemed feasible, then, given the entire momentum of modernism, the outcome of Hiroshima was unavoidable.

Within policymaking circles there was never any serious doubt that the bomb would be used to maximum advantage when and if ready. It was, at the time, as the noted scientist Hans Bethe puts it, "a foregone conclusion." The motivations for use still remain cloudy after all these years, and different leaders undoubtedly endorsed use for different reasons. Surely there was some conviction at the time that using the bomb would end the war quickly on American terms, thereby saving lives, especially American lives. Also present were various ideas about the postwar context. Ending the Pacific war without Soviet help would give the United States a freer hand in shaping the future of the region, specifically in Japan and elsewhere in East Asia. Also, and this consideration was definitely present in the minds of some of Truman's senior advisors, most notably his ambitious anti-Communist Secretary of State, James F. Byrnes, the use of the bomb would go a long way toward inducing overall Soviet deference to American leadership in the postwar world.

In a quite distinct vein, Paul Fussell talks of Hiroshima as a way of "irrationally remembering Pearl Harbor with a vengeance."[4] The impulse to punish enemies who are portrayed as evil by destroying them remains a potent force in international relations. More recently, during the Iranian hostage crisis, a popular bumper sticker in the United States was "nuke the Ayatollah." Leaders are not immune from such sentiments, although the decorum of their role is such that they will normally not acknowledge such rockbottom motivations. Americans who feel wronged by the outrages of others have always seemed prone, quite self-righteously, to teach their international adversaries a bloody lesson they won't easily forget.

For our purposes, what is especially chastening about the use of atomic bombs against those two Japanese cities is that the military occasion was routine, certainly lacking in any compelling necessity. National survival was in no way at stake. Even the outcome of the war was patently clear, and possibly the atomic bomb achieved no more by way of war goals than saving a few weeks' time. Whatever the appraisal of the Hiroshima decision, there is common ground that it didn't take much for the United States back in 1945 to leap across the nuclear threshold. Of course, since Hiroshima a much stronger inhibition on nuclear weapons has developed, especially since the acquisition of nuclear weapons by rival states. How strong this inhibition is, is a matter of conjecture and controversy. Neither the United States nor anyone else has used a nuclear weapon to achieve a military victory or in the heat of international crisis, although a series of nuclear threats have been made by the United States in pursuit of specific foreign policy goals.

When the initial decision was made, the developmental process went forward with confidence and few regrets as one more act of war, as one more demonstration of American military and technological prowess at the expense of a hated enemy. The public accepted it in this spirit, believing at the time that it brought the war to a speedy end, thereby saving lives, liberating prisoners of war, restoring peace. Of course, once used, the starker longer term implications began to emerge rapidly. Immediately after Hiroshima political leaders in the West began to advocate some drastic steps to assure that such weapons were removed from the geopolitical scene.

In a thoughtful essay published on the thirty-sixth anniversary of the Nagasaki bomb, Kai Erikson poses what he regards as the overwhelming issue: ". . . What kind of mood does a fundamentally decent people have to be in, what kind of moral arrangements must it make, before it is willing to annihilate as many as a quarter of a million human beings for the sake of making a point?"[5] Let's not even address the premise of fundamental decency, certainly highly questionable from the point of view of domestic "losers," especially nonwhites, and of no relevance to our treatment of foreign "enemies," again especially nonwhites. The Hiroshima context informs us that it does not take much, at least in the setting of general war, to prepare Americans, and one suspects other similar states with pretensions of geopolitical "greatness," to inflict atrocities on enemy societies in order to make a point. In a sense, at least for the West, such a capacity has a hallowed heritage. The Old Testament God seemed always ready to plunder an enemy people unto the last woman and child for the sake of His chosen people. In other words, moral arrangements for genocide and atrocity have long enjoyed a high cultural stature and are presumably imprinted on our civilization in a manner that is so deep that it is hidden from active consciousness.

Of course, there were some mildly inhibiting "moral arrangements" associated with international law and morality, religious scruples, and the like. What is surprising, however, is how weak these inhibitions were in the context of waging "a just war" against those "Japs." The degree of incoherence was intense, considering that only months later the United States Government was to set up a court for the trial and punishment of Japanese civilian and military leaders who violated the laws of war in a manner much less significant than the violations associated with the atomic attacks. Our moral arrangements permitted us to engage in indiscriminate terror against the civilian population of Japan, while holding Japanese leaders accountable for adherence to the letter of the law. This double standard enables the moral arrangements of a fundamentally decent people to do virtually anything provided only that there is bipartisan domestic consensus in support of the main tendency of foreign policy. When that consensus erodes, as it did after the Tet Offensive in the Vietnam War or late in the Korean War, then and only then do the moral arrangements inhibit that particular group of leaders charged with carrying out what has become, by virtue of the elite split, a *controversial* policy.

What is significant for our purposes here is that the use of atomic bombs against Japan never has become, in this sense, "controversial." Even more to our point, the overall policy governing possible *future* use of nuclear weapons has started to be controversial only in the last few years.

Perhaps it is true that the sanction of a popular, general war was required. Surely during the latter Vietnam years there were various forms of "testing" going on to assess whether a policy of bombing (nonnuclear) the dikes in North Vietnam, endangering the lives of several million Vietnamese, would be "acceptable" to world public opinion and to the American people. It is a tribute to the achievement of the peace movement, I believe, to raise sufficient doubts in the mind of American policymakers as to whether they could get away *domestically* with an atrocity on such a scale in the Vietnam context. These doubts were further reinforced by military doubts about the effectiveness of such tactics. As always, it is not possible to apportion weights for this forbearance, especially in a context where leaders are reluctant to admit (even to themselves) the mix of factors influencing their behavior.

What does seem disturbingly clear, however, is that the moral arrangements, in Kai Erikson's sense, currently exist for the massive use of nuclear weapons in the course of a general war with the Soviet Union, or even in response to some provocation perceived as grave by our leaders at the time. Indeed our entire doctrine of national security rests on the *credibility* of our willingness to use such weapons if vital national or alliance interests are seriously jeopardized. Other nuclear weapons states as well, most notably the Soviet Union, have in place comparable moral arrangements. Since Hiroshima, in a sense, every public expression of support for nuclear disarmament has involved some impulse to undo these atrocity-producing moral arrangements that continue to make it easy for our leaders, and political leaders generally, to contemplate recourse to nuclear weapons as just another "option" in a crisis situation.

At the end of World War II, in the immediate postwar context, there seemed to be a brief political resolve to remove nuclear weapons from the scene. World leaders, including the American president and the British prime minister, insisted on the importance of acting quickly. If such internationalization did not occur dire consequences were predicted. Even such an archrealist as Winston Churchill on August 16, 1945 told the House of Commons "we must remold the relationships of all men, of all nations in such a way that these men do not wish, or dare, to fall upon each other for the sake of vulgar, outdated ambition or for passionate differences in ideologies, and that international bodies by supreme authority may give peace on earth and justice among men."

Several factors converged at the time. A widespread sense of the agony of major war existed and supported moves by political leaders to relinquish national sovereignty for the sake of future peace. The United Nations was founded on the basis of such sentiments, which were shared on the surface, at least, by all important governments. Further, the wartime alliance prevailed in an atmosphere in which victory was viewed as a confirmation of moral superiority. The continuation of that atmosphere might have been expected to be dramatically sustained by the national renunciation of atomic weaponry. Especially the United States, with its idealistic tradition, was strongly inclined to neutralize any shadows cast by its use of the bomb by now demonstrating a willingness to take steps to assure its prohibition in the future.

Additional factors were encouraging, as well. The Soviet Union lacked the bomb and was thought to be a decade or more away from developing it. Therefore it was assumed in the West that it was not immediately necessary to trust the Soviets and, at the same time, since they would otherwise be at the mercy of the American nuclear monopoly, it was supposed that they had an enormous incentive to agree to a Western proposal for the international control of atomic energy.

As we know, things didn't work out this way. True, the United States, after considerable internal bickering, put forth the so-called Baruch Plan in 1946. This proposal called for the international control of the entire gamut of nuclear technology and capabilities. But its way of vesting control by stages of unspecified duration assured the United States an indefinite edge in nuclear technology that could have been quickly converted into military capabilities in the event that the underlying agreement broke down. At the same time, as other international experiences involving liberal projects have demonstrated, the president cannot always successfully commit the United States to international undertakings. The most famous instance is, of course, Woodrow Wilson's failure to persuade the United States Senate to ratify the Versailles Treaty, since it included the Covenant of the League of Nations. More alive in our memory, surely, is the difficulty that Jimmy Carter had with the Panama Canal Treaties and, later, with SALT II. Looking back, it is far from assured that if the Soviets had leaped to sign the Baruch Plan as presented, that two-thirds of the United States Senate would have gone along. A great debate would surely have ensued, with military and conservative groups strongly mobilized in opposition. Deep, dark questions about the nature of World Communism and of real Soviet intentions would have surfaced. Nationalists and jingoists would have harangued the public about the lunacy of giving away our best weapons in a world of power polities.

Of course, the Soviets never put us to the test. They were themselves too much part of the world power game to take risks with our "idealism." The Soviet Union was an extreme instance of a powerful state with a self-help orientation. Stalin had prevailed in a bitter domestic struggle, partly by advocating the thesis of "communism in one country," a stress upon Soviet insularity that accentuated a fortress mentality that was already an ingrained feature of Russian history. As a rising superpower, the Soviets seemed disinterested in international undertakings that would freeze them into a position of permanent vulnerability and strategic inferiority. The Soviet leadership was totally unwilling to put its trust in others, especially in relation to state matters of security.

Historical assessment never yields assured conclusions. Yet I think the best available evidence suggests there never was a really good opportunity to close down the opening of the nuclear arms race. At most there was a short-lived impulse to explore Soviet receptivity to a plan that would not quickly, or perhaps ever, jeopardize American nuclear preeminence.

The situation might have been different after World War II if any of the following conditions had existed: (1) If the Germans had developed and used the bomb, especially against American and British cities, then the *necessity* for international control would have been more deeply and widely felt on the victors' side; (2) if the Soviet bomb development program was either comparable to the United States' attainment or so markedly inferior that the Soviet leadership saw no prospect in the foreseeable future of neutralizing the American atomic advantage, then Soviet receptivity to the American plan and American willingness to forego its sovereign rights might have been greater; (3) if the United States had developed and used more fission bombs of the Hiroshima type over a longer period or moved ahead to "the Super" (H-bomb, later known merely as "nuclear weapons") in World War II and used it against Japan, the devastation might have been great enough to shift around the priorities for postwar reconstruction that existed in 1945.

With the failure of the Baruch Plan, there was a return to traditional international politics. The United States possessed a monopoly on the relatively small arsenal of atomic bombs that was gradually augmented in the 1945–1949 period until it reached about one thousand. The Cold War commenced in a serious way with Churchill's "iron curtain" speech at Fulton, Missouri, in March 1946, the setting forth of the Truman Doctrine of containment in 1947, and the formation of opposing military alliances in Europe toward the end of the decade. In these initial years after 1945, there was no set doctrine governing the use of atomic bombs beyond this fundamental molding pattern of Soviet conventional superiority and easy geopolitical access to Europe versus the United States' atomic superiority, foreign bases, and global military mobility. Such a pattern has remained at the center of international politics ever since.

Note that limits were placed on the role of atomic weapons. No serious attempt to roll back Soviet domination over Eastern Europe was made by way of atomic threats. Presidential approval was required even in combat situations. No serious consideration was given to preventive war scenarios (counseled at the time by right-wingers and given serious behind-the-scenes support by a few official advisors).

Actually, the Soviet explosion of an atomic device of its own in August 1949 came as a shock. The Soviet Union was way ahead of what Western leaders supposed to be its timetable. It is possible that had the Soviets' progress been more correctly understood, a strong temptation to launch the sort of preemptive attack that the Israelis carried out against Iraqi nuclear facilities at Osirak in 1981 might have existed.

The main actual effect of this abrupt ending of the United States' atomic monopoly was to exert pressure on American leaders to keep decisively ahead. This partly meant adding to the stockpile, but mainly it meant going ahead with the controversial Super. Going ahead with the Super marked the transition from the atomic to the thermonuclear age.

The Super was controversial because it seemed to carry the destructive capabilities of weapons makers beyond all rational limits. Whereas the standard atomic bombs of World II variety had an explosive magnitude of 20,000 or so tons of TNT, the Super could (and would) attain magnitudes of 1 to 35 million tons, with even larger capabilities possible. Put differently, a Super would have an explosive yield of 50 to 1750 Hiroshima Equivalents. On such a scale, the terroristic character of warfare could no longer be doubted. The belief that weaponry far more destructive than the Hiroshima bomb was needed for purposes of national security suggests the degree to which the political framework of war had been superceded, or that the compulsion to stay ahead produced bizarre measures of superiority.

The General Advisory Commission, a body headed by J. Robert Oppenheimer consisting mainly of leading scientists to advise the Atomic Energy Commission on policy questions, met to discuss the Super on October 29, 1949, a few months after the Soviet test explosion. At that time their unanimous conclusion opposed the development of the Super. Although they believed that such thermonuclear devices were technically feasible, they argued that the economic burden of such development would interfere with the ongoing, more militarily important program of expanding the number and types of fission bombs. Also they believed that the only Soviet targets that could conceivably warrant bombs on such a scale were Leningrad and Moscow; everything else of value for even the most drastic war effort could be adequately destroyed by A-bombs. Finally, and of most importance at the time to the commission, was the conviction that the moral standing of the United States would fall if such weapons were developed.

More entrenched and professional bureaucratic forces organized a counterattack that quickly succeeded. The questions of military effectiveness were resolved in favor of the Super, and the moral question was easily put aside, even by scientists, many of whom were easily induced to overcome their qualms and embrace the prospect of participating in a new technological frontier where the interface between knowledge and power might have such a dramatic impact on human affairs. On the basis of seven minutes of Cabinet-level discussion, President Truman announced the decision to go ahead (". . . we have no other course") with the super-bomb on January 31,

1950, and there was little public expression of opposition.

In some respects this rather obscure decision represented, as it has sometimes been described, the real "quantum leap" in the relationship between violence and policy. For with the fusion bomb there was no conceivable way to avoid the genocidal and ecocidal "side-effects" of allegedly "military" uses, at least if land targets in populated areas are involved. Indeed the circumference of the area devastated and the scale of fallout meant that indiscriminateness of fantastic magnitudes had become inherent in the warfare of the future. For *any* conceivable military target per se, such as troop concentrations, naval formations, or even industrial centers, the earlier A-bomb based on fission technology was more than sufficient, as Hiroshima itself so grimly demonstrated.

The global context was different in 1950 than it had been five years earlier at the time of Hiroshima. At the earlier time, the atmosphere of the wartime alliance influenced the tone, if not the substance, of foreign policy. By 1950 the Cold War was the cornerstone of foreign policy, meaning that hostility toward and distrust of the Soviet Union established the national mood. The Soviet development of an atomic bomb ahead of schedule was attributed, in part, to their espionage network and reinforced our fear that they might get ahead of us without our ever even realizing it until too late. In fact, this sense of "opening up" the closed Soviet society as a condition of our security has led the Soviet Union's leaders to fear that we were using "inspection" and "verification" demands in arms control negotiations to collect targeting information. Again the differing circumstances of the two superpowers led to two antagonistic sets of perceptions. Our image of the Soviet Union's world revolutionary crusade led us to suppose that its closed society was a potentially lethal weapon in the ongoing struggle for global supremacy, while the U.S.S.R.'s image of our insistence on practicing diplomacy from a position of nuclear superiority and encircling overseas bases led it to believe that our emphasis on inspection was part of a larger, continuing plan to destroy it as a rival power, or at least to reduce it to international impotence by nuclear blackmail. Very likely both sets of perception, reflecting the different positions of the two states, contained substantial insights.

Another persisting feature of the nuclear national security state also was exhibited by the momentous decision to build the H-bomb. The citizenry and, even, Congress were effectively denied any voice or role, despite the absence of any pressing emergency or a circumstance of war. The go-ahead was reported to the American people in a rather routine presidential announcement, its significance gradually filtering to the public but in a manner that discouraged general understanding. Early in the atomic age the antidemocratic premise was tacitly adopted—that crucial decisions bearing on nuclear weapons development and strategic doctrine should be determined within the Executive Branch on the basis of secret and technical information. The cumulative effect of this concentration of authority is to subvert the healthy relationship envisioned by the Constitution between government and citizenry in the area of policy most crucial to the future well-being of American society. In effect, this characteristic nonaccountability and noncontroversiality of nuclear weapons policy naturally inclines policy in the directions favored by the militarist cast of mind, which enjoys a permanent presence in the bureaucratic structure that seems virtually unchallengeable even by *elected* political leaders, including the president, given the political climate and economic configuration of power that has up to this point existed in this country.

If the United States Government associates the protection of its national interests with a circumstance of strategic advantage (at whatever level of overkill!), then the conditions for an endless arms race exist unless the Soviet Government is prepared to allow Washington to control the play. Policy makers in Moscow must seek parity (or an edge), if they hold beliefs similar to those of their Washington counterparts, or even if they don't! In the latter instance, because if the United States believes it has a usable advantage then even if it would be irrational for American leaders to follow through on such a basis, the Soviet Union might be victimized (as would, of course, the United States) by such irrationality and hence must build more missiles to discourage any illusion of advantage. These interactions are deadly serious even if grounded on absurd reasoning.

This supposed "linkage" between strategic levels and assertiveness in foreign policy is impossible to validate or invalidate. As a result it can be sustained indefinitely by bureaucratic momentum that accepts the inevitability of conflictual relations and is averse to assuming the risks associated with a cooperative approach. And, in fact, if we act on the basis of such assumptions about linkage, then there is a self-fulfilling component added on. If strategic strength (or weakness) correlates with "resolve" toward Third World threats or crisis confrontations, then assertiveness may indeed follow from a perception of strategic buildup. And if it does, then the Soviet Union will be induced to undertake its own buildup to discourage such assertiveness. If one follows the drift of security debate and foreign policy behavior since the 1950s, it seems to reflect the reality of this psychological dimension of strategic armaments, even though these levels are virtually unrelated to any discrete change of superpower vulnerability.

Note also that such a calculus of gain establishes a precedent that touches on the sovereign discretion of other states. The Soviet Union reasons, apparently, in a similar manner vis-à-vis China, India vis-à-vis Pakistan, and on and on. The acquisition of a nuclear edge seems like a legitimate means to pursue national interests in a world system whose operative rules are shaped by the behavior of the leading states. Thereby is nurtured one of the other nightmares of the nuclear age—gradual proliferation of the weapons capability to additional states and, hypothetically, beyond even states, to other political actors, including possibly at some point terrorist groups.

The H-bomb decision is, in retrospect, so decisive because it showed once and for all that despite the menace of nuclear war, the statist imperative of staying ahead, or seeming to, remains deeply ingrained.[6] It is only necessary to add that, in all probability, *any* state that had found itself with the sort of power advantages that accrued to the United States as a result of its competitive success in harnessing the atom would have acted similarly to conserve the advantage for itself. Surely there is no evidence that the Soviet Union would have been more farsighted or restrained had it been the nuclear innovator. That is, the moral and political arrangements that exist here in the United States are inadequate for the imperatives of the nuclear age, but no more so than arrangements elsewhere.

CHAPTER 16

The Soviet Factor:
A "Useful" Enemy

The vector of nuclear intentions is, of course, the Soviet Union. More and more Americans grasp the tragic flaws bound up with nuclearism and yet they support the nuclearist path as the lesser of evils. Pushed, the majority of Americans would rather take their chances with nuclear war than expose the country, or even its world position, to Soviet aggression. A rigidifying either/or mentality that can only envisage pacifism as an alternative to nuclearism confines choice and creates a national and species destiny.

"Hatred is like rain in the desert—it is of no use to anybody" is an African saying that speaks directly to our nature as human beings. Revealingly, hatred is of great use to the makers of foreign policy for powerful states. It builds a positive sense of "we" identity on the ground of our negative sense of "them." The image of sacrificing money, convenience, even life to oppose a common enemy has been used over and over again to summon a population to war and war preparations. To conceive of another people, members of the same species, as an enemy usually embodies elements of hatred and fear as well as issues of conflict and opposition. To the extent hatred and fear are present, peaceful relations are far more difficult to establish. Hatred, whether directed at another people, its leaders, or its ideology, may also be part of the essential moral and psychological preparation to wage nuclear war, implying a willingness to inflict and endure such severe suffering. As such it becomes essential to resist the manipulation of our emotions and the construction of our essential identity around the imagery of the hated enemy. In effect, the wisdom of the African saying should become a practical guide for international politics without, of course, any expectations that conflict will thereby disappear or that it will not continue to be necessary to oppose and defend against various political evils.

For Americans the presence of the Soviet Union in the world is enough to explain nuclear arms racing, making the nuclearist path seem inevitable, even if increasingly acknowledged as tragic. Presumably the architects of defense policy in the Kremlin see the world scene in reverse, confronted by a militarized United States poised to devastate the Soviet homeland if it were not for the constraining impact of Soviet armed might. Each side regards its own militarism as essentially reactive, as a defensive necessity given the character, designs, and capabilities of its rival. These mutually reinforcing images of an aggressive enemy are part of what makes nuclearism, a special aggravated case of militarism, such a rigid reality.

Historically it is useful to remember both that the United States and the Soviet Union fought together as allies against the common enemy of fascism and that virtually as soon as that enemy disappeared from the earth each victorious superpower began to treat the other as an enemy. Throughout the history of international relations states have seemed always to consider the main foreign states as either "allies" or "adversaries." This pattern of relations suggests that the idea of the enemy state may be strongly encouraged by the structure of international political life and that changes in this structure may be indispensible if there is to be any hope for building over time a world liberated from nuclearism.

Part of what keeps normal people—that is, people without any inclination to risk the nuclear death-trap—from deep questioning and opposition on matters of national security is their acceptance of the reality of the Soviet challenge. In effect, many Americans believe that unless we are prepared to surrender to Soviet tyranny, it is necessary to keep our nuclear defensive guard high. This means, at least, matching weaponry, and this produces, like it or not, a readiness for major war, a reliance on nuclear weapons, and an embrace of the nuclear arms race.

Often peace movement militants oppose the American reliance on nuclear weaponry and defense spending without seeming to take account of the existence of the Soviet challenge, and this disturbs many mainstream citizens who are worried by both the danger of nuclear war and the Soviet challenge. To this extent the movement can be dismissed as naive, pacifist, or utopian. The Soviet menace is generally perceived as real and must be addressed. In this regard most Americans continue to associate the security of their nation with a sufficiency of military prowess. For centuries such an image of security has been imprinted upon human consciousness. In relation to the Soviet Union it is specifically interconnected with the ideological legacy of more than sixty years of anti-Communist, anti-Marxist, antirevolutionary encounters and propaganda. To shape a politics of response to nuclearism requires us to include the Soviet Union in our appraisal of various risks and probabilities. And further, it is necessary, I think, to premise our concern with an acknowledgment that Soviet society and bureaucratic socialism more generally present us with an unpleasant version of collective life, something to be avoided for ourselves.

But to perceive the Soviet state in this manner does not further imply that Soviet leaders are hell-bent on world conquest, come what may. Currently Soviet leaders seem, on balance, more inclined to establish a moderate framework for international relations than do their American counterparts. There are several important reasons for this greater receptivity: The aged Soviet leadership tasted the bitterest fruits of war within its lifetime (20 million dead, 20 million wounded in World War II; famine, devastation of large areas; a cruel occupation); the Soviet Union started the nuclear arms race from a position of definite inferiority and has been untainted by the use or overt threat to use such weapons; Soviet defensive interests, partly because of geographical considerations, do not seem dependent on ever threatening first use of nuclear weapons (even along its contested China border); the absence of Soviet interests in the maintenance of the colonial order (except in East Europe) or of a favorable overseas climate for markets, investments, and multinational corporate activity puts their foreign policy into alignment with the phenomenon of national revolution that continues to sweep across the Third World (although Moscow's recent search for foreign bases and commitment to maintain Marxist-Leninist regimes once in power is producing an interventionary diplomacy as exhibited by its relationships with Cuba, Afghanistan, and Ethiopia).

Others, as we shall see, evaluate the Soviet presence in the world in far more alarmist terms. The realistic prospects for reducing militarism and nuclear dependency depend critically on how we in the United States assess the Soviet challenge. This process of assessment is beset by ideological difficulties, as well as by a series of vested interests that find it useful to maintain the Soviet Union as our implacable "enemy." It is also beset by the strong appeal to common sense contained in the question "Well, what if you're wrong?" Nuclear arms racing, for all its costs, is viewed intuitively by many as a sort of ultimate insurance policy, overcoming reliance on the thin reeds of Soviet moderation or defensive dispositions and validated by the avoidance of nuclear war since 1945. The basic trouble with such justifications of nuclearism is that this form of insurance vastly increases the risks it is expected to alleviate and helps sustain conditions favorable to the occurrence of ultimate catastrophe.

Modern militarism is not a professional enterprise entrusted to small armies that carry out state policy. Since the Napoleonic wars of the early nineteenth century the prosecution of war has depended on the ideology of nationalism, on mass mobilization of support for costly war efforts, and, increasingly, on the blurring of combat distinctions between what is civilian and what is military. The image of "total war" expresses this essential development, and the strategic doctrines of the nuclear age represent a sort of terrorist culmination of prenuclear developments that extends its sway even to periods of so-called "peace." Beneath such phrases as "massive retaliation" and "mutual assured destruction" lies a *public* commitment to destroy with the push of a button an entire foreign society in a peculiarly horrifying way that includes long-lasting radiation effects, contamination of food and water for indefinite periods, and, quite possibly, irreversible environmental effects that pose a threat to the entire planet. Even the Nazis felt the necessity to keep "the final solution" hidden from their citizenry!

This American willingness to embrace a policy of genocide and ecocide has, to be sure, been presented as a defensive necessity, as the best that can be done given the nature of the challenge we face, given a world of rival states distrustful of one another. This selling of nuclearism has involved a subtle, complex, cumulative process that resembles, in its essential content, the original justification for using the bomb at the end of World War II. It goes back, in other words, to two intertwined realities: the absolute character of war (in the end, anything goes that helps achieve victory) and the unscrupulousness of the enemy (abstracted in such a way to minimize the concreteness of the victims and to discourage feelings of empathy across belligerent boundaries).

The ideological preparation for nuclear war centers on nurturing a hatred for "the enemy." This nurturing is especially necessary for the United States, with its democratic political forms that include the accountability of leaders by way of elections and with a cultural identity that emphasizes the goodness of the nation, sometimes described as American exceptionalism. In geopolitical terms the United States seeks to mask its "natural" identity as a leading state with an extensive global role and farflung interests by claiming that when it goes to war it is to destroy evil as well as to promote state interests. This mask was first loosened and then partially restored by the Vietnam experience; a large portion of the public, including those who were sent to fight, rejected "the mission" of the war and have been slow to accept that kind of mission again, as the lack of popular support for intervention in El Salvador demonstrates. This public reticence, also expressed by opposition to a revival of the draft, is what our militarists decry as "the Vietnam syndrome." At the same time, since the mid-1970s there has emerged a greater public willingness to fight for wealth as well as ideals. Even our leadership seems at a loss to find a moral rationale for the American military resolve to oppose revolutionary movements hostile to Western interests that might emerge in the oil-producing Persian Gulf. Nevertheless, the main reality is that the mobilization of resources and sentiments for war remains organized around the central idea of an enemy that is evil and whose evil will eventually encroach upon our independence, and even our territory, unless we are militarily prepared. Part of this composite image of evil incorporates the idea of "aggressor," as it is the enemy who endangers peace by threatening to launch a military attack. In that respect World War II provides a powerful text for this homily—it was Hitler who cast treaties aside, who trampled gleefully upon his Munich appeasers and resorted to war in the spirit of reckless expansionism, and it was imperialist Japan that attacked Pearl Harbor out of the blue. American leaders of all persuasion drew several central lessons from Munich and Pearl Harbor—appeasement doesn't work, aggression must be resisted with force of arms, and a foreign enemy will not hesitate to launch a surprise attack that is as crippling as possible. Under pre-1945 conditions even these lessons could have been absorbed without transforming the society, stage by stage, into a nuclear national security state, involving also the distortions of "a permanent war economy." Prior to nuclearism the United States indulged in "peace" without appearing to jeopardize its national security. The only plausible enemies were far away. We were protected from the recurrent ravages of war by our relative geographical isolation, and we often prescribed isolationism, at least in relation to Europe, as a source of both national virtue and national advantage (for instance, George Washington's celebrated edict against "entangling alliances").

Modern technology has deprived us of this possibility. Our oceans no longer offer us much of a buffer and, indeed, are an arena of danger, being patrolled by enemy submarines capable of delivering nuclear warheads to our cities in a matter of minutes. Since we are confronted by a powerful enemy we must remain constantly at the ready, especially as there is no way to protect our people or society from devastation no matter how many weapons we possess. Also, since any successful expansion by our enemy encourages the enemy's further expansion (aggression begets aggression; the recurrent imagery of falling dominoes), we must resist on a global scale to the extent practicable. And since the important factors in this competition are power and resources, the alignment of a foreign society with our enemy is as much a loss as if it was conquered on the battlefield. As a result, farflung alliances, military bases, and naval operations are all parts of our "defense," as is intervention in foreign civil strife.

Initially the Soviet menace has at various stages been intertwined with a broader ideological confrontation between capitalism and communism, between freedom and totalitarianism, between the modernized North and the developing South. From the moment of the Russian Revolution (at least the October Revolution), the United States joined in perceiving the ideology of communism as a mortal threat. We participated in an abortive effort, joining with several European allies, after World War I to destroy that revolution and for years afterward refused to enter even into normal diplomatic relations with the Soviet leadership, refused, in the parlance of international law, to recognize the Soviet Government. Later, and for decades, we did exactly the same thing in response to Mao's victory in China, including a prolonged arm-twisting foreign policy effort to deny the Communist government its natural place as China's representative in the United Nations.

During World War II we joined, of course, with the Soviet Union in an antifascist alliance, and it was the collapse of that alliance that set the stage for the current climate. There are many explanations of how the Cold War got started, which side was primarily responsible, and what kind of conflicts of interest existed to threaten major war. Many sensitive interpreters of historical trends, going back at least as far as Alexis de Tocqueville, anticipated that a rivalry between the United States and the Soviet Union, because of their respective size, resource endowments, impenetrability, and strategic positions, would come to dominate international political life at some point. World War II undoubtedly accelerated the process, leaving the old European centers of power and conflict devastated and exhausted, unable even to hold onto their overseas colonial possessions. The Soviet Union was also badly bruised by the war itself, but its huge armies had swept to victory against Germany. The Soviet leadership transformed military occupation into political vassalage throughout Eastern Europe, which helped rekindle the anticommunism of the West, especially in the United States. Furthermore, the Soviet military presence in Eastern Europe threatened a helpless, broken Western Europe with invasion and subversion. These threats were magnified by the large Soviet-oriented Communist Parties in France and Italy. In a different dimension, the colonial order was collapsing under the rising pressures of national revolutionary movements. These anticolonial victories were largely seen by the United States as accretions to Soviet power, especially after Mao's 1949 victory in China. The United States saw itself confronted with an expanding monolithic world revolutionary movement orchestrated from Moscow, probing for weaknesses in Western defenses throughout the world.

Against this background the Cold War emerged, its initiation being often associated with the Truman Doctrine in 1947, declared in the context of a Western defense of the national integrity of Greece and Turkey in the face of alleged Communist subversion and external pressure. At this time also was enunciated the famous organizing image of "containment," given its original formulation in a famous dispatch ("the long telegram") written by George Kennan from his diplomatic post in Moscow. The important "moral" element in this dynamic of unfolding conflict was the perception of Soviet-led communism as an aggressive force in the world that could be "contained" only by defensive resistance. There have been learned discussions about whether Kennan meant the same thing by containment as did the various American political leaders who construed its mandate in largely military terms. Nevertheless, from the late 1940s American foreign policy has been supposedly organized around this central tenet of defensiveness.

Important, also, was the portrayal of the evils of Soviet society, an inhuman political system that tormented its citizenry with cruelties and bureaucratic tedium. Gulag revelations of the extensiveness of the Stalinist death camps, post-Stalinist repression of dissidents, and periodic Soviet interventions in Eastern Europe to destroy the strivings of the people by way of restoring stability to Communist rule has lent credibility to the claim that our rival embodies evil in the primary sense that it is worth fighting and dying to avoid such a political fate for ourselves. In this regard it is not surprising that American leaders view as "contemptible" such European slogans as "better red than dead." Such a response to the threats posed by Communist expansionism is regarded as sure of evidence of moral decadence by any committed cold warrior. Paul Nitze's formulation captures the spirit of the United States' image of the Soviet challenge: "The Kremlin leaders do not want war; they want the world. They believe it unlikely, however, that the West will let them have the world without a fight."[1] It is interesting that Nitze has been entrusted by the Reagan Administration with the task of negotiating a European arms control agreement with the Soviet Union, a choice that expresses the current official outlook.

It is against this background that the American public reliance on nuclear weaponry has been erected. It has been generally accepted, in large part, as a defensive necessity, given Soviet advantages of position and manpower in relation to the crucial sectors of the world outside the territory of either superpower (especially Western Europe and the Persian Gulf). In the background also are contentions about "the balance of power" and about the Soviet mentality. With respect to balance, it has been argued that any shift in alignment, especially with respect to Europe or the Persian Gulf, threatens world peace by upsetting the balance of power (of course, this is self-serving in the extreme as the balance is never disturbed by defections on their side) and, therefore, must be opposed by all possible means (including at times covert operations to prevent pro-Soviet governments from coming to power, if possible). The threat to inflict nuclear annihilation has been accepted as essential to keep Moscow in check, but to be effective altogether it must be reinforced by local capabilities that can resist low levels of Soviet military pressure and even by a willingness, as necessary, to engage in nuclear war–fighting.

This overall image of Soviet aggressiveness is, it is argued by the most militant on our side, rooted in Marxist-Leninist ideology. Soviet leaders have endorsed their commitment to the world revolutionary process, they lend support to "wars of national liberation," and they have, at great expense to their own people, armed well beyond levels of armament required for prudent defense. Especially in the recent period since 1970, during the supposed time of détente, while the United States allegedly slowed its pace of arms racing, the Soviet Union has been portrayed as forging ahead in quest of strategic superiority.

With this sense of things, during the Carter presidency conservative forces in the United States mounted a blistering public relations offensive. As well documented by Jerry Sanders a close student of special interest politics, in his forthcoming book *The Peddlers of Crisis*, very deliberate organized efforts were made by individuals with close Pentagon ties to make the American people feel that détente, the SALT process of arms control negotiations, nonmilitary priorities, and budgetary restraints were hobbling our capacity to deal with the growing threat of Soviet military power. This grim view was further reinforced among critics from the right by their belief that geopolitical trends were definitely adverse. Colin Gray, professional strategist and skillful advocate of nuclear war–fighting preparations, argues the case for a Western military response:

> . . . the most pressing, dangerous, and potentially fatal fact of the real world—namely, that we are at the mid-stage of a shift in relative power and influence to the Soviet Union that is of historic proportions, and which promises, unless arrested severely, to have enduring significance. . . . The rise in Soviet standing in the world, which may be traced almost exclusively to the increase in relative Soviet military capabilities, both dwarfs other concerns in its immediacy and seriousness, and renders other problems far less tractable.[2]

The assessment was more or less accepted by pre-Reagan official documents of the United States Government, including the annual military posture statements issued by the Department of Defense after 1978. They pointed to the Soviet boldness of sending proxy Cuban troops to Ethiopia and Angola to assure Moscow-inclined victories in both countries, and subsequently they somehow connected the outcomes of the Iranian and Nicaraguan revolutions with Washington's absence of "resolve," a favorite word. And, finally, the Soviet invasion of Afghanistan in late December 1979 was seen as final confirmation of a new balance of forces in a strategic region, posing further threats to the oil-producing Persian Gulf, as well as a dangerous first use of Soviet troops in combat roles in a Third World country.

The active dissemination of this alarmist view of global developments was promoted from many sources—the Pentagon and its corporate allies, the strategic think tanks, the emergent "new" Right, the *Commentary* neo-conservatives, a growing sector of Congress—and it was endorsed by such influential foreign policy heavyweights as Henry Kissinger and Zbigniew Brzezinski. Perhaps the most effective organ of cold war revivalism was the Committee on the Present Danger, organized in March 1976 by a grouping of prominent private citizens, most of whom had earlier served high up in the government, led by Paul Nitze, Eugene V. Rostow, and several retired generals, and who were to be returned to eminence by Reagan's 1980 electoral victory. The effect of this concerted campaign was to alter the public climate of debate in the late 1970s, putting the moderate approach of the early Carter years on the defensive. Big business also joined the chorus; reading the editorial columns of *The Wall Street Journal* meant receiving the same message as set forth in the handouts of the Committee on the Present Danger. *Business Week* devoted its entire March 12, 1979, issue to "the decline of American power," with a dramatic cover portraying a tearful Statue of Liberty.

It was in this atmosphere that Ronald Reagan, an effusive supporter of the Committee on the Present Danger, mounted his successful presidential campaign. A central theme of Reagan's appeal to the electorate was to cut social services and increase defense spending. This appeal was popular with both the middle classes and business, which believed that inflation and the declining productivity of American industry were associated with the defective economics and misguided ethics of the welfare state gone soft as well as with profit-eating environmental and antitrust regulation. Resurgent capitalists were determined to rebuild profit margins and growth rates by squeezing the poor, rolling back wages, and neglecting the

The Soviet Factor: A "Useful" Enemy

environment. Reviving fears of a foreign enemy threatening our way of life was helpfully diversionary.

Whatever the causes, this revival of East–West tensions moves us closer to nuclear war, economic collapse, environmental crisis and, as such, contributes to the actuality of American decline and makes us, in objective and subjective terms, less, not more, secure. The picture being presented to the American people is put together with half-truths and the selective use of information and analysis. The Soviet Union is not, in any reasonable sense, riding the crest of history. Soviet power, as much as American power, is in a condition of decline. Soviet leaders are beset with an adverse set of circumstances that pose serious dangers to their current position. They are surrounded by enemies, the defection of China in the 1960s representing an enormous shift in the balance of power in a westward direction made credible by Chinese nuclear capabilities, huge armies, implacable hostility, and revisionist demands with respect to the four-thousand-mile long border. The Afghanistan invasion has turned into a Soviet nightmare with little light at the end of the tunnel. The Polish workers' movement has once again deeply exposed Moscow's morbid fear of genuine socialism, while once again discrediting Soviet claims of respect for the sovereign rights of the countries in Eastern Europe. Soviet encouragement and support of martial law in Poland (imposed late in 1981) has both embarrassed and antagonized most Communist parties around the world, weakening the overall Soviet stature in the Third World. Even the Cuban role in Africa does not promise any permanent extension of Soviet influence. Of course, the Soviet Union is a global presence at this stage and as such will find favorable opportunities in various settings to extend its influence, but on balance its situation is precarious and deteriorating. In my judgment, the

U.S.S.R.'s militarism, like ours, is a response to a perceived reality of overall political, economic, and cultural decline. Soviet leaders are likely to fear "the barbarians" at their gates at least as much as we do. And further, without excusing or ignoring the cruelty and grinding inefficiency of Soviet rule, there are no solid reasons to regard Soviet military power as anything more than a defensive capability that is designed, among other things, to deny us a free hand in areas of interest to them.

This conclusion seems especially persuasive with respect to nuclear weaponry. Remember that all along the Soviet Union has been "a poor second" straining to catch up, stay abreast, convince us of the futility of limited nuclear war; during this period of prolonged vulnerability the Soviet leadership was quite aware of the mutual suicide that would be the main result of nuclear war. Khrushchev and Brezhnev have repeatedly made clear their understanding of the importance of avoiding a superpower breakdown. It is the Soviets who have modified Marxist-Leninist thinking by insisting that "peaceful coexistence" is the proper relation of opposed political systems and ideologies in the nuclear age. George Kennan, among others, persuasively questions the view that "the Russians are such monsters" that they would, even if they could do so safely, "launch upon us a nuclear attack, with all the horrors and sufferings that that would bring." Kennan rejects the view, on the basis of his long observation of Soviet behavior, "that our Soviet adversary has lost every semblance of humanity and is concerned only with wreaking unlimited destruction for destruction's sake"[3] These observations are entitled to added weight, I think, because Kennan is not someone who has been oblivious to the Soviet danger (he is after all the father of containment, even if he has disowned the more militarist versions of his progeny) or someone with an idealist faith in the peaceful proclivities of human nature (indeed he cynically accepts spheres of influence as integral elements of international order and is skeptical about experiments in international cooperation).

Correlating American decline in a world setting with either the insufficiency of military power or with Soviet aggressiveness is sheer mystification. The main challenge to the preeminent position of the United States in the world is the continuing dynamic of national revolution and development in the Third World, rising energy costs, and the decay of critical sectors of American industry relative to European and Japanese competition. A militarist response in these circumstances represents a failure of analysis that actually worsens the American geopolitical situation. The current United States effort to crush the national revolutionary process in Central America is straining all credulity when it tries to justify American involvement by reference to Soviet arms provided revolutionary forces from Cuban sources. As has often been demonstrated, the outcome of civil strife depends overwhelmingly on internal factors, with the government forces usually having a big advantage when it comes to the scale and quality of weaponry. Whatever weapons a guerrilla movement gets from abroad are seldom likely to be a critical factor in the struggle for political control.

The Soviet dissident brothers Roy and Zhores Medvedev diagnose, correctly, I think, the collapse of détente and the rejection of the SALT II treaty: "We think the principal cause of the return to confrontation was the fact that SALT II did nothing to redress the disadvantages of the United States in the Third World, where America had suffered yet another setback after its failures in Indochina and Angola—the Iranian revolution."[4] Well, of course strategic arms control cannot help the United States in the Third World, even in the unlikely event that Moscow were inclined to link the two kinds of concerns. Moscow, too, lacks control over national revolutions, as events in Afghanistan suggest. Indeed the Soviet

Union cannot even provide assured control over the revolutionary process in countries where a Marxist-Leninist leadership is in power, as the defection of Yugoslavia, China, and the various opposition movements in Eastern Europe suggest. In reaction to this basic pattern (alongside the proposed deployments of new missiles in Europe), West–West tensions have also risen. West German trade relations with the Soviet bloc have given them a major economic stake in détente. The ex-colonial powers increasingly believe that accommodation with the governments of successful national revolutionary movements is possible on a mutually acceptable basis. Indeed traditional allies of the United States, most notably France under Mitterand but also the Netherlands and the Scandinavian countries, are not willing to defer any longer entirely to American statecraft, even in Central America, as is evident in their sale of arms to the Sandinista government in Nicaragua despite vigorous opposition from Washington. Such European penetration of an American sphere of influence suggests the forming of new patterns of multipolar diplomacy (independent of either superpower) that will further obstruct the militarist approach currently prevalent in the United States. In addition, some richer Third World countries—for instance, Algeria and Libya—are extending support to the Sandinista government.

What seems evident is that the Soviet Union serves as no adequate excuse for continuing the nuclear arms race. There are wider human and global interests that should not be ignored. The Soviet challenge can and must be met without threatening first use of nuclear weapons or proceeding to develop further, even more destabilizing weapons systems. In a typical public statement the Soviet leader Leonid Brezhnev said, "It is madness for any country to build its policy with an eye to nuclear war"[5]. There is every reason to act as if the Soviet Union appreciates this madness, and the peace movement

The Soviet Factor: A "Useful" Enemy

has prompted some comparable statements from Washington. Of course, appropriate deeds on both sides are called for at this stage. To remove the madness we do not have to trust the Soviet Union (nor they us), but we do require a political climate that challenges the entrenched positions of nuclear militarists on both sides. Such a challenge on the American side will almost certainly have to be preceded by a powerful grassroots movement outside the formal framework of politics; on the Soviet side the challenge will have to be mounted by a faction of the Politburo and then win wider support throughout the command structure of the topheavy Soviet bureaucracy.

In the end, more than challenging nuclearism is required. It will be necessary to work toward the adoption of new conceptions and structures of security that rest on a mutual disarming process. Such a process cannot occur unless realism can be divorced from nuclearism.

CHAPTER 17

Passivity— The Enemy of Peace

An extraordinary passivity envelops the nuclearist solution to peace. As a society and as a species we find ourselves virtually "waiting for the apocalypse." Leaders as well as citizens have felt helpless to challenge nuclearism in any serious way.

This helplessness represents both a state of mind and a set of circumstances. The mental attitude is shaped by the acceptance of war as endemic, if not to the human condition, then at least to the conduct of international relations. And if war is endemic, then reliance on the most destructive weaponry available follows to the extent that our political lives are organized around sovereign states. As such, the circle is complete, nuclearism appears inevitable, although its form can be more or less moderate depending on the play of domestic politics (hawks versus doves as foreign policymakers). However, no mainstream political formation has yet dared bring into question the main postulates of nuclearism.

Passivity—The Enemy of Peace

Nuclearism is also a reflection of a set of domestic and international circumstances. Powerful social, economic, and bureaucratic interests are joined in a militarist coalition of support for nuclearism. On an international level, the global role of the United States and the fact that our main rival possesses nuclear weapons make it seemingly impossible to dislodge nuclearism from our collective lives.

The one glimmer of exception relates to crisis and breakdown. There is some historical basis for believing that international reforms come, if at all, after great wars: the Peace of Westphalia (1648) after the Thirty Years War; the League of Nations after World War I; the United Nations after World War II. There is posed a question: Must we sit around waiting for the apocalypse or is the traumatic impact of a near-miss sufficient to shatter the nuclearist consensus? Underneath this question is another: Since even the postwar reforms of the past have not transformed the violent core of international conflict, is there any reason to hope that reforms in the future can lead us down a liberating path?

These issues can be illuminated by a brief consideration 1962 Cuban Missile Crisis, the only instance since 1945 when it was widely believed in East and West that we were at the brink of World War III. There were other geopolitical (Berlin crises of the late 1950s; nuclear alert during the 1973 Middle East War) and accidental (computer false alarms) near-misses, but they passed quickly and were hushed up by the government and media so as not to undermine public confidence in nuclearism.

Even aside from the impetus created by crises, there has been some sentiment at high levels of government to manage the risks of nuclearism. This managerial perspective has produced arms control, which should be contrasted with disarmament. In arms control policies and agreements are favored that reduce the risks of nuclearism, while in disarmament nuclear-ism is itself the target. American leaders have disagreed over the merits of various arms control measures but have not in any serious way ever proposed moving beyond arms control to disarmament. As such, official reforms have had as their objective making the world safer for nuclearism and should not be confused with reforms that might try to overcome nuclearism.

The major participants in the Cuban Missile Crisis defi-nitely believed that the world teetered for days on the edge of nuclear war. If Khrushchev had not backed down, or if the Soviet Union had enlarged the scope of crisis by moving aggres-sively in a context where *it* had a local advantage, as would have been the case had it occupied West Berlin, nuclear war-fare could have easily resulted from a rapid series of actions and reactions. A more aggressive Soviet response to the Ameri-can position had been widely expected. As an indication of the pessimistic mood, the British Foreign Office unanimously ex-pected, after hearing President Kennedy's October 22 speech establishing a partial blockade of Cuba, that the Russians would be in West Berlin by the following day.[1]

I will not raise questions here about the imprudent behavior of both superpowers that allowed war risks to rise so high on that occasion. Why did the Soviet Union use deceit and decep-tion to provoke an American response, especially in a geo-graphic setting of traditional American influence? Why were so many missiles contemplated (nine launch sites with four launching pads apiece) and why were intermediate-range (2100 mile) as well as medium-range (1100 mile) missiles part of the plan, if the Soviets were, as they claimed, merely trying to de-fend Castro's Cuba against possible subsequent U.S.-launched attacks? Clearly the Soviet Union was trying to rectify quickly and relatively cheaply an unfavorable strategic balance at the time, and possibly seeking, as Castro later told a foreign correspondent, to strengthen the overall position of international socialism.

The United States also seemed partly responsible for bringing the crisis about. After all, giving backing to the CIA-sponsored Bay of Pigs invasion by anti-Castro exiles in April 1961 created an atmosphere of apprehension that encouraged the Soviet Union to do something more in defense of Cuba. Furthermore, the United States had for a decade located "offensive" missiles on sites (Turkey, Italy, England) as close to Soviet territory as Cuba is to ours, seemingly establishing a precedent for provocative deployments. And then there was Kennedy's rejection of Khrushchev's offer in the midst of the crisis to terminate plans for the Cuban missile base in exchange for the face-saving removal of a far smaller force of obsolete Turkish missiles, which were supposed to have been removed by the time the confrontation in Cuba took place but for obscure bureaucratic reasons were still present in Turkey.

This Cuban confrontation revealed clearly that both leaders of the superpowers were prepared to seriously risk nuclear war in order to achieve their geopolitical goals, that is, goals related to image and position rather than to such ultimate issues of security as the defense of national territory, vital allies, or even critical resources. Kennedy's refusal to take the Turkish missiles out, however obsolete, was related both to maintaining U.S. freedom to engage in overseas nuclear deployments and to demonstrating an American resolve and capacity to squeeze the Soviets so hard for stepping across the line of moderation that they would be made to endure the humiliation of backing down. In the background also were domestic political forces that seemed to have played their part in stiffening Kennedy's spine. Congressional elections were coming up. According to the polls, Republicans were scoring heavily with attacks on the Kennedy Administration for its weak foreign policy, for its vacillations in response to Soviet challenges, and for its bungling of efforts to get rid of Castro. Voltaire's remark that "everything essential is invisible" helps us understand the rationality of irrationality at work; clearly the political position of the Kennedy/Democratic Party leadership would be greatly enhanced—as it was—by a dramatic Soviet defeat.

The analysis of the Cuban Missile Crisis itself is not my concern here. Rather I want to explore the weight of the realization that the policies being pursued brought the world alarmingly close to nuclear war. We know that at the time this closeness was on the minds of the citizenry. In fact, some Americans left the country, many others stocked up on food, and there were frequent "farewell" parties given with the ironic intention of preparing for the end of the world. Although the gravity of the situation was hidden from the Soviet people, there are many indications that their leadership was extremely worried that a general war could have erupted. When the Soviet Union acceded to the American demands, there was in the United States a celebration of a big Cold War victory, but there was also a sigh of relief.

There was a sense that the world was lucky to be still intact. In his letter of October 28 agreeing to dismantle Soviet missile facilities and remove "offensive" weaponry, Khrushchev writes "If we, together with you . . . succeed in eliminating this tense atmosphere, we should also make certain that no other dangerous conflicts, which could lead to a world nuclear catastrophe, would arise." And, more specifically, the Soviet leader urged a revived "exchange of views on the prohibition of atomic and thermonuclear weapons, general disarmament, and other problems relating to the relaxation of international tension."[2] Now, "exchange of views" may seem a tame offering, given the depth of anxiety surrounding the crisis, but it should be realized that Khrushchev made this proposal in the face of a humiliating

Passivity—The Enemy of Peace

Soviet retreat in a context of confrontation. Major leaders, especially if ideological adversaries, do not traditionally propose constructive responses in such diplomatic settings. Khrushchev's willingness to do so is a recognition of that special "common interest" in avoiding nuclear war that binds even "enemies" to one another.

Kennedy's direct response, on the same day, was similar in tone: "It is my earnest hope that the governments of the world can, with a solution of the Cuban crisis, turn their urgent attention to the compelling necessity for ending the arms race and reducing world tensions." More concretely, Kennedy replied in a gradualist vein: "I agree with you that we must devote urgent attention to the problem of disarmament. . . . Perhaps now, as we step back from danger, we can together make real progress in this vital field. I think we should give priority to questions relating to the proliferation of nuclear weapons, on earth and in outerspace, and to the great effort for a nuclear test ban."

In actuality, of course, there was unprecedented energy devoted in the months and years ahead to the development of negotiable measures of arms control. The rationale for this effort was that it would contribute to the stability of the nuclear balance, as then constituted, and reduce, if possible, the risks of war arising from miscalculation or accident. A series of agreements were produced in the 1960s and early 1970s that went forward on a separate track from the confrontational side of the Cold War, which was largely restricted in this period to various encounters in the Third World, especially Indochina.

Interestingly, the first Soviet-American bilateral arms control agreement involved the so-called "Hot Line" Agreement establishing a direct communication link between the two superpowers. This agreement became effective in July 1963 and arose from the realization during the Cuban Missile Crisis that in the nuclear age it was absolutely essential to have safe and reliable means of communication at all times. Such a realization supplanted an earlier tendency of antagonistic states to disrupt their communications during times of crisis.

Other arms control agreements followed rapidly one upon another. The Limited Test Ban (1963), prohibiting all atmospheric testing, was properly hailed as a dramatic achievement, reducing significantly the health hazards posed by fallout from weapons tests. Note that the arms race was not inhibited very significantly, if at all, as testing could (and did) continue by way of underground explosions. Also, the refusal of France and China to go along with the test ban treaty suggested the growing complexity of a world in which states additional to the superpowers possessed nuclear weapons and would not subordinate their plans to the game plan set by Moscow and Washington. At the same time the ban, although limited, was definitely a step in the direction of peace and sanity and was enormously popular with the American public, which seemed at the time to believe, without much grounds for doing so, that this agreement made nuclear war much less likely.

The most direct acknowledgment of the Cuban Missile Crisis came some years later in the form of the Soviet-American Agreement on the Prevention of Nuclear War (1971). Here both superpowers entered a formal agreement in which they promised to act "to prevent the development of situations capable of causing a dangerous exacerbation of their relations, as to avoid military confrontations, and as to exclude the outbreak of nuclear war between them." In some sense the respective governments agreed, in effect, not to allow crisis situations of the 1962 variety to arise in the future, even to the extent of agreeing to conduct foreign policy and international behavior with such goals in mind. This agreement was declaratory.

Neither government was obliged to do anything specific. At the same time the lingering sense of fragility occasioned by the missile crisis remained active in the political consciousness of the leaders of the two superpowers, who were, in their overall relations, moving rapidly to establish détente and consider the Cold War ended. Of course, such a declaratory statement of intention is vulnerable to a shifting of the political mood and can be cast aside without any adverse consequences. Now another decade later the priority given earlier to the avoidance of nuclear war in a crisis situation seems all but forgotten. What counts again is the military edge.

The Outer Space Treaty (1967) and the Seabed Arms Control Treaty (1971) were not altogether successful attempts to place certain domains out of bounds in the nuclear arms race. Such agreements were seen as safety devices related to the idea that each superpower might otherwise spend lots of money and effort to hedge against the other side gaining an advantage. It suggests what has become one of the strong irrational articles of faith built into the nuclearist mind-set, namely that security depends on doing virtually anything the other side decides to do.

The Non-Proliferation Treaty (NPT) (1968) was an important attempt to restrict the number of nuclear weapons states as much as possible. All along the conviction has been that the superpowers, in addition to their mutual interest in avoiding war against one another, had a second major shared interest in avoiding the spread of nuclear weapons to additional states. The Soviet Union has consistently denied even its closest allies direct assistance in developing a weapons option. In the late 1950s this denial was one major cause of early tensions in the Sino-Soviet relationship. Overall, the idea of nonproliferation can be seen in at least two ways. One involves general considerations of stability, the fewest possible states with fingers on the nuclear trigger. The other involves a new type of international status relations in which the existing nuclear weapons states seek to maintain a definite position of dominance in world affairs.

In the NPT nuclear weapons states pledged to pursue arms control and disarmament in good faith as part of the bargain by which nonnuclear states were induced to accept the commitment to renounce their weapons option. To some slight extent the bilateral Strategic Arms Limitations talks (SALT) of the 1970s could be understood as a fulfillment of this pledge, but with the breakdown of the SALT process as of 1980, there is little evidence that the nuclear weapons states intend seriously to renounce, or even moderate, the arms race, much less contemplate nuclear disarmament. Even at its best SALT mainly involved placing high ceilings on agreed-upon categories of weapons systems and could not properly be understood as involving a renunciation by the superpowers of their weapons option, or even of their commitment to augment their overall military strength through a continuous series of innovations in nuclear weaponry.

The relevant point here is that the arms control process that flowed out of the Cuban Missile Crisis did produce a series of generally useful agreements *within* the abiding framework of nuclearism. The very spectacle of Soviet-American negotiations was also reassuring to a certain extent, helping to establish an international climate of calm that allowed détente to emerge in the early 1970s.

At the same time the arms control process bred several forms of disillusionment that also reveal the character and dominance of nuclearism. To negotiate an arms control agreement successfully it was necessary to convince the most militarist segment of the government that the new step served their image of the security interests of the country. In each major instance this meant, in practice, making side concessions to domestic militarism that often nullified the overall value of the agreements themselves. To obtain their grudging support for the test ban, for instance, the American military had to be promised an extensive program of underground tests including assurances that major forthcoming innovations, such as MIRVs and the Polaris submarine, would be developed at an accelerated rate. In other words, despite high expectations created by the treaty, in actual fact the pace of the arms race was really quickened; this was the price paid to win domestic political support. A comparable process appears to have taken place in the Soviet system. The politics of arms control within one's own country meant that one step forward internationally toward control meant at least one step backward nationally in the direction of pressing forward faster with new and often destabilizing weapons systems. Finally, the SALT agreements helped to allow the nuclear hawks to seize the initiative, contending that SALT I was an unfair treaty in which the Soviet Union got the better of the bargain and questioning whether arms control was not itself dangerous as it leads the United States to be unduly complacent about its long-run strategic interests. Such a backlash has led us to the present moment of heightened tensions, renewed preoccupation with East–West relations, suspended strategic arms control negotiations, and a greatly increased defense budget.

Without a supportive political climate, one that exerts sufficient pressures to neutralize the military-industrial complex, nothing fundamental by way of transformed security policy can be achieved. The basic flow of the nuclear arms race persists. As a result the impact of a crisis may be salutory on the short-term atmosphere of hostility, but it seems incapable of altering the overall danger of nuclearism. It removes or reduces certain risks, but it adds others.

Step by step as we enter the 1980s the arms race proceeds at a rapid pace and includes a mindless rush to develop and deploy unstable (first-strike) weapons systems. The only positive residue of the Cuban Missile Crisis, the concrete possibilities of communications under any set of circumstances as a result of the hot line, is the probably abiding sense that direct confrontations by the superpowers in tense circumstances should be avoided, or at least prudently managed. Even this degree of restraint cannot be assured. There are influential strategic thinkers on our side who argue, even in public, that "an occasionally necessary confrontation" must occur from time to time so that potential nuclear antagonists can clarify for one another unacceptable kinds of behavior.

The opportunity to see clearly created by a nuclear near-miss serves, at most, managerial purposes. But as the Reaganites have proclaimed, any effort to manage risks must properly be subordinated to overall strategic relations. Or understood differently, the worst risk is nuclear weakness relative to rivals or strategic role. As long as this militarist calculus retains its hold on power-wielders, the nuclear arms race will go on and the fundamental peril cannot be removed, although there may be times when the danger appears to have receded.

Some insist that only an extraordinary jolt can summon the energy to challenge the Machiavellian world picture, and that this jolt must involve the actuality of nuclear catastrophe. A near-miss, however dramatic, is not enough, not nearly enough.

Somehow a conviction is widely held that the survivors of a nuclear breakdown will reconstitute what is left of political life on the planet in a new, wiser way. Usually this vision of "rescue" involves the development of a new framework for world order, typically combining total disarmament with world government. Often also adherents of this view of transformed politics are quite content under current arrangements to press the case for military advantage by way of nuclear armaments. If pushed, for instance, Herman Kahn and Edward Teller—hard-line strategists and cold warriors—often claim an underlying faith in utopia in the wake of Armageddon.

An extreme variant of this mode of thinking is encountered in literatures of fantasy. There the theme of a galactic enemy is developed as the necessary basis for the unification of political life on earth. One variant of this theme involves a deliberate conspiracy of earthlings to make political leaders throughout the world fear an imminent attack from an enemy civilization based on a distant planet. The conviction here too is that such external intervention is required to break the iron grip of the old ways. Also this view incorporates the related idea that patterns of identification broader than family, tribe, and neighborhood depend on the cohering impact of an enemy external to the community for which security is provided. This image of unity through hatred and fear is an imaginary extension of the history of international relations. The idea that planetary unity depends on an external threat is an important psychological insight into the inability of political leaders to find a path that leads beyond nuclearism. It is essentially a pessimistic assessment of the human prospect as it acknowledges impotence and depends on a wholly implausible scenario of extraplanetary rescue.

Only slightly less pessimistic is an outright utopian position—namely that the current crop of world rulers can be persuaded to subscribe to a plan for global disarmament and that such a plan, if adopted, could be implemented by popular consent. The utopianism of such a vision is less the blueprint for a disarmed, peaceful world than the expectation that the antagonistic forces of world militarism would somehow evaporate into thin air.

To conclude, reforms induced by near-misses cannot hope

to do more than strengthen the impulse to manage risks more prudently. The formalization of this impulse produces arms control arrangements. These arrangements are constrained by the framework of nuclearism and must also be generally acceptable to those militarist outlooks well entrenched in the governments of all leading nuclear weapons states.

More decisive steps may become possible in the event of an actual breakdown of the deterrent system. This possibility should prompt citizens and others to work out images of a denuclearization process so that if the tragic moment of nuclear weapons use should occur, then at least it can eventually be turned to human advantage.

But are we condemned to such a passive destiny? There is no solid reason to accept a fate that consists of waiting for the end, and hoping that when the moment arrives, it will not be the end after all. Some suppose that a third world war will administer such a shock to the senses of the peoples of the world that they will awaken with a start to demand the abolition of war as a human institution and, with it, the abolition of nuclear stockpiles once and for all. Such a vision embodies a careless phantasy, as the social and political remnants of nuclear war are likely to be incapable of anything more ambitious than a primitive and ruthless struggle for physical survival.

CHAPTER 18

Constraining and Liberating World Pictures

We are often unwitting captives of certain organizing beliefs, attitudes, and ideas that lend coherence to our experience. In a stable cultural circumstance one image of coherence, called here world picture, clearly predominates, although others coexist at the edges of any complex civilizational experience. A predominant world picture provides a shared framework for legitimate leadership and collective action.

Premodern world pictures were shaped in the main by a mythic sensibility that emphasized human dependence on divine and natural forces. The modern world picture has rested upon underlying ideas of science, especially Newtonian physics, about the nature of reality. Applied to political life, the modern world picture rests also on the basic postulates of a godless universe and a rapacious human nature restrained in its appetites by societal pressures.

Perhaps it was Nicollò Machiavelli who most effectively set forth the modern world picture as applicable to politics in his short treatise of 1512 entitled *The Prince*. Although the enigmatic Florentine diplomat-scholar's true intentions have puzzled scholars for centuries, the clarity of Machiavelli's prose and the cynical direction of his thought have given his formulations of a world picture great authority. Essentially Machiavelli writes in the spirit of guiding a political leader, urging an amoral zeal in the pursuit of state interests under all circumstances. In effect, this world picture emphasizes the separation of human society into distinct political communities and accepts the inevitability of ceaseless struggle among such communities for ascendency. War becomes the arbiter of history, and the goals of war should be pursued by a proper leader without scruple or inhibition. Machiavelli's position does not encourage the prince to embark upon mindless cruelty or foolish adventures. The Machiavellian world picture emphasizes rationalism in the sense of relating means to ends in a prudent, self-interested fashion. A benevolent leader seeks neither more nor less than his capabilities permit and is careful to avoid needless or inflamed resistance at home or abroad.

This Machiavellian world picture still dominates the thinking and behavior of virtually every political leader of the world. It has been thoroughly adopted by the forces of nationalism that have been rampant in our century. At present political leaders of sovereign states, whether Marxist or non-Marxist, East or West, North or South, are all more or less adherents of the Machiavellian world picture. There are a few fundamentalist exceptions, such as Iran's Khomeini, Libya's Qadaffi, and Israel's Begin, who, to different degrees, appear to lead on the basis of absolutist precepts, backed up by invocations of divine providence;

240

such leadership is contemptuous of the Machiavellian stress on relations of proportionality between means and ends.

Nuclearism represents a desperate attempt to adapt the technology of mass destruction to the ongoing predominance in leadership circles of the Machiavellian world picture. Deterrence by way of nuclear weaponry strives to relate means to ends in such a manner as to prevent imprudent warfare and maintain a rationalist confidence that separate sovereignties can avoid self-destruction without reliance on idealistic illusions about human nature or political behavior.

So long as the Machiavellian world picture predominates, it constrains human freedom to overcome the mortal dangers and to remove the terrible burdens of nuclearism. Its acceptance of war, of unconditional state power, and of the finality of partial human identities confines rigidly the political imagination and dooms any project of social and political reconstruction. To combat nuclearism it is a matter of urgent necessity to loosen the constraining grip of the Machiavellian world picture on the political leadership of the planet.

But by what means? A variety of competing world pictures have been operative in human affairs. I have already suggested that religious fundamentalism represents one alternative world picture, in its essence more frightening by far than the Machiavellian orientation as it repudiates diversity and is unrestrained by prudence. If ever backed up with nuclear weapons capabilities, the fundamentalist's world picture would greatly increase the likelihood of global conflagration.

There are, fortunately, also more encouraging forces at work. All along a more cosmopolitan image of human nature and destiny has been embodied in the great world religions and civilizations. Even Machiavellian leaders generally acknowledge the weight of this competing imagery through rituals of deference to more universalist ideals. A holistic world picture that experi-

ences the interrelatedness of life on the planet as the fundamental reality is struggling to be born at this stage of history.
The rise of the biological sciences to a position of preeminence
among the sciences, and the displacement of physics, can be
understood as laying a possible foundation for a new politics
because of the emphasis of some influential biologists on the
links between cooperative traits of a species and the species
success in waging struggles for survival. This possibility is further encouraged by practical and visionary considerations.

Practically, the peoples of the world are awakening to the
dreadful fragility of ordering arrangements based on the Machiavellian world picture. As matters now stand, this awakening is mainly rendered as fear and negation. There is as yet no
confidence in the sustaining power of a holistic world picture.
As such, we live in a period of transition; the old ways no longer
work, but new ways have not yet become available. It is a time
of terrible danger and of awesome opportunity. Although the
struggle against nuclearism is the most dramatic dimension,
other struggles confirm the judgment that the Machiavellian
world picture can no longer satisfy human needs or cravings.
As a species we have rediscovered our dependence on respect-
ing the tolerances and cherishing the expansiveness of our natural surroundings. A growing ecological consciousness is fash-
ioning a holistic world picture quite independent of nuclearist
forebodings. Beyond this, the global scale of business and technology, the cosmic drift of spiritual revival, and the sense of
the earth as seen from space are erasing the boundaries of separation and distinction that are such a vital aspect of the Machiavellian world picture.

We cannot in any way calculate the prospects for a healing,
holistic world picture. Its influence is being resisted by all those
forces that retain their footing by managing the old order of
separate, warring sovereignties. A world picture often retains

its influence long after its usefulness has vanished because it has grown so closely identified with the legitimacy of ruling interests and structures. It is largely the power grounding of the Machiavellian world picture that explains its continuing predominance in our time, and it is this power grounding that must be challenged if our struggle against nuclearism is to have "a politics."

There is a final observation. Within the framework of a world picture there are a range of viewpoints possible that may bear critically on short-run viability. More concretely, there are a range of "nuclearisms" that flow from the perpetuation of the Machiavellian world picture. Therefore, at the same time that we work to fashion and strengthen the emergent holistic world picture, we need also to devote our energies to strengthen the more prudent variants of nuclearism. Proposals to cut back on the nuclear weapons stockpile, to renounce nuclear first uses, and to freeze the arms race can be understood as contributions to stability within the persisting nuclearist framework of the Machiavellian world picture.

Moving beyond nuclearism depends on a longer, more fundamental cycle of liberation, including the rise to predominance of a holistic world picture reinforced by a new leadership, by appropriate mass beliefs and values, and by a new network of institutional arrangements—that is, in short, by a new world order.

The horizons of the possible have not yet been tested. To retain the Machiavellian world picture precludes a necessary testing and helps explain why such an exemplary Machiavellian as Henry Kissinger is consumed by despair and fatalism. Given the realities of our circumstances a hopeful posture toward the future increasingly depends on seizing our freedom to create new political possibilities according to the mandate of a holistic world picture.[1]

CHAPTER 19

Obtain the Possible: Demand the Impossible

Participation in the surging popular movement of opposition to nuclearism is making many people more hopeful about the future. Yet this new hopefulness is often closely connected to an arousal of fear and anxiety, and is certainly fragile, being vulnerable to disillusionment. The present spirit of the antinuclear movement is captured by W. H. Auden's words:

"We who are about to die demand a miracle." Demanding a miracle is itself an affirmation of life, exhibiting, at the same time, an uplifting clarity about the gravity of the danger.

The miraculous applies to freeing the planet of nuclearism altogether. Such a prospect seems beyond the horizon of what is possible. Complete nuclear disarmament is not really plausible so long as leaders hold a Machiavellian world picture, and perhaps, so long as the organization of political life is based upon grossly unequal sovereign states competing militarily for scarce resources. Common sense illustrates the difficulty of achieving total nuclear disarmament in the world as we know it, even assuming good will on the part of the main governments, which it is misleading to assume either for ourselves or our adversaries. Suppose we imagine a situation in which nuclear disarmament had been agreed upon and implemented, but national sovereignty and the war system remained. It seems inconceivable that a government faced with the prospect of defeat in a major war, yet retaining the knowledge and technology to reconstruct nuclear weaponry would refrain under such conditions. Realizing this prospect, a government would assume that its adversary might try to evade the disarmament agreement at least to the extent of retaining a small hidden stockpile as a hedge against a rearmament race or nuclear blackmail. To prevent this evasion of a disarmament treaty, given the grave consequences at stake, would require a highly reliable system of verification, itself a nonnegotiable barrier to agreement, given the apprehensions associated with sovereignty. But more than this, since the bomb cannot be disinvented and since the technology will become more and more accessible, it must be supposed that any political actor faced with the prospect of defeat would revive at the onset of crisis its nuclear weapons option. When these considerations are understood, it becomes clear that war, in general, not nuclear weapons in isolation, must become the inevitable focus for any serious effort to overcome *nuclearism.* Like the Zen archer, the dedicated antinuclearist must aim above the target to strike the bull's-eye.

To get rid of war, however, requires a new type of world order, including a far stronger sense of human identity to complement and complete the various partial identities of nationalism, religion, race, and ideology. The end of war implies, in effect, the displacement of Machiavellianism by a holistic world picture.

For all these reasons, then, it seems impossible, as matters now stand, to achieve nuclear disarmament, despite its necessity. As long as nuclear weapons remain a central basis of national security, the danger of their use will condition our experience—at times mitigated, at other times, such as at present, magnified. Additionally, reliance on nuclear weapons inevitably concentrates antidemocratic authority in governmental institutions and builds such a strong permanent disposition to engage in ultimate war as to negate the atmosphere and structure of genuine peace. We can never taste real peace again until we find the means to eliminate nuclear weapons altogether.

Yet we need not wait. There are many things we can do to make the world safer and saner, thereby also creating opportunities for more fundamental changes to occur. We can greatly reduce the risks of nuclear war, as well as dramatically reduce the drain upon the world's precious resources. It is possible to foster a political climate in which leaders are induced to take steps, gradual and partial in character, but highly significant in their cumulative effect. The antinuclear movement, while finally demanding the impossible, is tactically focused on attainable goals: freezing the arms race, renouncing first use options and limited war doctrine, opposing the deployment of specific weapons systems (for example, neutron bomb, Pershing II, cruise missile), establishing nuclear weapons free zones (such as the Indian Ocean, the Korean peninsula, Europe), prohibiting all further flight testing of missiles, and underground testing of warheads.

These tactical goals will themselves not be easy to attain. There are powerful, vicious, mystifying, and self-mystifying social forces tied up with the reign of nuclearism. Politicians are surrounded by advisors who contend that whatever danger of nuclear war exists is attributable to their enemy, and preserving "peace" depends on achieving nuclear superiority for oneself. There are, in other words, as Robert Lifton has discussed, powerful nuclear illusions that keep the arms race going and oppose by all available means popular demands for minimizing the dangers of nuclear war. Some nuclearists in and close to power centers will surely resort to a mixture of deceit, nominal accommodation, infiltration and provocation, and outright repression before giving way to democratic peace pressures. The antinuclear movement, without losing its enthusiasm, will have to develop a politics of struggle and resistance if it hopes to achieve major results. There is no assured way to get from here to there, even if there is defined in the relatively limited terms of stabilizing the role of nuclear weaponry.

Also, bureaucracies are unfortunately more durable than either politicians or popular movements. Politicians can respond to shifts in mood and might even be persuaded to implement serious antinuclear goals. We see that beginning to happen here and in Western Europe and Japan. It is an impressive tribute to the extraordinary vitality and strength of the antinuclear movement. Yet the roots of militarism are deeply embedded in the huge, implacable structures of governmental bureaucracy and reach out to encompass powerful, privileged sectors of the economy, including parts of the media. If past behavior is any guide, this faceless, durable bastion of nuclearism is certain to organize a variety of responses to the popular movement, perhaps even largely behind the backs of the main politicians, hoping to disillusion, or at least outlast, protest activity. Consider the following: Stalin was repudiated, but Stalinism remained, not exactly as before but essentially a regrouping of the same forces to maintain a basically repressive relationship between the Soviet state and the Soviet people. Bureaucracies are notoriously hard to reform so long as they remain intact.

Since popular movements are difficult to sustain (Americans

being particularly prone to quick disillusionment), it is essential that its guiding spirits possess and impart a vision of what needs to be done, and how to do it. There is a special requirement present here, as well. To oppose nuclearism effectively does impose a difficult and special requirement that we connect tactical demands with a commitment to perseverance in pursuit of essential long-range objectives. Either without the other will collapse: the moral passion that gives grassroots politics its edge depends largely on an overall repudiation of nuclearism in any form, while the emphasis on attainable goals builds needed popular confidence that victories over nuclear forces are possible, that ordinary people can mobilize and wield decisive power, and that a path can be eventually found to overcome once and for all, the nuclear menace.

Most current action within the peace movement is dedicated, whether deliberately or not, to *stabilizing* rather than *eliminating* nuclearism. The goal is to force a shift from certain *adventurist* forms of nuclearism (arms race, counterforce strategy, first-strike options, limited war and war-fighting scenarios) toward some variant of a *defensive* nuclear posture (nuclear weapons are retained, but their role is strictly limited to providing protection against nuclear blackmail and surprise attack by an enemy state).

Recalling the discussion of world pictures, it seems evident that the shift toward a more defensive nuclear posture can be achieved by stages and can partly rely on the methods of politics-as-usual, including the logic and dynamics of the Machiavellian world picture. It is not surprising, then, given the self-destructive dangers of adventurist nuclearism, that many prominent Machiavellian "realists" are beginning to lend their support to popular demands for greater moderation when it comes to nuclear weapons policy. These welcome defections from the upper ranks of policymakers greatly enhances prospects for influencing formal institutional policies. A stifling consensus is replaced by a political process consisting of pressures and counterpressures that reflect the interplay of special interest groups, social forces, and competing images of realism. At the center of dispute is the proper content of national self-interest and security requirements in relation to the various facets of nuclear weapons policy.

Only within the altered climate created by the popular movement, do we find élite figures advancing their own proposals for moderation. In the late 1970s militarist forces within and without the governing structure had succeeded in dominating policy with a predictible heightening of East-West tensions and quickening of the arms race. Only the unexpected reactions of public opinion, alarmed about rising nuclear war risks created a serious possibility of challenging nuclear adventurism at the level of national debate. The tricontinental peace movement now enables even mainstream politicians and journalists to consider openly, and even support, policies designed to move toward more moderate roles for nuclear weapons. At this point it is astonishing to observe even an avowedly militarist president clamoring aboard the arms control band wagon. It may well turn out to be an optical illusion. Strong grounds for skepticism remain. The Reagan forces could merely be riding out the antinuclear storm, hoping to calm things down enough to go forward with their basic thrust toward nuclear superiority and an interventionary foreign policy. It seems realistic, rather than cynical, to suppose that the current American leadership would like to place the onus of the arms race on Soviet shoulders so as to convey the sense that the United States has tried and failed, and now has no choice but to proceed with a further military buildup. However it may also be possible that the drive to remain in the White House will convince even confirmed cold warriors and superhawks that dramatic progress toward stabilizing nuclearism can alone bring them victory on the domestic scene. Everyone recalls that it was that impeccable anti-Communist, Richard Nixon, who in 1972 turned a conciliatory visit to Red China into a great electoral triumph. Ironies never cease. Now it may be the turn for an ardent militarist like Reagan to deliver the goods on arms control and world peace.

While it is important not to be duped by powerfully entrenched militarist interests, it is also desirable to be receptive to changes by leaders, however opportunistic their motivation. In one sense, the popular movement against nuclearism has achieved substantial success when it rewards peace-minded leadership at the ballot box. In fact, shifting the calculations of politicians is the most hallowed democratic method of reorienting policy and should be respected. Beyond even this kind of healthy pragmatism, however, lies a more genuine possibility of shifting the inner balance of feelings operative among our war-makers. Even the most ardent militarist admits that a nuclear war would be a disaster, and some part of his being must be touched by efforts to minimize these risks.*The distinctiveness of the nuclearist menace is that all of us, including even nuclearists and their families, are potential victims in the fullest sense. The kind of benefit that some derive from positions, power, wealth, and influence associated with present patterns of nuclearism would be forever destroyed by the personal tragedy brought about by nuclear war. Conversions among the élite have already taken place, and there must always be a readiness to welcome with open arms those who genuinely renounce nuclear-

---

*There is a deep self-mystification that interferes with such awareness. Militarists continue to believe that the path to peace is to deter the other side by being even stronger and that the path to war is to tempt enemies to commit aggression. This obsolete mind-set, which has elements of insight, needs to be understood, analyzed, and discredited as effectively as possible. As long as it dominates the thinking and feeling of policymakers and opinion-shapers, it will allow those in power to oppose peace forces in good faith.[1]

ism. In this central sense, the anti-nuclear movement, despite its destiny of struggle, has no permanent or inevitable enemies. What blocks many from recognizing their own deeper affinities with the peace forces, aside from their preoccupation with defending special interests, are certain insulating thought-forms that have grown up over the centuries to bolster the militarism of the Machiavellian world picture, despite its growing absurdity as a rational ground for security. I have in mind here, particularly, the paradoxical idea, enchanting to foreign policy specialists and former national security advisors, that peace is most effectively pursued through preparation for war. This posture toward war and peace enables one to reconcile ethical and survival concerns with the most adventurist forms of nuclearism. As such, it inhibits a recognition of the dangers of the nuclear arms race, allowing at most tactical adjustments in response to political pressure. The contrary position taken by the antinuclear movement is that preparations for war are themselves a cause of war, that arms races have through international history displayed an overall tendency to heighten tensions, produce crises, and lead to wars.

I think it is particularly important to challenge the mental armor of nuclearism at this stage. For this reason, it seems useful to highlight the immorality, illegality, and illegitimacy of nuclear weapons and tactics.[2] Such an emphasis is also consistent with a series of United Nations General Assembly resolutions declaring that "the use or threat of use of nuclear weapons should . . . be prohibited, pending nuclear disarmament."[3] The most effective way to push ahead on this front is through a global insistence on a no-first-use policy pertaining to nuclear weapons, an insistence that earlier might have prevented a nuclear arms race altogether (see discussion, pp. 162–64), but even now could contribute greatly to a more stable world.[4] Such a step would make the crucial acknowledgment that these weapons can never be legitimately threatened or used for the ends of state power, however helpful it may seem in a particular set of circumstances. It would be beneficial to have such a declaration of no-first-use solemnized in a formal statement subscribed to by all governments. Part of the appeal of such a no-first-use arrangement is its simplicity: it is equal, easy to negotiate or can consist of unilateral declarations, requires no monitoring or verification, and contributes to overall security. The importance of this step is not only as an official statement of policy but also to persuade governments to abandon the forward or battlefield deployment of nuclear weapons, especially in Western Europe. A government of a superpower is unlikely to make a declaration of this sort in solemn form without adapting its war plans and deployment patterns.

Some Western specialists say that Europe, South Korea, or the Persian Gulf cannot be defended without threatening to respond to conventional attacks with nuclear weapons. There are many reasons to believe that the new conventional weaponry that is becoming available, including the latest in precision guided munitions and antitank technology, can meet defense requirements at current levels, or less, of expenditure. Contrary to the protestations of nuclearists, it is not necessary to militarize further other dimensions of domestic and world politics to compensate for taking this large step toward the stabilization of nuclearism. Note, also, that a no-first-use posture is fully compatible with a wide range of other arms control proposals, including the nuclear weapons freeze, prohibitions on new weapons system and further testing, creation of nuclear free zones, restraints on conventional weaponry, and a diplomacy of nonalignment for countries formerly allies of one or the other superpower.

Some critics complain that a no-first-use pledge is worthless, consisting of mere words, lacking any provision for sanctions, enforcement, or verification. Its verbal character, they argue, creates a one-sided trap for the more peace-minded states in the world, while placing no obstacle whatsoever in the path of an aggressor government. Here again the reasoning of defenders of the nuclear status quo seems poor. Except for possibly the United States, no other country has the slightest incentive other than in a situation *in extremis* to threaten or use nuclear weapons. If the United States were to adopt a no-first-use posture, it would certainly at the same time alter accordingly its contingency plans and capabilities, while the fear of what a beleaguered country might do if at the edge of survival and in possession of nuclear weapons seems almost irrelevant. Of course, no regime of restraint can promise perfect compliance. All rules of inhibition are susceptible to violation in any situation where political survival is deeply threatened, and yet even here, the situation would be no worse than what exists without the declaration. The importance of no-first-use thinking and practice is to discourage resolving crises by the temptation of recourse to nuclear threats. Even with a no-first-use orientation firmly in place, it will remain dangerous to press hard for military victory in conflicts touching on the vital interests of states that retain nuclear weapons or are closely aligned to such states. The Falklands/Malvinas War of 1982 vividly shows the helplessness of international society as a whole when the "honor" of sovereign states is drawn into questions, especially if a military confrontation is popular at home and officials of the adversary governments are eager to distract criticism with an overseas side-show. This helplessness has resulted in a stream of costly, senseless wars over the course of history, perhaps World War I being the clearest major instance in our century. No rule of conduct can hope to do more in a world of sovereign states than build a framework of inhibition that over time reshapes attitudes and expectations about the role of nuclear weapons, and by such alteration builds new possibilities for futher denuclearization.

If moderate postures (that is, as a weaponry of ultimate recourse when total defeat is in prospect) evolve into purely defensive nuclear postures (that is, a weaponry retained only as protection against the nuclearism of others), then a fundamentally different situation would exist. True, even a defensive conception of nuclear weaponry might produce various forms of anxiety about whether the capabilities and intentions of the other side could not mount a successful disarming first strike (thereby destroying the hedge), and such speculation, possibly induced by maliciously false intelligence reports, could, if believed, create renewed pressures to resume the nuclear arms race despite the adoption of declarations of prohibition, freeze arrangements, and a host of other arms control measures. As long as the weaponry continues as an existing part of the security package then the structure of nuclearism, however contained, will cast its long shadow across our lives, posing in some form risks to human survival, impairing democratic relations between state and society, and, very likely, inducing a tensed reliance on nonnuclear militarism to offset the diminishing role of nuclear weaponry in an unchanged global political context. A central source of persisting anxiety will be the forward march of technology, making the weaponry of mass destruction more and more accessible to virtually all governments and discontented groups; the problems of proliferations will remain and jeopardize any international framework based on purely defensive conceptions. Furthermore, so long as the war system persists, a purely defensive posture for nuclear weapons would always be drawn into question whenever a government possessing nuclear weapons was facing the prospect of a major military defeat. Worthy and ambitious as is the shift to a purely defensive posture, it cannot hope to be entirely stable, and yet, as Jonathan Schell tirelessly underscores, the weaponry cannot be disinvented. We again confront here the apparent unresolvable tension between our need to get totally rid of this weaponry and the apparent impossibility of doing so. This tension expresses in clearest form the specific nature of the nuclear trap. History must be reversed, but history, by its nature, is irreversible.

Yet the finality of this formulation may itself be a trap set by ourselves, by our way of thinking. Nuclear weapons may "disappear" when other arrangements render them "irrelevant," when, for instance, the defense of our national boundaries relies no more on military capabilities than does the security of Pennsylvania in its relationship to New Jersey or Ohio. We get a glimpse of this possibility in the mutual relations of Western European countries since 1945 or of Canada and the United States in this century.

To overcome nuclearism, as such, requires quite a different sort of action than increasing the rationality and prudence of existing political leaders or of moderating institutional arrangements. It rests on the live possibility of establishing an orientation toward security that is not wedded to militarist strategies of geographical defense. It presupposes, in other words, supplanting the Machiavellian world picture with some version of a holistic world picture. Such a process would automatically transform the role and character of political institutions, eliminating a society's dependence on the existence of an enemy to achieve identity and coherence. A holistic world picture defines group coherence positively by a capacity to satisfy basic human needs of all people without damaging the biosphere or weakening reverence for nature. This holistic alternative is struggling in various ways to emerge in our thought and action, although as yet its influence seems weak and marginal, often expressing itself more in relation to ideas about diet and health than reshaping our sense of the political. It is important for the movement against nuclearism to grasp that realizing its goals is inseparable from the triumph over time of this holistic orientation. At this stage, this understanding may require nothing more substantive than a receptivity to such a possibility and a clarity about the desirability, yet limited horizons, of actions designed to diminish the dangers of nuclearism in its current forms.

There are a few additional orienting comments about action that flow from an acceptance of the long-range necessity for holistic politics.

Contra utopianism.

A holistic vision does not imply a blueprint for the future, much less does it imply covert support for the project of world government or for the formation of a superstate; only in the process of gaining ascendency can the holistic world picture evolve appropriate institutional forms, but we can anticipate that they will not be reproductions on a global scale of the sort of governmental arrangements now associated with the sovereign state. Decentralization of power and authority will be paramount, as will efforts to coordinate economic, social, and cultural relations without reliance on bureaucratic oversight. New technologies for dispersed participation in shaping and sharing information may be one of the keys helpful for unlocking the future. Finally, the holistic prospect is not cut off from historical processes of evolution, as is the case with utopias that are posited as fully wrought solutions. We require a politics, as well as an imagery, of transformation.

Obtain the Possible: Demand the Impossible

Contra militarism.

Militarism is difficult to define clearly. It involves both a state of mind and a set of supportive societal arrangements. The essence of modern militarism is a comprehensive reliance on instruments of violence in the pursuit of national security. Militarism is also tied to technology. A militarist state of mind does far less damage, as a rule, under conditions of primitive technology, although even this direct assertion needs to be qualified. If, as is the case in the nuclear age, the consequences of militarism are catastrophic, then even the unabashed militarist is inhibited to a certain extent. Militarist guidance of foreign policy without any nuclear weaponry on the scene would undoubtedly have already produced World War III by now.

The rejection of militarism is wider than the rejection of nuclearism, but it is integral to it. And, in fact, the rejection of nuclearism without the substantial modification, if not outright rejection, of militarism is, finally, a futile project. Although nuclearism represents something that reaches far beyond the mere application of military technology according to the dictates of the Machiavellian world picture, its incorporation of specific weapons of war proceeded within this traditional framework. It may not be necessary, at least at the outset, to confront militarism with pacifism, but overcoming militarism will eventually depend on the existence of nonviolent alternatives to achieve security for peoples and nations.[5] One important way to dilute militarism is to confine military capabilities and foreign policy to the strict circumstance of *defensive necessity*, as well as to draw distinctions between the defense of governments and of people. Of course, defense is an elastic concept, but my intention is to emphasize a real change of heart that seeks to restrict sharply the role of military weapons of all kinds.

The arrival of a sheriff in a western town during the early part of the last century brought a different kind of order *only* if the expectations about violence changed for most of the inhabitants. Without such a shift the new *forms,* and even *capabilities,* could not enhance security in the community and might indeed have produced a reliance on higher levels of violence on all sides.

Unless antinuclearism evolves in the wider setting of antimilitarism there is conjured up the prospect of a renunciation of the nuclear option combined with a vast buildup of conventional weaponry, a revival of the draft, an enormous peacetime army deployed around the world, thus creating an overall darkening prospect of major wars fought with weaponry of far greater savagry than used in World War II, as well as the persisting prospect of nuclear rearmament. The kind of popular momentum created by antinuclearism would, if it succeeded, also move naturally in an antimilitarist direction, questioning the ethics and viability of interventionary diplomacy and realizing the need to diminish those nonmilitary causes of war related to food and energy supplies, world poverty, and environmental decay.

Contra a Narrow Agenda.

There is a view frequently found among antinuclear activists that their concerns can be treated apart from others, arguing that the removal of the danger of nuclear war constitutes the necessary ground that must achieved first if other social and political challenges are ever to be faced. This insistence on priority, however well conceived, tends to misunderstand the political conditions that must come to exist if an antinuclear movement is to achieve even limited success in both East and

West. We need to consider what quality and quantity of social forces must be mobilized to challenge effectively the nuclear national security state in both superpowers. When we do this it becomes obvious, I think, that labor and minority discontent, peace activism by leading church groups, popular demands for liberty and social justice, attacks on the corruptions and repressiveness of the bloated state create bonds of transnational dimension that can also easily become bearers of antimilitarist and antinuclearist sentiments. The success of Polish Solidarity, as most leaders in the European Nuclear Disarmament movement understood, would strengthen their prospects; its defeat would be demoralizing and debilitating, in part constituting a reassertion of the primacy of Soviet militarism and an uncertainty about whether a Western-centered movement for peace is not, in the end, self-defeating.

If antinuclearism succeeds in influencing policies of nuclear governments it will be because it prevails through struggle, a struggle that includes the persuasiveness in debate of antinuclear forces. Persuasiveness is an important instrument to mobilize portions of the citizenry and to sow doubts in the nuclearist consensus, but it is by itself not nearly enough. Coalitions must be struck with social forces animated by discontent about the *status quo*. The nuclear national security state has grown into a powerful apparatus of coercion that can be and would be trained upon any opposition movement that threatened its dominion. The more broadly conceived the movement, the harder to break its will and morale.

It is pure illusion to suppose that there exists an apolitical and nonmilitant path to a nuclear-free United States or world. It is a further illusion to suppose that a political path can be discovered that is not beset by obstacles and struggle. Prospects for a nonviolent struggle toward these ends is likely to depend, in large part, on how broadly based and strongly motivated such an oppositional movement can become. In this regard, the particular characteristics of the movement need to be understood by its various segments. On the one side, are the present fragments of the American political elite and generally conservative professionals, including doctors, lawyers, and engineers that have formed their own antinuclear pressure groups. On the other side are present more militant groups that oppose nuclearism as part of a wider struggle against the modern state and its injustices. In between are an array of other orientations, including a wide variety of positions emanating from church activism on the nuclear issue. The capacity of the overall movement to grow more powerful and successful will depend greatly on the wisdom of its leaders, especially their ability to regard the diversity and multileveled character of the antinuclear movement as an expression of democratic vitality rather than as an indication of disunity and weakness.

Contra Secular Absolutism.

Over time the modern state, even in societies proudest of their democratic identity, has adopted absolutist prerogatives and moved steadily in authoritarian directions. Nowhere is this tension between democratic creed and antidemocratic practice more evident than in relation to nuclear weapons diplomacy. The same leaders who insist that the major stake in international conflict is the fate of democratic governance have steadily eroded democratic content in the name of national security.

It is well to recall the early American antipathy to peacetime military establishments of any kind, phrased as opposition to so-called "standing armies." Even Alexander Hamilton, in so many ways an architect of governmental centralism, joined in the then prevalent belief that, as set forth in Federalist Paper

No. 8, the standing armies of Europe and their perpetual readiness to engage in war "bear a malignant aspect to liberty and economy" for the country involved.[6] The founders of the American republic believed that advantages of geography and of political ideology would provide the United States with a general circumstance of security without militarism.

A similar disposition underlay, of course, the preoccupation with creating checks on possible abuse of presidential powers. The entire Constitution was drafted in light of the central doctrine of "the separation of powers" and the closely aligned notion of "checks and balance." The founders of our republic sought to avoid, above all else, a re-creation in some new format of royalism and of leaders, who like the kings of old, could claim to rule by divine right. The American idea was to limit presidential authority by combining rules of substance with restraining procedures. Indeed, given the stern religious teachings of early America, including a preoccupation with original sin, the constitutional framework was conceived as a buffer against weakness and evil inherent in the human condition. The requirement that Congress participate in a declaration of war was specifically intended to prevent the president from having the power to commit the country unilaterally to war.

Over time there have been many encroachments on this conception of peacetime governance, a variety of accommodations to practical necessity without any formal adjustments by way of constitutional revisions. The avoidance of standing armies gave way to an expanding permanent military establishment. The Executive Branch claimed various privileges to keep national security information secret. The Congress and the public tolerated, even encouraged, a variety of recourses to armed force without prior declarations of war, American involvement in the Korean and Vietnam wars being the most spectacular instances.

All these tendencies helped to set the stage for the advent of nuclear weaponry that has put a permanent seal of inevitability on the imperial presidency. The nuclear national security state is a new, as yet largely unanalyzed, phenomenon in the long history of political forms. Being constantly ready to commit the nation (and the planet!) to a devastating war of annihilation in a matter of minutes on the basis of possibly incorrect computer-processed information or pathological traits among leaders creates a variety of structural necessities that contradict the spirit and substance of democratic governance: secrecy, lack of accountability, permanent emergency, concentration of authority, peacetime militarism, extensive apparatus of state intelligence and police. No king ever concentrated in his being such absolute authority over human destiny, not just in relation to his own people but for humanity as a whole. War as the sport of presidents has become the ironic, dreadful descriptive circumstance, an outcome brought about by the combined impact of the growth of statism and of the characteristics of the technology of war now available to leaders of the superpowers.

Indeed nuclearism has caused a cultural, as well as a political and constitutional, breakdown. The unconditional claim by finite, fallible human beings to inflict holocaustal devastation on an unlimited scale for the sake of national interests and on behalf of any particular state is an acute variety of idolatry—treating the limited and conditional as if it were unlimited and unconditional. Our religious leaders have been slow to respond, complacent in their own secularism, and have tended to acquiesce in whatever powers the state claims for itself beneath the banner of national security. An encouraging recent sign is a dramatic weakening of deference to secular absolutism within the religious community when it comes to nuclear weapons policy. An increasing number of spiritual leaders with an array of denominational backgrounds are speaking out, to date mainly on the pernicious nature of nuclear weapons but also in strong support of individuals who stand apart from the state in a posture of resistance.

The erosion of democracy, while serious, is by no means final. In fact, if popular forces succeed in altering nuclear weapons policy it will have an overall revitalizing effect on our entire political process. Thomas Jefferson, always dubious about the capacity of constitutional arrangements ("a mere thing of wax"), put his trust for the maintenance of democratic vitality in "an energetic citizenry." One of the features of the nuclear national security state is to demobilize the citizenry as totally as possible on the most crucial questions facing the society. Only an energetic citizenry can hope to modify the political climate sufficiently to create space for new leadership and different directions of official policy. To combat nuclear militarism in the United States certainly requires an even more energetic citizenry reinforced by a cultural and religiously active appreciation that the authority of the state has degenerated into a new and acute species of idolatry.

At this time political analysts are in a position comparable to that of seismic specialists called upon to predict the intensity and date of an expected earthquake. There are many warning tremors. The political fault lines are so wide and deep that when it comes, the eruption could shake the strongest institutional foundations, but we cannot be sure whether this shattering of our order will come sooner or later, or what precise form it will take.

On a more concrete level, a distinction can be drawn between proximate goals that can be stated quite concretely and more distant goals that will have to be specified as they are approached. The essence of an antinuclearist orientation, given the realities of the world as we know it, involves a renunciation of the nuclear option combined with the retention of a limited number of nuclear weapons as an instrument of ultimate resort, confined in its potential role to a nuclear retaliation to a nuclear attack. The ethics and politics of this renunciation should help center a popular movement in the United States and would, I feel confident, find a resonant response elsewhere, including the Soviet Union. Such an expectation is not based on any perception of untapped altruistic energies being set loose. Quite the contrary. Selfishness would lead other countries to join with us in this process of nuclear renunciation, partly because it is the United States alone that has made such a strong investment over the years in maintaining the nuclear option against all challengers. I would not want to pretend that this dynamic of partial renunciation will come about easily. Its realization would represent a profound reversal of field with respect to the lineaments of security in the nuclear age.

If antinuclear sentiments take command, even more ambitious goals would then seem attainable: namely a determined assault on "the war system" in its totality, including national and transnational subsystems of special privilege, exploitation, and repression. In effect, the pursuit of humane governance is a goal on all levels of social organization from the family to the world. Such an animating vision may never be fully attainable, but its pursuit seems implicit in any serious engagement to work toward liberating our planet and our species from the nuclear curse that has been laid so heavily upon it.

This great struggle for global transformation encompasses normal politics, but it is also far broader than any strictly political experience, resembling more the emergence of a new religion or civilization on a global scale than a change, however radical, in the personnel or orientation of political leaders. In essence, as the transformation proceeds, the ground of politics will shift, and by shifting, will cause turmoil and confusion as new tendencies grow stronger, while the old structures, despite being undermined, remain in place and may through the desperate efforts of their stalwarts, embark on even more aggressive and adventurist paths. The avoidance of a crash landing of the old order is obviously a high priority under these circumstances. One form of constructive politics in such a setting are forms of thought and action that incorporate positive aspects of the past rather than insisting on its utter repudiation of a complete break. The pain of transition could be considerably eased by regarding attitudes of reconciliation as a cardinal virtue alongside those of perseverance and commitment.

Some words by James Douglass, theologian and antinuclear activist, provide a concluding vector: ". . . a way of stopping the world in an end-time of global violence is, above all, a way not of speculation but of practice—a way of living and acting out a day-to-day personal and communal struggle for a liberating, transforming truth for humanity. . . ."[7] There are many paths that ascend the mountain, but we dare not any longer evade the challenge of the long, difficult climb. The vision from the peak will surely be a holistic panorama. And yet, there is no real suspense. In the most profound sense the holistic world picture is available to all of us now; we can simply cease to be Machiavellians whenever we choose. Each individual withdrawal of energy and consent strengthens collective capacities to fashion life-sustaining alternatives for the society as a whole. If only we are alert, all of us have this extraordinary vitalizing opportunity to create together a postnuclear history.

In Darkness—
Toward Light

To embrace nuclearism is quite literally to descend into darkness. If survival of a nuclear attack is imaginable at all it is generally associated with being crowded into a specially designed shelter burrowed deeply into the earth. A few elaborate shelters exist that are selectively available to the top leadership of our government, isolated, set in darkness, and providing only the most minimal kind of protection against exposure to damage from nuclear attack. Despite sharp reductions of funds for such vital necessities as food stamps and student loans, the present administration proposes to spend more than $4 billion on nuclear shelters and evacuation plans, at once acknowledging a serious expectation of nuclear war and committing the country to a set of so-called "precautions" that are ludicrously incapable of providing genuine protection in the event of nuclear attack. We can only suppose that a lethal mixture of extreme cynicism and frightening complacency explain why our elected leaders would offer the American people such hollow answers to a real fear and risk of nuclear war.

The Kyoto Central Hotel in Japan has recently promised patrons three extra weeks of life in the event of a nuclear war even if the entire world should be destroyed. In describing the reasoning that lies behind this new "service" that takes the form of a huge lower basement shelter equipped to take up to 3,000 guests, hotel manager Ryuzo Kutami, explained:

> This is the first hotel in the world to construct a modern nuclear shelter of this proportion. The shelter was built in line with our policy of providing our guests with the best service and facilities.
>
> The shelter was built because our president, Ryuzo Ikeuchi, is pessimistic about the future. He is convinced a nuclear war will break out.[1]

In essence, we as citizens can choose to build "shelters" and wait in various ways for the end of life on the planet, or we can join in a struggle to make life secure in the daylight. It will take a special effort of will to recover the vitality of our identity as citizens with a shaping role in the destiny of our country.

To sink into the despair of shelter-safety is to confirm the wider subordination of the human spirit to the relentless forward march of technology. Technological relentlessness has become an even greater threat to human freedom than political tyranny. It binds our eyes and minds tightly closed with its basic message of helplessness. This fatalistic outlook disastrously neglects our special capacity for symbolization, that is, for projecting images and possibilities that give direction to human freedom. We can posit a benevolent and attainable future through our imaginings, a liberating beginning in consciousness that can influence our actions. We, as a species, are not necessarily trapped by nuclearism provided we do not subscribe to some variation of that deterministic claim that since nuclear weapons exist, we are forever condemned to be dependent upon them.

The antinuclear movement starts from the contrary premise that a world without nuclear weapons is a possibility, and that this possibility can only be realized through a massive human effort of international scope to challenge and supplant the current wisdom of leading governments. Despite acute apprehensions about the danger and effects of nuclear war, most grassroots protest activists are generally hopeful, claiming, or reclaiming, life at its core. The Dutch peace movement's self-conscious rejection of *doomdanken* or "doomthinking" is a typical expression of this affirmative spirit. A report written by an American observer of European peace efforts notes that "With the aid of the arts, particularly satire and humor, the entire mood of the peace movement is transformed from sullen preoccupation with death and destruction, to an endorsement of life. Every country we visited had plays, posters, concerts, statues, songs, jokes and parties, celebrating life, an end to the terror of nuclear destruction, continuity in human civilization."[2] This energizing restorative quality is experienced as soon as one accepts responsibility for acting in the world to overcome nuclearism. There was a similar sprit of celebration and renewal in New York City on June 12,1982, when more than 750,000 people gathered in the largest antinuclear demonstration ever held. They rallied to affirm human life as well as to demand an end to the nuclear arms race—indeed the two goals are one.

We understand the antinuclear movement as a groping toward light. Implicit is the insistence that human beings can refuse to be nuclear guinea pigs any longer for the uncertain and macabre workings of the war system. It is also an insistence on ending the hostage status of the peoples of the world. This movement is carrying antinuclear thinking into the world in the shape of constructive and committed action. No one can promise at this stage that nuclearism can be successfully challenged. As we have indicated, the roots of nuclearism are embedded deeply in the soil of privilege, power, and profits. They are also embedded in our political consciousness, anchoring that great misconception that the security of the country from foreign enemies continues to depend in the nuclear age upon having a larger number of weapons of destruction than our enemy. All the specialized talk about the comparative size and quality of nuclear weapons arsenals obscures the central truth that nuclear war would be an overwhelming catastrophe for both the stronger and weaker sides.

There are many resources of society that are now for the first time being devoted to the struggle against nuclearism and this is most encouraging. For the first time, prominent church leaders from many denominational backgrounds are beginning to associate opposition to nuclearism with religious duty. Furthermore, professionals, especially doctors, but also lawyers, scientists, engineers, and artists are using their specializing skills to promote antinuclear causes. For instance, doctors have dramatized the extent to which the damage effects of a nuclear attack would overwhelm medical capacities, scientists and engineers have exposed dangerous implications of various weapons systems, and lawyers have raised questions about the legality of nuclear weapons and the constitutional and ethical implications of allowing leaders to rely on unlawful weapons.

Somewhat surprisingly, universities have been slow to respond. There are, as yet, few courses that train students at various levels of education to grapple with the challenge of nuclear war. We believe an enormous opportunity exists to increase the awareness of young people and to stimulate their inquiry into prospects for peace, including nonviolent approaches to diplomacy and national security. There are curricular beginnings in the form of a few modest programs on world order and peace studies, but much more could be done with a subject matter that has both such a vital practical importance and offers such rich rewards for interdisciplinary collaboration.

Even less has been done to involve organized labor in the struggle against nuclearism. True, a few labor leaders have spoken out against the nuclear arms race and have explained how current levels of defense spending are injurious to the economic health of the country and the situation of most workers. Yet labor as a whole remains largely inert, failing to realize the extent to which nuclearism threatens their future as workers and citizens.

As the raising of consciousness within the antinuclear movement proceeds, the relevance of the global setting grows stronger. Already Soviet doctors have joined with American doctors in joint statements and other cooperative ventures. At large peace demonstrations, foreign delegations and speakers are playing ever more prominent roles. There is a growing sense of solidarity across national boundaries despite different tactical goals in different regions. As matters now stand, the Europeans emphasize problems of "limited nuclear war," the Americans stress the nuclear arms race, and the Japanese underscore their opposition to nuclear weapons as such. There is, however, unity beneath this diversity, a shared insistence on a nuclear-free world, and a gathering appreciation that national boundaries and identities are becoming relatively less important.

An encompassing vulnerability creates the foundation for a

new type of politics of struggle in which a main objective is to turn enemies into allies. As even the most confirmed militarists are also potential victims of nuclearism, there are grounds for believing that genuine changes of heart can occur, and we have been strengthened in these beliefs by the role in the peace movement being played here and abroad by high-ranking former military officers. We must allow governments, as well, the space to move away from nuclearism, by welcoming and rewarding any genuine initiatives for peace without losing a skeptical sense that official proposals in the nuclear weapons area may be put forward mostly, or even only, for the sake of scoring propaganda points. In this regard, we take positive note of the significant pledge never to use nuclear weapons first that Leonid I. Brezhnev made on behalf of the Soviet Union in his June 15, 1982 message to the United Nations, and we are disturbed by our government's dismissal of the proposal without offering any constructive response of its own. To dismiss as cynical propaganda whatever the other side puts forward is to tighten still further the noose of self-entrapment that is the essence of nuclearism. We regard it as essential to mount pressure on both superpowers to explore seriously and fairly any proposals from any source that offer humanity some greater prospect of averting nuclear catastrophe.

This potential constituency of the entire world, conceived of as a real project, not a sentimental piety, could also help clarify the contours of a less militarist, nonnuclear conception of security. The central idea of securing peoples lives against danger could be greatly advanced by the demise of nuclearism. Working to assure that the basic human needs of food, energy, housing, health, and education for all people are realized would also help establish security by removing some of the causes of war. Gradually using international institutions on a regional and global level for peacekeeping roles could further diminish the war-making function of the modern state. In such a setting, training citizens in resistance skills could both strengthen the democratic foundation of genuine security and weaken the case for militarist approaches.

We are not so foolish as to believe that this quest for postnuclear security will be achieved quickly or easily. At every stage, powerful temptations to abandon the quest will be present: at times, we will be made fearful of the other side, at other times, we will be reassured by gestures of arms control. Direct tactics of counterattack are also likely to be relied upon by nuclearists, including an array of efforts by the state to destroy the credibility and will of peace forces. The antinuclear movement may also be split by a dispiriting tendency of governments to respond to pressure by shifting resources into nonnuclear forms of militarism.

There are already some indications that the government is becoming nervous about the mounting challenge to nuclearism. For instance, recently the White House warned the Pentagon that any prosecutions of young Americans for failing to register for the draft might inflame antinuclear forces and, if any trials are held, they should be located in remote parts of the country. John S. Herrington, assistant secretary of the Navy, put the situation this way: "My feeling is that felony prosecutions at this time may have an awful lot to do with the antinuclear movement. I think we ought to proceed really cautiously on this particular point. This would be a real rallying point. I am not in principle against felony prosecutions for this. . . . I think the cases should be quiet; and pick the right jurisdiction so you don't end up in New York or Chicago, and end up in Omaha or somewhere like that for your first few trials."[3]

In another development, a top official sent a memorandum for presidential consideration in May 1982 advocating a concerted media blitz as a response to the antinuclear challenge. The memorandum analyzes the movement in adversary terms as consisting of "such perennial elements as the old-line pacifists, the environmentalists, the disaffected left, and various communist elements," but then goes on to admit that there is also "participation, on an increasing scale in the U.S. of three groups whose potential impact should be cause for concern. They are the churches, the 'loyal opposition,' and, perhaps most important the unpoliticized public."[4] Such a frank admission of anxiety about the exercise of citizen rights by "the unpoliticized public" is suggestive of how ingrained antidemocratic attitudes in relation to nuclear weapons policy have become in Washington.

For a broadly based popular movement to persevere in such an atmosphere will demand qualities of sincerity, courage, and hope. Building confidence in the security of our personal and collective lives without reliance on nuclear weapons depends on a citizenry alive to its own power to resist broadly all forms of encroachments on freedom and independence, whether originating within or without national boundaries, a resistance needed, in any event, to revitalize the basic spirit of democracy.

We end, then, on a Jeffersonian note—a call to action directed at our fellow citizens and at kindred spirits in every country to join in this epic struggle to liberate the planet from the menace of nuclearism.

Robert Jay Lifton
Richard Falk

APPENDIX

Nuclear War's Effect on the Mind[1]

"Scenarios" about fighting, recovering from, or even "winning" a nuclear war tend to be remarkably vague about the psychological condition of survivors.

Some commentators simply assume that survivors will remain stoic and begin to rebuild from the ruins in a calm, disciplined way. Others seem to attribute that rebuilding to a mysterious, unseen hand. Usually absent is a reasoned estimate, on the basis of what experience we have, of how people might actually be expected to behave.

Recently physicians and other scientists have been making careful projections of the effects of nuclear war, and all raise severe doubts about general claims of recovery.

A twenty-megaton bomb, for instance, if detonated over New York City, Chicago, or Leningrad, would vaporize, crush, incinerate, or burn to death almost every person within a radius of five or six miles from the center of the blast—two million people, perhaps. Within a radius of twenty miles, a million more or so would either die instantly or would suffer wounds from which they could not recover. If the bomb exploded on the ground, countless others who live miles away, far beyond the reach of the initial blast and searing heat wave, would be sentenced to a lingering death as radioactive fallout drifted quietly down onto people, buildings, water and food supplies, and the earth itself.

But that picture, harsh as it seems, is inadequate even for a limited nuclear war and certainly for a full-scale one. New York City, say, would be hit by many warheads, as would other cities, industrial centers, and military targets—hundreds of warheads, maybe thousands.

One has to try to imagine 100 million or more people dead, and lethal amounts of radioactivity scattered over huge areas.

And the survivors? Would they panic? Would they help one another? What would they feel and do?

In Hiroshima, survivors not only expected that they too would soon die, they had a sense that *everyone* was dying, that "the world is ending." Rather than panic, the scene was one of slow motion—of people moving gradually away from the center of the destruction, but dully and almost without purpose. They were, as one among them put it, "so broken and confused that they moved and behaved like automatons. . . . a people who walked in the realm of dreams." Some tried to do something to help others, but most felt themselves to be so much part of a dead world that, as another remembered, they were "not really alive."

The key to that vague behavior was a closing off of the mind so that no more horror could enter it. People witnessed the most grotesque forms of death and dying all around them but felt nothing. A profound blandness and insensitivity—a "paralysis of the mind"—seemed to take hold in everyone. People saw what was happening and were able to describe it later in sharp detail, but their minds, they said, were numbed.

Hiroshima and Nagasaki, however, can provide us with no more than a hint of what would happen in the event of nuclear war. A single weapon today can have the power of one thousand Hiroshima bombs, and we have to be able to imagine one thousand of those exploding in the space of a few minutes. Moreover, in the case of Hiroshima and Nagasaki—and this is absolutely crucial—there was still a functioning outside world to provide help.

In a nuclear war, the process of psychic numbing may well be so extreme as to become irreversible.

Imagine the familiar landscape turning suddenly into a sea of destruction: Everywhere smoldering banks of debris; everywhere the sights and sounds and smells of death. Imagine that the other survivors are wandering about with festering wounds, broken limbs, and bodies so badly burned that their features appear to be melting and their flesh is peeling away in great raw folds. Imagine—on the generous assumption that your children are alive at all—that you have no way of knowing whether the radiation they have been exposed to has already doomed them.

The suddenness and the sheer ferocity of such a scene would not give survivors any chance to mobilize the usual forms of psychological defense. The normal human response to mass death and profound horror is not rage or depression or panic or mourning or even fear; it is a kind of mental anesthetization that interferes with both judgment and compassion for other people.

In even minor disasters, the mind becomes immobilized, if only for a moment. But in the event of a nuclear attack, the immobilization may reach the point where the psyche is no longer connected to its own past and is, for all practical purposes, severed from the social forms from which it drew strength and a sense of humanity. The mind would, then, be shut down altogether.

The resulting scene might very well resemble what we usually can only imagine as science fiction. The landscape is almost moonlike, spare and quiet, and the survivors who root among the ruins seem to have lost contact with one another, not to mention the ability to form cooperating groups and to offer warmth and solace to people around them.

In every catastrophe for which we have adequate records, survivors emerge from the debris with the feeling that they are (to use anthropologist Anthony Wallace's words) "naked and alone . . . in a terrifying wilderness of ruins."

In most cases—and this, too, is well recorded in the literature of disaster—that sense of isolation quickly disappears with the realization that the rest of the world is still intact. The disaster, it turns out, is local, confined, bounded. Out there beyond the peripheries of the affected zone are other people— relatives, neighbors, countrymen—who bring blankets and warm coffee, medicines and ambulances. The larger human community is gathering its resources to attend to a wound on its flank, and survivors respond to the attention and the caring with the reassuring feeling that there is life beyond the ruins, after all. That sense of communion, that perception that the textures of social existence remain more or less whole, is a very important part of the healing that follows.

None of that will happen in nuclear war.

There will be no surrounding human community, no undamaged world out there to count on.

No one will come in to nurse the wounded or carry them off to hospitals. There will be no hospitals, no morphine, no antibiotics.

There will be no succor outside—no infusion of the vitality, the confidence in the continuity of life, that disaster victims have always needed so desperately.

Rather, survivors will remain in a deadened state, either alone or among others like themselves, largely without hope and vaguely aware that everyone and everything that once mattered to them has been destroyed.

Thus survivors would be experiencing not only the most extreme forms of individual trauma imaginable but an equally severe form of collective trauma stemming from a rupture of the patterns of social existence.

Virtually no survivors will be able to enact that most fundamental of all human rituals, burying their own dead.

The bonds that link people in connecting groups will be badly torn, in most cases irreparably, and their behavior is likely to become muted and accompanied by suspiciousness and extremely primitive forms of thought and action.

Under these conditions, such simple tasks as acquiring food and maintaining shelter would remain formidable for weeks and months, even years. And the bands of survivors would be further reduced not only by starvation but also by continuing exposure to radiation and by virulent epidemics.

For those who manage to stay alive, the effects of radiation may interfere with their capacity to reproduce at all or their capacity to give birth to anything other than grossly deformed infants. But few indeed would have to face that prospect.

The question so often asked, "Would the survivors envy the dead?" may turn out to have a simple answer. No, they would be incapable of such feelings. They would not so much envy as, inwardly and outwardly, resemble the dead.

Robert Jay Lifton
Kai Erikson

REFERENCES

Section I / Imagining the Real

CHAPTER 1 / THE WORLD OF THE BOMB

1. Herman Kahn, *On Thermonuclear War* (Princeton: Princeton University Press, 1961), p. 86.
2. Alia Johnson, "Why We Should Drop the Bombs!", *Evolutionary Blues*, Vol. 1, No. 1, 1981, p.1. Copyright *Co Evolutution Quarterly.*

CHAPTER 2 / NUCLEAR ILLUSIONS

1. Edward Teller with Allen Brown, *The Legacy of Hiroshima,* (Garden City: Doubleday, 1962), pp. 244ff.
2. Robert Jay Lifton, *The Broken Connection: On Death and the Continuity of Life* (New York: Touchstone Books, 1979), pp. 147–62, 330–334. See also, Jerome D. Frank, *Sanity and Survival* (New York: Vintage, 1968).
3. Desmond Ball, "Can Nuclear War be Controlled?" in Adelphi Paper no. 169, The International Institute for Strategic Studies, London (Autumn, 1981).
4. *Boston Globe,* 11 November 1981, p. 1.
5. Teller, *Legacy of Hiroshima,* p. 244.
6. Herman Kahn, *On Thermonuclear War* (Princeton: Princeton University Press, 1961), pp. 42, 71.
7. Colin S. Gray and Keith Payne, "Victory is Possible," *Foreign Policy,* (Summer 1980): 14–27.

CHAPTER 3 / SECURITY—THE ULTIMATE PSYCHOLOGISM

1. Dexter Masters, *The Accident* (New York: Knopf, 1965 [1955]), p. 41.
2. Edward Shils, *The Torment of Secrecy: The Background and Consequences of American Security Policies* (Glencoe, Ill.: Free Press, 1956), p. 42.
3. Spencer Weart, *Nuclear Fear,* unpublished manuscript. Subsequent quotations and information concerning Marie Curie are also from Weart.
4. Greg Herken, *The Winning Weapon: The Atomic Bomb in the Cold War 1945–1950* (New York: Knopf, 1980), p. 98.
5. Masters, *The Accident,* pp. 370–71.
6. Jonathan Schell, The *Time of Illusion* (New York: Knopf, 1976), p. 344.
7. Ibid, pp. 381–85.

CHAPTER 4 / IS HIROSHIMA OUR TEXT

1. Robert Jay Lifton, *Death in Life: Survivors of Hiroshima*, (New York: Basic Books, 1982 [1968]), pp. 22–23.
2. Ibid, p. 54.
3. Lifton, *The Broken Connection: On Death and the Continuity of Life*, (New York: Touchstone Books, 1979), p. 171.

CHAPTER 5 / THE BOMB IN OUR SCHOOLS—AND IN US

1. Michael J. Carey, "Psychological Fallout," *Bulletin of the Atomic Scientists*, 38 (January 1982):20–24.
2. John E. Mack, "Psychological Trauma," *The Final Epidemic: Physicians and Scientists on Nuclear War*, ed. Ruth Adams and Susan Cullen, (Chicago: Educational Foundation for Nuclear Science, 1982), pp. 21–34; and William R. Beardslee and John E. Mack, "Children and the Impact of Nuclear Advances," unpublished manuscript.
3. Ibid.
4. *New York Times*, 17 March 1982.

CHAPTER 6 / THE IMAGE OF EXTINCTION

1. *New York Herald Tribune* editorial, 7 August 1945.
2. Robert Jay Lifton, "On Death and Death Symbolism: The Hiroshima Disaster," originally in *Psychiatry* 27 (1964):191–210. (Reprinted in *History and Human Survival*, pp. 156–86.)
3. Jonathan Schell, *The Fate of the Earth* (New York: Knopf, 1982).
4. Spencer R. Weart, "Nuclear Fear," unpublished manuscript.

CHAPTER 7 / A WAY OF SEEING

1. Robert Jay Lifton, *The Broken Connection* and *The Life of the Self: Toward a New Psychology*, (New York: Simon & Schuster, and Touchstone Books, 1976).

CHAPTER 8 / A BREAK IN THE HUMAN CHAIN

1. Margaret Mead, "The Information Explosion," *New York Times*, 23 May 1965.
2. Paul Tillich, *The Courage to Be* (New Haven: Yale University Press, 1952), p. 190.
3. Hilton Kramer, "An Artist Emerging from the 60's Counter Culture," *New York Times*, 13 December, 1981.
4. Loren Eiseley, "Man, the Lethal Factor," manuscript.
5. Edgar Snow, "Interview With Mao," *New Republic*, 27 February 1965.

References

CHAPTER 9 / NUCLEAR FUNDAMENTALISM

1. Vergilius Ferm, *An Encyclopedia of Religion* (New York: Philosophical Library, 1945), p. 491; and George M. Marsden, *Fundamentalism and American Culture* (New York: Oxford University Press, 1981).
2. Robert Jay Lifton, "The Appeal of the Death Trip," *New York Times Magazine*, January 1979, pp. 26–7, 29–31.
3. Marsden, George M. *Fundamentalism and American Culture*, quoted in David Martin, *Times Literary Supplement*, 18 April, 1981, p. 1461.
4. Robert Jay Lifton, *Revolutionary Immortality: Mao Tse-tung and the Chinese Cultural Revolution* (New York: W. W. Norton, 1971 [1968], p. 95.
5. In Leslie R. Groves, *Now It Can Be Told: The Story of the Manhattan Project* (New York: Harper, 1962), pp. 437–38.
6. William James, *The Varieties of Religious Experience* (London and New York: Longman's, 1952), p. 150.
7. William L. Lawrence, *Men and Atoms* (New York: Simon & Schuster, 1959), pp. 116–119, 197, 207, 242, 250, and 319.
8. Edward Teller, *The Legacy of Hiroshima* (Garden City: Doubleday, 1962); and Stanley A. Blumberg and Gwinn Owens, *Energy and Conflict: The Life and Times of Edward Teller* (New York: Putnam, 1976).
9. Nuel Pharr Davis, *Lawrence and Oppenheimer* (New York: Simon & Schuster, 1968). p. 230.
10. Letter to James Conant, in *Energy and Conflict*, p. 207.
11. Martin J. Sherwin, *A World Destroyed: The Atomic Bomb and the Grand Alliance* (New York: Knopf, 1975), p. 118.
12. Sherwin, *World Destroyed*, p. 200.
13. Norman Moss, *Men Who Play God: The Story of the H-Bomb and How the World Came to Live With It* (New York: Harper & Row, 1968), p. 54.
14. Lawrence, *Men and Atoms*, p. 250.
15. *New York Daily News*, 29 January, 1982.
16. Ralph E. Lapp, *The Weapons Culture* (New York: Norton, 1968), p. 11.
17. Lawrence, *Men and Atoms*, p. 319.
18. Quoted in Gar Alperovitz, *Atomic Diplomacy: Hiroshima and Potsdam* (New York: Simon & Schuster, 1965), pp. 276–79.

CHAPTER 10 / ON NUMBING AND FEELING

1. Alice Kimball Smith, "Behind the Decision to Use the Atomic Bomb: Chicago 1944–45," *Bulletin of the Atomic Scientists*, October 1958, pp. 3–10, 11.
2. Eugene Rabinowitz, "Five Years After," *The Atomic Age*, ed. Morton Grodzins and Eugene Rabinowitz, (New York: Basic Books, 1963), p. 156. (Includes next two quotations.)
3. Robert Jay Lifton, *Death in Life: Survivors of Hiroshima* (New York: Basic Books, 1982 [1968] p. 54.
4. Judith Eve Lipton, M.D., personal communication.

References

CHAPTER 11 / IMAGINING THE REAL

1. Robert Jay Lifton, *Home From the War: Vietnam Veterans—Neither Victims Nor Executioners* (New York: Simon & Schuster and Touchstone Books, 1973).
2. Lionel Tiger, *Optimism: The Biology of Hope* (New York: Simon & Schuster, 1979) p. 57.
3. Clifford Gertz, *The Interpretation of Cultures* (New York: Basic Books, 1973), pp. 83–47.
4. *Times Literary Supplement,* 18 December, 1981, p. 107.
5. Thomas Merton, *On Peace* (New York: The McCall Publishing Co., 1969), p. 167.

Section II / Political Anatomy of Nuclearism

CHAPTER 12 / TAKING STANDS

1. All quotations are from Henry A. Kissinger, *Years of Upheaval* (Boston: Little, Brown, 1981), p. 1195.
2. For earlier work along these lines see Richard Falk, *Legal Order in a Violent World* (Princeton, N.J.: Princeton University Press, 1968), esp. chapters XII and XIII, pp. 374–413; *A Global Approach to National Policy* (Cambridge, Mass.: Harvard University Press, 1975), chapters 2 and 3, pp. 29–53.

CHAPTER 13 / NUCLEARIZING SECURITY

1. *New York Times,* 21 April, 1982, p. B24.
2. David C. Gompert, "Approaching the Nuclear Future" *Nuclear Weapons and World Politics,* ed. David C. Gompert, et al. (New York: McGraw-Hill, 1977), pp. 4–5.
3. Jerome Kahan, *Security in the Nuclear Age: Developing US Strategic Arms Policy* (Washington, D.C.: Brookings Institution, 1975), p. 2.
4. On this reasoning see Richard Falk, "Renunciation of Nuclear Weapons Use," *Nuclear Proliferation: Prospects for Control,* ed. Bennett Boskey and Mason Willrich (New York: Dunellen, 1970), pp. 133–145.
5. Mary Kaldor, "Nuclear Weapons and the Atlantic Alliance," *democracy* 2 (1982): 17–18; Dan Smith, *Defence of the Realm in the 1980's* (London: Croon Helm, 1980).
6. Robert W. Tucker, *The Purposes of American Power,* (New York: Praeger, 1981), p. 102
7. Ibid.

References

8. Lawrence W. Beilenson and Samuel T. Cohen, "A New Nuclear Strategy" in *The New York Times Magazine*, 24 January 1982, pp. 34, 38, 39.

CHAPTER 14 / NUCLEAR INTENTIONS

1. Thomas J. Downey, "Against Trident II," *New York Times*, 11 February, 1982, p. A35.
2. Lynn E. Davis, *Limited Nuclear Options, Deterrence and the New American Doctrine*, Adelphi Papers No. 121, (London: Institute for Strategic Studies, 1975/76), p. 1.
3. Bernard Brodie, *Strategy in The Missile Age* (New Jersey: Princeton University Press, 1959), p. 213.
4. Both statements quoted in Milton Leitenberg, "Presidential Directive (P.D.) 59: United States Nuclear Weapon Targeting Policy," *Journal of Peace Research* 18 (1981): 311.
5. Iklé, "Can Nuclear Deterrence Last Out the Century," *Foreign Affairs* 51 (1973): 281.
6. Louis René Beres, "Tilting Toward Thanatos: America's 'Countervailing' Nuclear Strategy," *World Politics* 34 (1981): 31.
7. Harold Brown, "Remarks Delivered at Convocation Ceremonies for the 97th Naval War College Class," U.S. Naval War College, Newport, Rhode Island, 20 August 1980, p. 7; for clarification of P.D. 59 see Louis René Beres, "Presidential Directive 59: A Critical Assessment," *Journal of the US Army War College* 11 (1981):19–37; Leitenberg, "Presidential Directive (P.D.) 59."
8. Quotations from Steinbrunner in "Nuclear Decapitation," *Foreign Policy* 45 (1981–82) p. 21.
9. Ibid, pp. 21–23.
10. Jonathan Schell, *Fate of the Earth* (New York: Knopf, 1982), p. 183.

CHAPTER 15 / EMERGENT NUCLEARISM

1. Quoted from "Niels Bohr's Memorandum to President Roosevelt, July 1944," reprinted as an appendix in Robert Jungk, *Brighter than a Thousand Suns* (New York: Harvest/HBJ, 1958), p. 344; also sensitive to the longer-term dangers was the so-called "Franck Report" of seven leading nuclear physicists that were sent to the secretary of war in June 1945 to warn about the consequences of a nuclear arms race and to urge governmental consideration of a demonstration explosion in an uninhabited place. For text see Jungk, pp. 348–360.
2. Pierre Teilhard de Chardin, *The Future of Man* (New York: Harper Colophon Books, 1964), p. 151.
3. Discussion based on Martin J. Sherwin, *A World Destroyed: The Atomic Bomb and the Grand Alliance* (New York: Knopf, 1975).
4. Paul Fussell, "Thank God for the Atom Bomb. Hiroshima: A Soldier's View," *New Republic*, 22 & 29 August, 1981, p. 28.
5. Kai Erikson, *New York Times Book Review*, 9 August, 1981, p. 22.
6. For detailed consideration of the story to build the Super see Gregg Herken, *The Winning Weapon: The Atomic Bomb in the Cold War 1945–1950* (New York: Knopf, 1980), pp. 304–337.

References

CHAPTER 16 / THE SOVIET FACTOR: A "USEFUL" ENEMY

1. Paul H. Nitze, "Strategy in the Decade of the 1980s," *Foreign Affairs* 59 (Fall, 1980) p. 90.
2. Colin Gray, *The Geopolitics of the Nuclear Era* (New York: Crane, Russak, 1977), p. 3.
3. "Two Views of the Soviet Problem," *The New Yorker*, 2 November 1981, p. 62.
4. "A Nuclear Samizdat on America's Arms Race," *The Nation*, 16 January, 1982, p. 44.
5. *New York Times*, 4 February, 1982, p. A1.

CHAPTER 17 / PASSIVITY THE ENEMY OF PEACE

1. See Bernard Brodie, *Escalation and the Nuclear Option* (Princeton, N.J.: Princeton University Press, 1966), p. 49.
2. For text of Khrushchev's letter see Robert F. Kennedy, *Thirteen Days: A Memoir of the Cuban Missile Crisis* (New York: W.W. Norton & Co., 1969), p. 208.

CHAPTER 18 / CONSTRAINING AND LIBERATING WORLD PICTURES

1. For elaboration see Richard Falk, *A Study of Future Worlds* (New York: Free Press, 1975); and Falk, Samuel S. Kim, and Saul H. Mendlovitz, eds., *Toward a Just World Order* (Boulder, Colo.: Westview Press, 1982).

CHAPTER 19 / OBTAIN THE POSSIBLE: DEMAND THE IMPOSSIBLE

1. For an important attempt along these lines see Richard J. Barnet, *Real Security: Restoring American Power in a Dangerous Decade* (New York: Simon and Schuster, 1981).
2. For an extended discussion see Richard Falk, Lee Meyerowitz, and Jack Sanderson, "Nuclear Weapons and International Law," World Order Studies Program, Princeton University Center for International Studies, occasional Paper No. 10, 1981, pp. 1–80.
3. The most recent formulation is contained in G. A. Resolution 36/91I, in Report A/36/751 (1981). It was adopted by a vote of 121 to 19, with 6 countries abstaining. The opposition included the United States and most of NATO, while both China and the Soviet Union voted in favor of the resolution.
4. For analysis to this effect see McGeorge Bundy, George F. Kennan, Robert S. McNamara, and Gerald Smith, "Nuclear Weapons and the Atlantic Alliance," *Foreign Affairs* 60 (1982): 753–768.
5. For an important effort to rethink security and foreign policy see Robert C. Johansen, *The National Interest and the Human Interest* (Princeton, N.J.: Princeton University Press, 1980); Johansen, "Toward a Dependable Peace: A Proposal for an Appropriate Security System," World Order Models Project Working Paper No. 8, (New York: Institute for World Order, 1978).

References

6. Jacob E. Cooke, ed., *The Federalist* (Cleveland, Ohio: World Publishing Co., 1961), p. 44.

7. James Douglass, *Lightning East to West* (Portland, Oregon: Sunburst, 1981), p. 65.

Conclusion / In Darkness—Toward Light

1. *Japan Times*, 5 April, 1982, p. 2.

2. Judith Eve Lipton, "Hollanditis: The European Peace Epidemic," mimeographed, 1982, p. 5.

3. George C. Wilson, "Prosecuting Draft Violators Seen Rallying Nuclear Foes," *Washington Post*, 19 May, 1982, p. A1.

4. "The Anti-Nuclear Battle Plan," *Washington Post*, 9 May, 1982, p. D1.

Appendix / Nuclear Wars Effect on the Mind

1. "Nuclear War's Effect on the Mind," *New York Times* 15 March, 1982; © 1982 The New York Times Company. Reprinted by permission.

INDEX

Abraham, 76
Absolutism, secular, 260–63
Absurdity: of air-raid drills, 51; of
civil defense measures, 55; encounters with, 128; levels of, 4–7;
of Machiavellian world picture,
251; of spiritual claims, 71
Academia: failure of, to address nuclear issues, 6; resignation-cyni-
cism of, 11
Action painting, 71
Actuality, nuclear, 46–47
Addiction, psychology of, 113
Adolescents: comments on nuclear
weapons by, 52–54; nuclear fear
of, 50
Afghanistan, Soviet invasion of, 171,
184, 211, 219, 221, 223
Africa, 8; Soviet and Cuban inter-
ventions in, 171
Aggression: of enemies, 214, 215; in-
direct, 159
Air-raid drills, 4; psychological im-
pact of, 48–52; self-deception in,
5
Alamogordo test, 90, 103, 149, 193,
194
Algeria, 224
American Psychiatric Association
Task Force, 52, 54
Angola, 223; Cuban troops in, 219
Antinuclear movement: agenda of,
258–60; antimilitarism and, 257–

58; on cause of war, 251; global
nature of, 270–71; hopefulness of,
268–69; Japanese, 132, 247; politics of struggle and resistance in,
247; Reagan Administration and,
249–50, 271–72; tactical focus of,
246, 248; Western European,
117, 121, 132, 156, 247, 258–59
Appeasement, 160, 214
Arab-Israeli war of 1973, 190, 227
Arkansas bomb accident, 60
Armageddon, 58; fundamentalist
reading of, 85
Arms control: following Cuban Missile Crisis, 231–34; militarism
and, 234–35, 238; see also Freeze
on nuclear weapons; No-first-use
policy
Arms Control and Disarmament
Agency, 35
Arms Control Policy, 227–28
Arms race, 145–46, 149–53, 155,
162, 166, 206, 210–11, 218, 249;
rapid pace of, 236; test ban treaty
and, 232
Asia, fundamentalism in, 84
"Assured Destruction" concept,
176, 180; see also Mutual assured
destruction
Atomic Energy Commission, 203
Auden, W. H., 244
Awareness, nuclear, 111–25, 143;
and renunciation of role of victim,

Index

China: Communist revolution in, 83, 215, 216; Nixon's visit to, 250; Soviet Union and, 206, 211; test ban treaty rejected by, 232; threats to use nuclear weapons in, 179

Christa, (artist), 72

Christianity, 70, 83; fundamentalist, 80

Chromosomes, abnormalities in, 43

Churchill, Winston, 106, 192, 198–99, 201

Civil defense measures, 54–55, 180–82, 189; Soviet, 172

Classification system, 139

Coalitions, antinuclear, 259

Coercive persuasion, 84

Cohen, Samuel T., 168

Cold War, 146, 233; arms control and, 231; beginning of, 201; Cuban Missile Crisis as U.S. victory in, 230; foreign policy of, 204; origins of, 215–16; revival of, 220; threats of use of nuclear weapons in, 179

Colonial order, collapse of, 216; see also National revolutions

Command vulnerability, 186–87

Commentary, 219

Committee on the Present Danger, 220

Communications systems, 186

Communism, ideology of, 215

Communist Parties, Western European, 216

Compartmentalization of knowledge, 26

Computers, "decisions" made by, 9

Conceptual art, 72

Congress, U.S., 138; alarmist view of global developments in, 220; Cuban Missile Crisis and, 229;

and decision to develop H-bomb, 205; declaration of war and, 140, 261

Conspiracy, secrecy and, 29

Constitution, U.S., 260

Containment, 216–17

Contamination, invisible, 40–44

Council on Foreign Relations, 147–48, 158

Counterforce thinking, 178, 180–82

Counterinsurgency war, policy of, 32, 159

Countervalue, 178

Craziness, children's perceptions of, 51

"Creationist science," 86–87

Credibility, 4, 25, 31–33

Crimes of War (Falk and Lifton), x

Cruise missiles, opposition to deployment of, 246

Cuba, Soviet interventionist policy and, 171, 211, 219, 221, 223

Cuban Missile Crisis (1962), 131, 179, 187, 227–32, 234, 236

Cults, 83–84

Culture: elimination of, 71; public symbols of, 122

Curie, Marie, 30

Darwinian principles of evolution, 86

Death: children's concepts of, 51; closing mind to, 275–76; conquest of, 95; imagery of, 49, 50; individual, acceptance of, 116; insensitivity to, 101; numbing in immersion in, 104; permanent encounter with, 39–40, 44

Death in Life (Lifton), 40

289

Index

Index

tage crisis in, 195; threat to use nuclear weapons in, 179
Iraq, Israeli preemptive strike against, 202
Isolation, 103
Isolationism, 214
Israeli, 84, 190, 240; 1973 war, 190, 227; preemptive strike against Iraq by, 202
Italy: Communist Party in, 216; U.S. missile sites in, 229

James, William, 89
Japan: antinuclear movement in, 132, 247; attack on Pearl Harbor by, 214; atomic bombing of, *see* Hiroshima *and* Nagasaki; Meiji Restoration in, 85*n;* radical communist students in, 83; shelters in, 267; war crimes trials in, 197
Jefferson, Thomas, 262
Jewish "biblical politics," 84
John, St., 76
John Paul II, Pope, 190
Johnson, Alia, 11
Johnson, Lyndon B., 179

Kahn, Herman, 5, 15, 19–21, 155, 237
Kaldor, Mary, 165
Kennan, George, 135, 216–17, 222
Kennedy, John F., 32, 154, 159, 179, 228–31
Khe Sanh, 179
Khomeini, Ayatollah, 84, 240

Khrushchev, Nikita, 222, 228–31
Kinetic art, 72
Kissinger, Henry, 31, 133–35, 190, 220, 243
Kistiakowsky, George, 90
Knowledge: compartmentalization of, 26; forbidden, 28; illusion of, 17–18
Korea, 184
Korean War, 140, 197, 261; pressures to use nuclear weapons in, 158; threats to use nuclear weapons in, 179
Kutami, Ryuzo, 267
Kyoto Central Hotel (Japan), 267

Labor, organized, 270
Language, domesticated, 106–7
Laos, 179
Lawrence, D. H., 76
Lawrence, William, 90, 95–97
Leach, Edmund, 122
League of Nations, 227; Covenant of, 200
Lebanon, landing of marines in, 179
Leukemia, 42; atomic bomb tests and, 121
Libya, 224, 240
Lillienthal, David, 30
Limited conventional war, doctrine of, 32
Limited nuclear war, 8; Carter Administration doctrine of, 97; credibility and, 32; illusion of, 14–17; nuclearism and, 91; policy shift to, 183–85; preparation for, 18; rebuilding of Hiroshima as argument for, 47; renunciation of doctrine of, 246; scenario of, 274–75;

Index

Music, 76
Mutual assured destruction (MAD), 178, 179, 181, 182, 186, 187, 212
MX missiles, 174
Mystery, 13

Nagasaki, 8, 44–47, 61, 88, 90, 137, 149, 164, 196, 276; numbing of survivors of, 104
Napoleonic wars, 212
National revolutions, 159, 164, 211; Cold War and, 216; and decline of American power, 223; Western Europe and, 224
National security, 24–25, 140, 205, 246; antidemocratic arrangements for, 139; children's comments on, 53; Executive Branch privileges and, 261; military-industrial complex as threat to, 161; permanent nuclear state of, 132; political legitimacy and, 138; secrecy and, 27; Super and, 203
National Security Council, 157
Nationalism, 212; Machiavellian world picture and, 240; see also National revolutions
NATO, 165
Nature, relationship to, 73–76
Nazis, 12, 26, 60, 61, 192, 212; Danish resistance to, 123; Thousand-Year Reich of, 82–83
Near-miss situations, 227, 236–38
Netherlands: antinuclear movement in, 268; Central American policy of, 224
Neurophysiology, 100
Neutron bomb, 97, 168, 169, 185; opposition to, 246

Nevada, atomic bomb tests in, 120–21
"New" Right, 219
New York Herald Tribune, 57, 89
New York Times Magazine, The, 168
Newtonian physics, 239
Nicaragua: anti-American revolution in, 171, 184, 219; Western European policy toward, 224
Nietzsche, Friedrich, 70
Nitze, Paul, 178, 217, 220
Nixon, Richard M., 32, 134, 179, 250
No-first-use policy, 135, 152, 162–64, 246, 251–53
Nonalignment, diplomacy of, 252
Non-Proliferation Treaty (NPT) (1968), 233–34
NORAD, 129
Nostalgia, politics of, 142
Nuclear free zones, establishment of, 246, 252
Nuclear utilization theorists (NUTS), 178, 181
Nuclearism, 87–99; arms control policy and, 227–28; awareness versus, 113; cultural breakdown caused by, 262; defined, ix; in development stage, 192–94; and development of Super, 202–7; of diplomacy, 94–95; and hatred of enemies, 208–10, 213–15; impairment of democratic political life by, 139; Machiavellian world picture and, 241, 243; mental armor of, 251; militarism and, 212–13, 257; modernism and, 190–91; moral arrangement of, 196–98; moralistic and legalistic endorse-

295

Index

Protection, illusion of, 18
Psychism, 86, 87
Psychoanalytic defense mechanisms, 103
Psychologism, 4; of security, 23–37
Purposes of American Power, The (Tucker), 166
Pynchon, Thomas, 77

Qadaffi, Muamar, 240
Quemoy, 179

Rabinowitch, Eugene, 102
Radiation, 278; acute effects of, 40–41; invisibility of, 13; long-term effects of, 41–46; minimizing fear of, 19; secrecy and dangers of, 30
RAND Corporation, 176
Rank, Otto, 7
Rapid Deployment Force, 184
Rationality, illusion of, 21–22
Reaction formation, 103
Reagan, Ronald, 16–17, 146–47, 156, 168, 171, 180, 217, 220, 249
Recovery, illusion of, 20
Red-baiting tactics, 156
Reductionistic moralism, 80
Reich, Wilhelm, 76
Religion: antinuclearism and, 259, 262, 269; Hiroshima and, 70–71; modernism and, 190
Religious conversion, 89
Religious images, 58, 61
Repression, 103
Republican Party, 229
Resignation-cynicism, 11

Resource depletion, 60
Restoration, mode of, 84n
Retaliatory capacity, 172–76, 188
Revolutionary fundamentalism, 83
Revolutionary nationalism, 159, 164, 211
Rickover, Hyman B., 96
Roosevelt, Franklin D., 60, 192, 193
Rosenberg, Ethel, 27, 139
Rosenberg, Julius, 27, 139
Rostow, Eugene V., 35, 220
Rumania, antinuclear demonstration in, 132
Russell, Bertrand, 35
Russian Revolution, 215
Rutherford, Ernest, 59

SAC headquarters, 129–32, 187
SALT-I, 235
SALT-II, 200, 223
Sanders, Jerry, 218
Saul of Tarsus, 76
Scandinavian countries, Central American policy of, 224
Scare tactics, 146
Schell, Jonathan, x, 58n, 189, 255
Schlesinger, James, 183, 184
Schools, air-raid drills in, 48–52
Scientism, 95
Scriptures, 80
Seabed Arms Control Treaty (1971), 233
Secrecy, 4, 25–31; antidemocratic arrangements for, 139; of nuclear intentions, 176; political legitimacy and, 138

297

Index

Secular absolutism, 260–63
Security, 23–37, 144–69; alternative idea of, 133; concept of, 4; credibility and, 31–33; defense spending and, 177; deterrence and, 148–49; international law and, 152–54; massive retaliation and, 157–58; no-first-use policy and, 162–64; nuclear option and, 164–68; paternalism and, 147–48; policy of terror and, 152; retaliatory capacity and, 175; revision of concept of, 113; secrecy and, 25–31; stability and, 33–37; strategic superiority and, 145–46, 149–51; and traditional imperatives of military power, 144–45; vulnerability and, 161; *see also* National security
Self, sense of, 78
Self-awareness, 112
Self-deception, 5
Senate, U.S., 200
Separation of powers, 260
Sexual repression, 63
Sexual secrets, 28
Shared awareness, 112
Shelter systems, 18–19, 55, 182; government spending for, 266; nuclearism and, 91
Sherwin, Martin, 193
Shils, Edward, 27
Shinto, 70
Simonds, Charles, 73
Sino-Soviet split, 160, 221, 224, 233
Skin disorders, 42
Slavery, abolition of, 123–24
Smith, Dan, 165
Smith, Gerald, 135
Snow, Edgar, 75
Social madness, 18, 22

Social security, 24
Soddy, Frederick, 29, 59–60
Solidarity, Polish, 132, 258–59
South America, 8
South Korea, defense of, 252
Soviet Union, 208–25, 249; aggressive image of, 218–21, 223; antinuclear propaganda of, 155, 156; appraisal of risks and, 210–11; arms control agreements with, 231–35; catch-up efforts of, 149–50, 153, 162; challenge to nuclearism in, 225; in Cold War, 204–5; conventional superiority of, 165, 166; in Cuban Missile Crisis, 228–31; declining power of, 221–24; and delegitimizing nuclear weapons, 162; deterrence and, 148, 157; first explosion of atomic device by, 202, 203; foreign policy behavior of, 205; as hated enemy, 208–10; ICBMs of, 161; ideological confrontation with, 215; and international institutions, 154; invasion of Afghanistan by, 171, 184, 211, 219, 221, 223; loss of strategic superiority to, 145; massive retaliation policy toward, 157–58, 160; militarism of, 259; missile buildup by, 166; mistrust of government information in, 143; moral arrangements of nuclearism in, 198; nuclear diplomacy and, 94–95; nuclear intentions toward, 170, 172, 176, 179; as nuclear power, 138; nuclear renunciation and, 263; and origins of Cold War, 215–16; portrayal of social evils in, 217; post-World War II, 199–201; proliferation of nuclear warheads in, 8; refined weapons technology of, 9; retalia-

298

Index